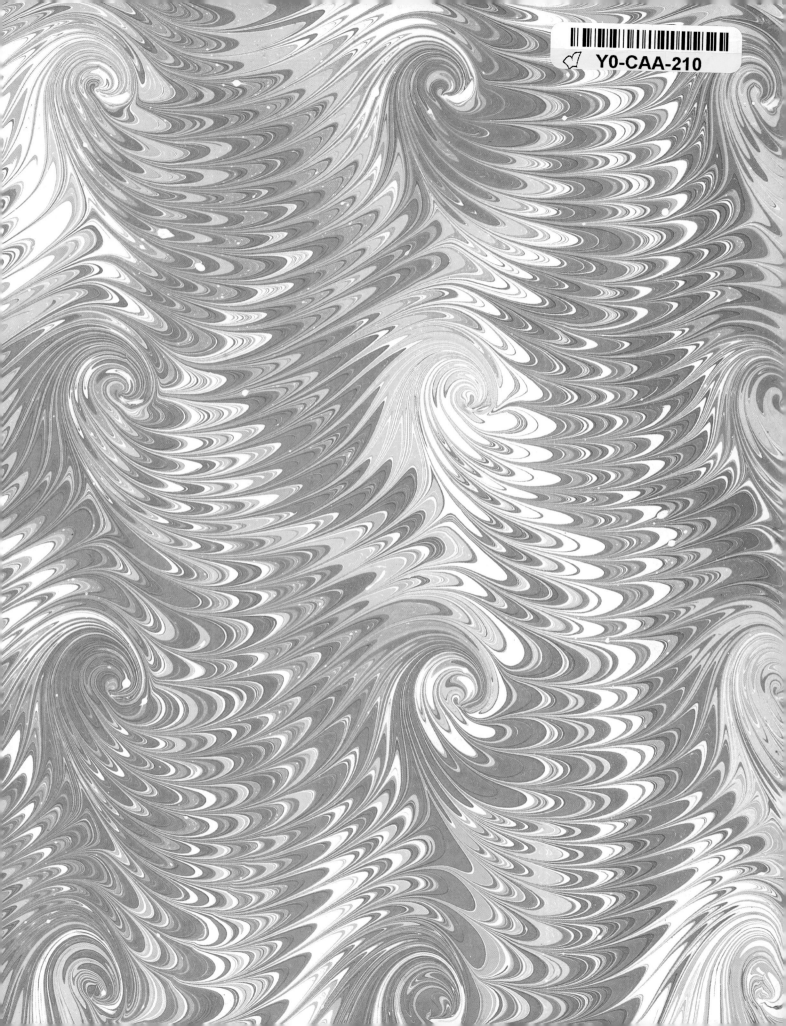

Twilight on the Lighthouses

Jim Gibbs

And God said, "Let there be light."

Schiffer Publishing Ltd

77 Lower Valley Road, Atglen, PA 19310

Dedication

To the intrepid, masterful and courageous builders of our Pacific Coast lighthouses who accomplished their work, often under the most adverse conditions.
And to Bob Schwemmer, maritime historian, writer, diver and friend.
Also to a host of wonderful lighthouse enthusiasts whom I've met through the years in writing about lighthouses and allied maritime subjects.

Front jacket photo:
Cleft of the Rock Lighthouse by commercial photographer Chad Ehlers.

Back jacket photos:
Upper left, Haceta Head; *Upper right,* North Head; *Left center,* Point Vicente; *Center,* New Point Loma; *Below center,* Haceta Head; *Right center,* Cape Arago; *Bottom left*, Old Point Loma; *Bottom right,* Pigeon Point.

Printed in China.
ISBN: 0-88740-930-X

Library of Congress Cataloging-in-Publication Data

Gibbs, Jim, 1922-
    Twilight on the lighthouses / Jim Gibbs.
        p.   cm.
    Includes bibliographical references and index.
    ISBN 0-88740-930-X (hardcover)
    1. Lighthouses--Pacific Coast (U.S.)--History. I. Title
VK1024.P3G5324   1996
387.1' 55' 0979--dc20   95-48454
                                    CIP

Published by Schiffer Publishing Ltd.
77 Lower Valley Road
Atglen, PA 19310
Please write for a free catalog.
This book may be purchased from
the publisher.
Please include $2.95 for shipping.
Try your bookstore first.

**We are interested in hearing from authors
with book ideas on related topics.**

Contents

Foreword

The twilight theme is not always a happy one, especially in the case of lighthouses. Still, in some ways it is a happy thought to know that the aging sentinels have become more popular with the general public than ever before. Even though their importance as aids to navigation is virtually over, many will continue on as monuments, like footprints in the march of time.

This work is a companion book to *Lighthouses of the Pacific,* published by Schiffer Publishing Ltd., in 1986. It is a pictorial view of the Pacific Coast lighthouses from a different perspective. The featured photographer is Keith Kammerzell, an affable gentleman, who along with his wife Judy, has made a hobby of filming the sentinels from the air as well as on terra firma. Traveling thousands of miles by plane, he not only has captured the lighthouses from a different angle but the surrounding seascapes as well—fascinating, sculptured natural strata, evergreen forests, sawtooth reefs and rolling surf. He has found that God's artistic hand blended with picturesque lighthouses make a delightful combination that blends in complete harmony.

Though Kammerzell is the principal photographer, others with the magic touch have also contributed to this work, with both photos and illustrations; among them Carole Reichel, Beverly Schreiber, Ed Peterson, Lee Forest, Merrie Holbert, Sam Foster, Don Sheldon, Bob Schwemmer, several Coast Guard photographers and some historic photos from the archives of time past. It is the earnest hope of the author and photographers that this book will further increase the public's interest in these classic structures.

With limited funds, the Coast Guard has been forced to back farther away from the lighthouses in favor of more demanding obligations. In turn, other government agencies and volunteers have stepped in, and in some cases have been able to open the towers to public visitation. Several situations exist and it is suggested that interested parties should check with the Chambers of Commerce in the settlement nearest the respective lighthouses to learn details, or contact whatever government agency or preservation group is in charge if visitation is desired. Numerous lighthouse societies and preservation groups have sprung up across the nation in an effort to save the remaining lighthouses. Some of our Pacific Coast lighthouses, no longer active as aids to navigation, are being used for other purposes; some have been aban-doned, some no longer exist and replicas of others have been constructed. Some of the Fresnel lenses that have been removed now serve as museum pieces along with other bits and pieces of lighthouse memorabilia.

A new epidemic has hit the nation called, "Lighthouse Fever," and it involves growing numbers of people that have a fascination with historical lighthouses. Changes in the status of lighthouses come about constantly. It is indeed sad to see many of the watchtowers go dark, ending an era that has been as much a part of Americana as baseball and apple pie. The fate of each lighthouse hangs somewhat in the balance, and it's anyone's guess what will transpire in the next decade. Twilight time is upon us where this facet of our nation's history is concerned.

I remember reading an article about lighthouses in 1948, which read: "It will be a sad day, sentimentally, when the lighthouse keeper goes ashore and leaves his post in the heartless but efficient care of a mere robot. But that day is coming when the guardian of the light will visit his station only once a month."

That article was written nearly 50 years ago and the prediction came true. Only one government light in the United States still has a keeper. For sentimental reasons, a Coast Guardsman is an attendant at Boston Lighthouse on Little Brewster Island, but only because it was the first place where an official light was established—in 1716.

As I write this book I have just returned from a visit to the Heceta Head and Yaquina Head lighthouses. Both towers have from their inception been blessed with beautiful, scintillating first order Fresnel lenses. Problems necessitated use of the auxiliary lights at the respective lighthouses. The public feared the big Fresnels would be permanently doused but they were finally relit. Other Fresnels have met the same fate. Pigeon Point Light in California was one of the first to leave the big Fresnel dark in favor of a small gallery beacon. Other classic optics have been moved to museums.

Like the classic lights, the foghorns of yesteryear—the steam whistle, reed, diaphone, diaphrams and sirens—have also been replaced by hi-tech long-range sound emitters powered by electromagnetically vibrated steel diaphrams, some with as many as six units on top of each other. Often they are started automatically by fog detectors, mechanisms more reliable than the human eye.

Site of America's first lighthouse—Boston Light on Little Brewster Island. The tower pictured here was erected in 1783 at the site of the original frame tower which was blown up by the British in 1776. The present tower was reconstructed and raised to its present height of 89 feet in 1859. It was here that Winslow Lewis first demonstrated his Argand lamp-parabolic reflector system which the federal government adopted in 1812, a system that lasted until the introduction of the Fresnel system of optics and lighting. Photo courtesy U.S. Coast Guard

Then there are the radiobeacons, radar beacons and radar reflectors, not to mention LORAN for long range navigation and a host of other innovative navigation aids capable of seeing through any kind of weather. Such instruments make the light and fog signal almost obsolete.

It was the beginning of the end for the classic optics of the Fresnel system when high intensity, high candlepower all-weather rotating airway beacons were installed in exposed positions or in the old lighthouse lamp rooms. Now even they, in some cases are becoming obsolete. Indeed it is a fast changing world, and with satellite navigation coming into its own, robot ships with refined nuclear power may be in the future. Only the good Lord knows how far mankind's intelligence and ingenuity can go.

True, the personal touch is gone; the friendly old light keeper is a lost occupation and the proud remaining lighthouses are monuments and symbols of the glorious past. Several of the great towers have already disappeared along with the traditional keepers of the lights. Many have already been reduced to the realm of memory, and memory is fragile stuff. Twilight time is upon us and time sometimes takes its toll.

How long will history remember Frenchman Augustin Fresnel? It was in 1822 that he invented the multi-prism lens with its dioptric and catadioptric characteristics. His contribution to history, the Fresnel lens, was five times more powerful than the reflector system then in use. But for maximum visibility, the light had to be placed high enough to compensate for the curvature of the earth. When set at 100 feet above sea level a light could be seen 18 plus miles at sea.

Lenses were in seven different orders, the smaller ones for harbors, estuaries and lakes, and the large first order lenses with more than 1,000 prisms in many cases, located on ocean front locations where the maximum visibility was needed. Light source was a lamp utilizing up to five concentric wicks, fueled initially by sperm or lard oil and later kerosene, and finally electricity. The prisms could focus the rays of such lamps into beams of 80,000 candlepower. By the 1930s, most lighthouses had been electrified and the constantly improved light sources could get up to almost three million candlepower in the largest lenses. To create the flash systems, lenses were replaced on "chariot wheels" and ball bearings and in some cases mercury baths. The multi-ton lenses could be turned with the push of a finger. Clockwork drives powered by a heavy weight that dropped through the trunk of the tower (prior to electricity) was wound by hand every four hours, from sunset to sunrise.

As wonderful as the lights were, they had their limitation. Fog, the bane of many mariners, allowed only the most powerful light to be seen less than a half mile. Thus the fog signals, so important before the advent of radio electronics with devices that could penetrate fog, became second hat. The first fog signals were rather primitive—gongs, cannon, bells, steam whistles—then came the sophisticated varieties like compressed air horns. Even the diaphones, diaphrams, and sirens have been replaced in most cases. Up until recent times, there was as many as 89 fog signals of various types sounding on San Francisco Bay and even more on Puget Sound. There has been a large evolution in both lights and fog signals on the Pacific Coast and even to a greater extent on the east coast.

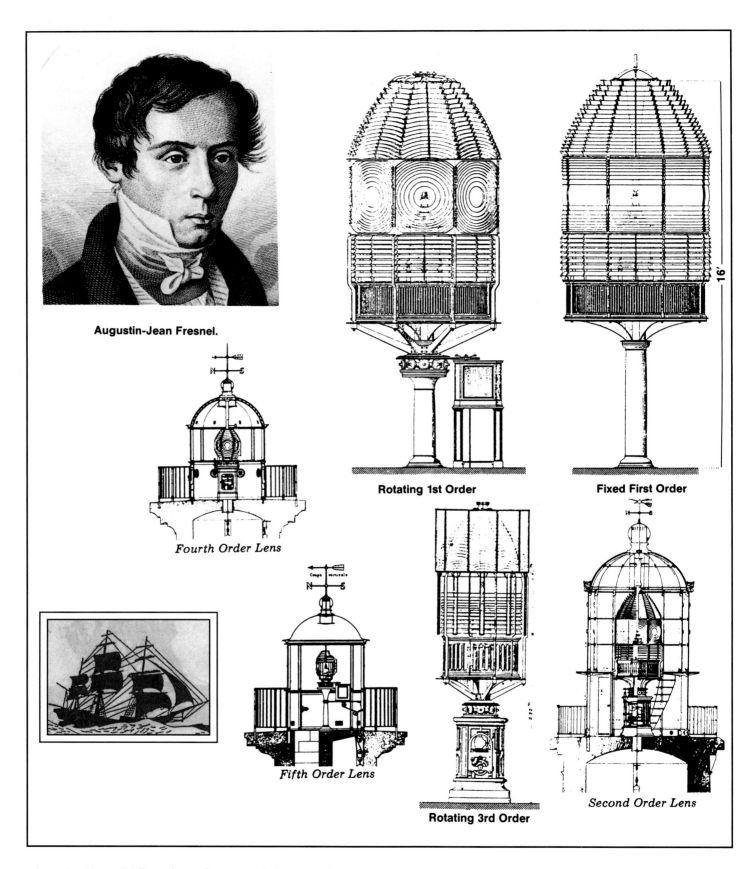

Augustin-Jean Fresnel.

Fourth Order Lens

Rotating 1st Order

Fixed First Order

16'

Fifth Order Lens

Rotating 3rd Order

Second Order Lens

Augustine (Augustin) Fresnel, was the renowned physicist and scientist who created the Fresnel lens which revolution-
ized the history of pharology and created a whole new era in the lighting of the worlds' marine beacons. The young
Frenchman found a way to reflect and refract a light into one central beam, beginning in the 1820s. Fresnel lenses
ranged from seventh order to first order, some samples depicted here.

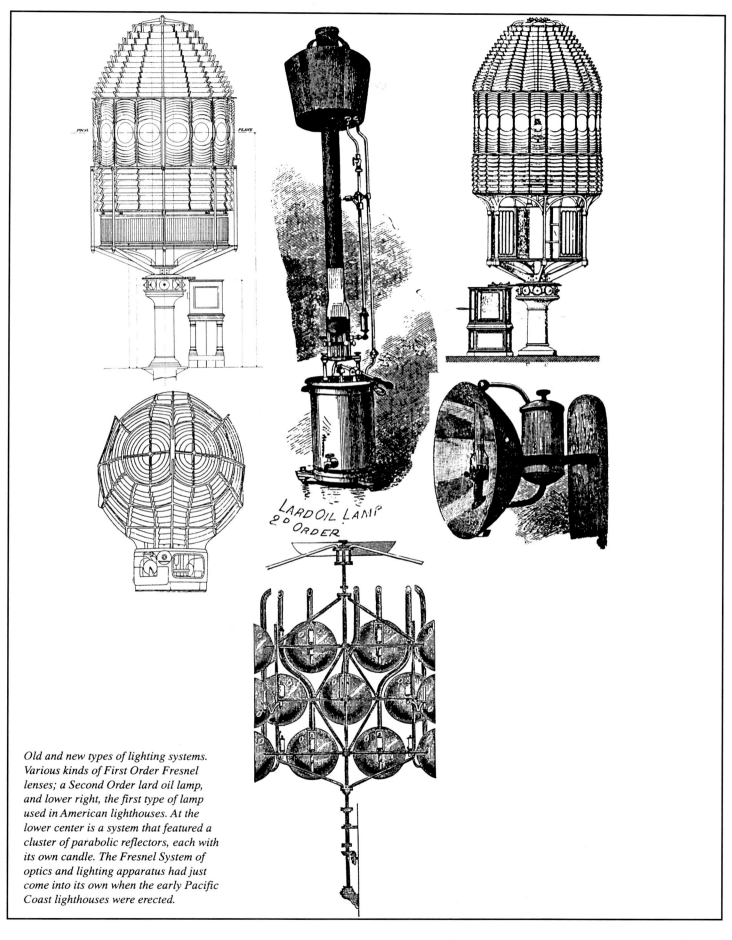

LARD OIL LAMP
2D ORDER

Old and new types of lighting systems. Various kinds of First Order Fresnel lenses; a Second Order lard oil lamp, and lower right, the first type of lamp used in American lighthouses. At the lower center is a system that featured a cluster of parabolic reflectors, each with its own candle. The Fresnel System of optics and lighting apparatus had just come into its own when the early Pacific Coast lighthouses were erected.

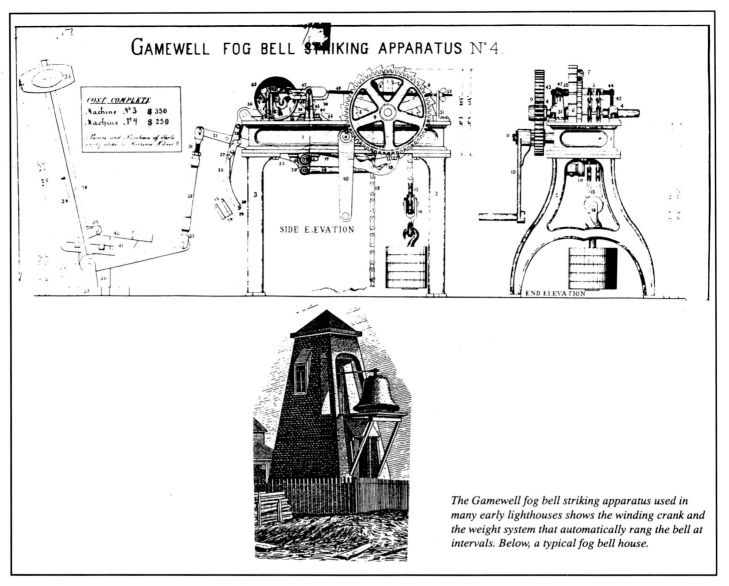

GAMEWELL FOG BELL STRIKING APPARATUS N° 4.

COST COMPLETE
Machine N°3 $350
Machine N°4 $250

Names and Numbers of parts exactly alike in Machines N°3 and 4

SIDE ELEVATION

END ELEVATION

The Gamewell fog bell striking apparatus used in many early lighthouses shows the winding crank and the weight system that automatically rang the bell at intervals. Below, a typical fog bell house.

Health was to bother Augustin Fresnel throughout his short life. His teachers thought the frail, bashful lad was slightly mentally retarded when at age eight he was a poor reader with a bad memory, unable to master a required foreign language. He did, however, excel in mathematics, so much so that he astounded his professors at age 16. In graphic arts and geometry he was brilliant.

He did graduate as an engineer, and after some very lowly jobs that had no bearing on his eventual genius he not only invented the beehive-shaped lens with dioptric and catadioptric concentric prisms with bullseyes, but also the fixed lens and the drum lens. He revolutionized marine lighting, making France the outstanding leader in the field for many years.

Fresnel died a young man, but his inventions opened the door to not only the improvement of lighthouses around the world, but also to the saving of many lives because of better lighting that prevented considerable shipwreck.

Standing solid against the thrashing ocean and violent winds, the old romantic lighthouses have been the source of yarns and stories spun beside cozy home fires on stormy nights, for lighthouses and their beams have always intrigued the imaginations of men, perhaps because they not only are wonderful to look upon but also inspire a sort of spiritual aura, similar to a great cathedral. People can find fault with just about anything in our present day but it is hard to find fault with a lighthouse.

The Coast Guard's oldest mission concerning federally provided public service is that of aids to navigation. During more than 200 years

in which the United States has operated navigation aids the basic endeavor, though revolutionized, is the same. The ninth act ever passed by the U.S. Congress included "...the necessary support, maintenance and repair of all lighthouses, beacons, buoys and public piers at the entrance to or within any bay, inlet, harbor or port of the United States for rendering the navigation thereof easy and safe..." That act was passed on August 7, 1789, and gave the Secretary of the Treasury authority over all navigation aids. The first lighthouse built by the federal government was completed in 1792 at Cape Henry. The first lighthouse per se, as mentioned earlier, was the Boston Light on Little Brewster Island in 1716, a publicly funded frame tower with an open brazier.

By 1840 our nation had 234 lighthouses and 900 lesser aids to navigation. Twenty years earlier an act of Congress had made the fifth auditor of the Treasury general superintendent of lights. For 33 years Stephen Pleasanton held that post, but marine lighting dragged well behind the European nations during that period and there was considerable mismanagement, and in many cases aids to navigation were insufficient.

In 1850, after numerous complaints from mariners, a systematic marking of all buoys came about, even numbers for the red buoys on starboard, and odd numbers on the black buoys on the port side.

The following year the most significant change came about with the creation of a Lighthouse Board, composed of two senior Navy officers, two Army Corps of Engineers personnel, two civilian scientists and one junior Navy officer. That Board was to last for 59 years, headed

The old style of river buoy is pictured here. The present day lighted buoys are much more streamlined and more compact than the old, but not nearly as much fun to watch as they rock and roll in their shackled positions.

Admiral William B. Shubrick, a well qualified gentleman, served as head of the U.S. Lighthouse Board from October 1852 until October 1871, during a period when a large share of the lighthouses were constructed on the Pacific Coast. The first official lighthouse tender, the Shubrick, *which carried the burden for decades on the Pacific Coast was named for the good admiral. In June 1910, Congress passed an act that reorganized the Lighthouse Service. The Lighthouse Board had been the complete authority for 58 years. Total lighted aids had increased from around 335 when the board assumed control to nearly 4,000, including minor lights and lighted buoys. Fog signals had increased from 49 to 457, and buoys from 1,000 to 5,300. The new 1910 act created the Bureau of Lighthouses, implementing a further reaching responsibility, increasing the number of districts and officials. The U.S. Coast Guard took over the Lighthouse Service in 1939.*

by such well known names as Admiral George B. Dewey and Admiral W.B. Shubrick, as well as others. It was early in that regime that the aforementioned significant change came about in lighthouse optics and lighting apparatus, a technological revolution—with the adoption of the Fresnel system of lighting. By 1859, all of the country's major lighthouses were fitted with the new optics.

Honed into an excellent system of navigation aids, equal to any other maritime country, the Lighthouse Board was not abolished until June 17, 1910. Through the years it had turned an unstable bureaucratic bramble into a well oiled operation. In earlier times a keeper could lose or gain his post depending on whether he was a Republican or Democrat.

In 1903, the Lighthouse Service had been transferred from the Treasury Department to the Department of Commerce and Labor, and seven years later a single commissioner was appointed to head the revitalized service. In 1939, President Franklin D. Roosevelt announced the transfer of the Bureau of Lighthouses to the U.S. Coast Guard. In 1967, the Coast Guard came under the Department of Transportation. It was a far cry from the original Boston Light when on July 23, 1715, the Massachusetts subjects of King George I of England carried out the building of the structure which was supported by a user tax. Today, after two and a half centuries, the site of the first lighthouse has been designated as a National Historic Landmark. It was also the locale of the first fog signal, a muzzle loading cannon.

America's first lightship was anchored off Craney Island in stormy Chesapeake Bay in 1820, a century after England's initial lightship, the *Nore*. The apex for the lightship in the United States came in 1909 when 56 were in use off America's shores. The first lightship on the Pacific Coast was the Columbia River Lightship, in 1892, the first of the five lightship stations off these shores. Some of the lightships, especially on the east coast, were later replaced by screw pile and caisson lighthouses. The advent of automation, in the 1960s and 1970s, spelled the final demise for the lightships, when offshore towers and super LNB buoys, totally sufficient and unmanned, took over. The lightships that escaped the scrap yards are now serving as museum ships in various American seaport cities.

For unknown reasons, no offshore light platforms replaced the lightships on the Pacific Coast as was the case on the east coast in the 1960s and 1970s. For a time, important lightship posts were taken up by LNB superbuoys but with the exception of the one off Blunts Reef, they too have been withdrawn in favor of lesser sized buoys. In the above photo in the 1960s the Frying Pan Lightship is being replaced by an offshore platform complete with light, fog signal, radio beacon and other innovations at a shoal area ten miles off the North Carolina coast. Note the Coast Guard helicopter on the landing platform, a quick and safe way to exchange personnel and to import supplies. Photo courtesy U.S. Coast Guard

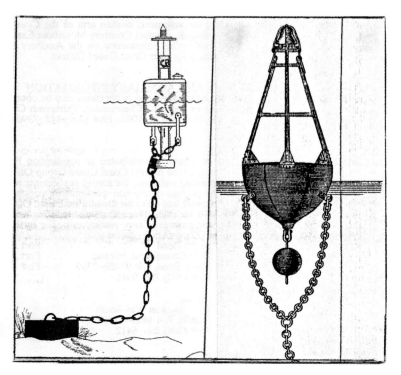

The old and modern types of buoys. At the right is the Browns type bell buoy widely used in days of yore. To the left is the modern type of buoy showing the method of anchorage.

LIGHTED BUOYS-1962 BUOY NOMENCLATURE
(9 x 32 LR BUOY PICTURES)

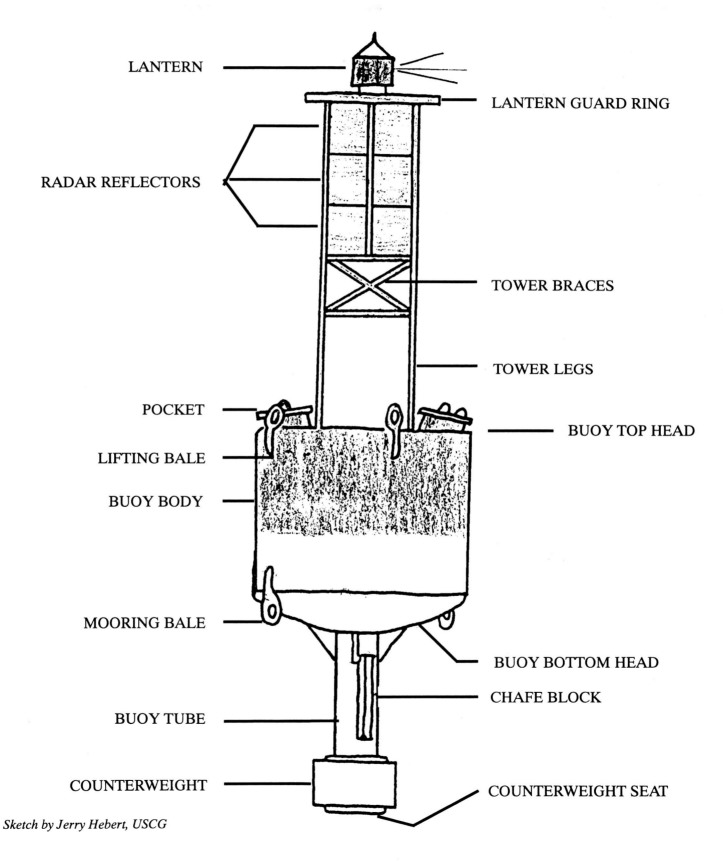

LANTERN

LANTERN GUARD RING

RADAR REFLECTORS

TOWER BRACES

TOWER LEGS

POCKET

BUOY TOP HEAD

LIFTING BALE

BUOY BODY

MOORING BALE

BUOY BOTTOM HEAD

CHAFE BLOCK

BUOY TUBE

COUNTERWEIGHT

COUNTERWEIGHT SEAT

Sketch by Jerry Hebert, USCG

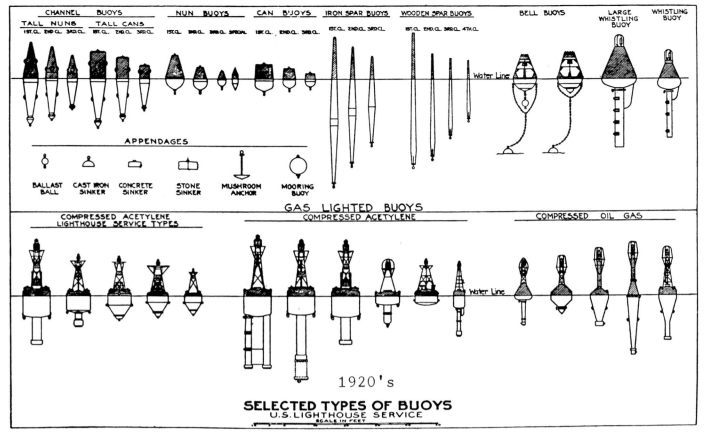

Everybody who goes to sea is familiar with buoys, those colorful iron and steel mechanisms that sway with the rhythm of the sea, mini-lighthouses, bell buoys, horn buoys, lighted buoys. Pictured here is the family of buoys of another time when their placement was the responsibilities of the U.S. Lighthouse Service tenders. Back then, many of the buoys were nuns, cans, spars and whistling buoys. Today the buoys are much more sophisticated, equipped with radio and radar devices along with lights and fog signals. In many ways they have become more important than the fading lighthouses as they usually mark channels across bars and into harbors.

Coast Guard buoy tender Sweetbriar W405, serviced buoys on the Northwest coast for several years.

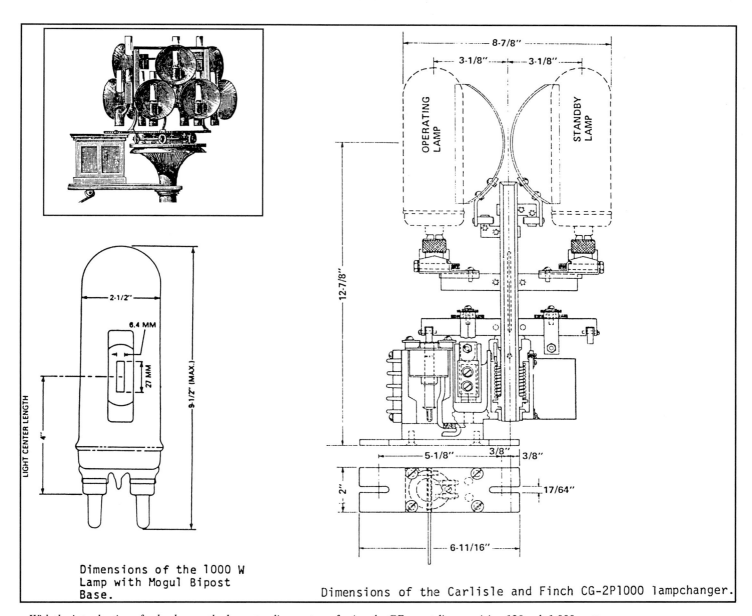

OPERATING LAMP

STANDBY LAMP

8-7/8"

3-1/8" 3-1/8"

12-7/8"

5-1/8" 3/8" 3/8"

2" 17/64"

6-11/16"

2-1/2"

6.4 MM

27 MM

9-1/2" (MAX.)

4"

LIGHT CENTER LENGTH

Dimensions of the 1000 W Lamp with Mogul Bipost Base.

Dimensions of the Carlisle and Finch CG-2P1000 lampchanger.

With the introduction of solar lamps, the long standing system of using the GE quartzline precision 120 volt 1,000 watt lamps may eventually come to a halt. The illustration shows the nine and a half inch high globe, each lamp supported by the Carlisle & Finch two place lampchanger. A secondary (standby) lamp automatically moves in place when the other burns out. Upper left hand corner, depicts the old parabolic reflector fixture with individual lamps in front of each silvered metal reflector. It was far inferior to the Fresnel system of lighting and was never used in lighthouses on the Pacific Coast.

A great advance in long range navigation came with the radio beacons and the sophisticated LORAN system which allows navigators to chart their courses with accuracy over great distances. Typical of such stations is the one on lonely Kure Island, 1200 miles west of Honolulu which supports a 625 foot LORAN antenna tower and quarters for a Coast Guard crew. To initiate the LORAN cycle, a controlling station designated as the "master" transmits a pulsed signal which is radiated in all directions. The signal travels on a straight line until received by a secondary unit called a "slave" station. Simultaneously, the signal goes to a position of any ship or aircraft in an area equipped with a LORAN receiver. At the receiver site the signal is converted to a visual trace displayed on the face of an oscilloscope, a device like a television screen. The LORAN receiver is arranged so the master signal appears below and slightly to the right of the master signal. The two signals are accordingly superimposed. When the result is before the receiver opera-

tor, he records a number from a direct reading counter on the set. The number in turn records how many millionths of a microsecond transpires between the time a master signal reaches a receiver site, and the slave signal triggered by the master signal, arrives at the same point. The receiver operator then consults a printed LORAN chart of the general area where he is stationed. The chart is overprinted with numerous hyperbolic lines, each of which represent a LORAN time difference. The lines are represented by microseconds. By matching his reading with the lines on the chart the operator determines that his position is located somewhere along the lines. By taking readings on two or more master slaves, the operator can determine his position with great accuracy. Daytime range is 750 miles but by night it is double that figure. LORAN C offers accuracy within a quarter mile even at ranges of 3,000 miles from the transmitting station.

If all of the above sounds complicated, you are not alone. Hi-tech innovations seem beyond the average human mind, but the strange thing about it all is that even the latest innovations become obsolete within a few decades. It is easy to see why the traditional lighthouse has reached its final role as an important aid to navigation. A majority of the minor lighted aids are now equipped with solar panels. And of course satellite navigation (GPS) is bringing about still another revolution in the field of navigation both on land and sea. And speaking of solarization, the U.S. Coast Guard has completed a program to solarize several of the major lighthouses. A new type of direct current lamp was developed that requires far less power. It consists of a 110 watt tungsten/halogen lamp that has an output equal to that of the 1000 watt AC lamps used in major lighthouses. The solar system requires a multi-panel solar array

and a heavy duty battery bank of over 2900 ampere hours. Advantages are many, including the ecological impact of diesel power being eliminated. Servicing is reduced as no fuel is required.

It is this writer's hope that the day will never come when in this increasingly hi-tech world a child will be sitting on his grandfather's lap and ask, "Grandpa, what's a lighthouse?"

There is an old saying, "Lighthouse keepers never die, their lights just slowly go out." Maybe that same thought applies to the nation's lighthouses as well.

—Jim Gibbs,
Cleft of the Rock Lighthouse,
Cape Perpetua, Oregon, 1996

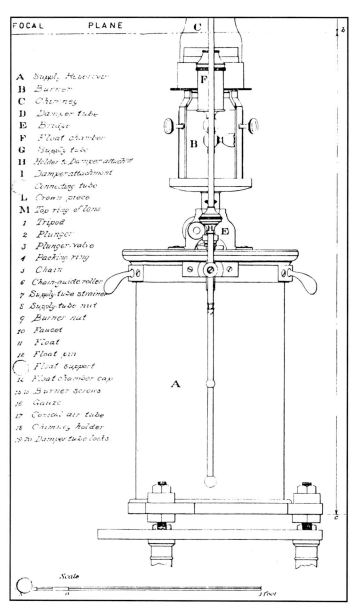

Exterior sketch of the lamp for a three-wick mineral oil lamp for a second order lens as of 1880. U.S. Lighthouse service sketch, U.S. Government Printing Office.

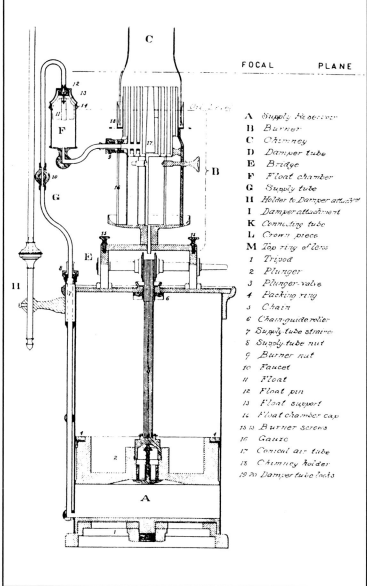

Interior sketch of the workings of a three-wick mineral oil lamp for second order lenses. U.S. Lighthouse Service, Instructions to Lightkeepers, 1880.

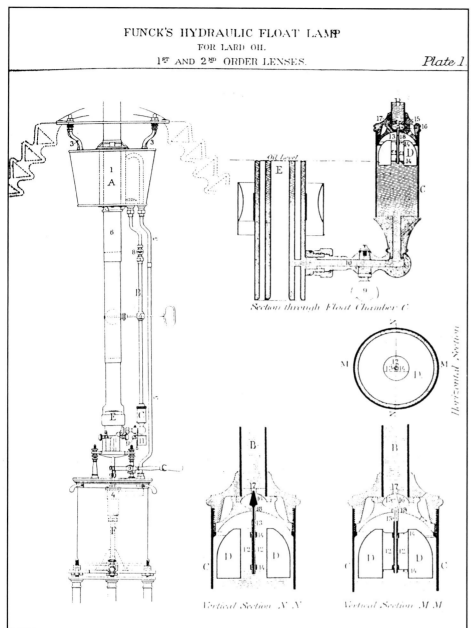

FUNCK'S HYDRAULIC FLOAT LAMP
FOR LARD OIL.
1ST AND 2ND ORDER LENSES.

Plate 1.

Funck's hydraulic float lamp for lard oil utilized in first and second order lenses, circa 1880s. U.S. Lighthouse Service, Instructions to Lightkeepers.

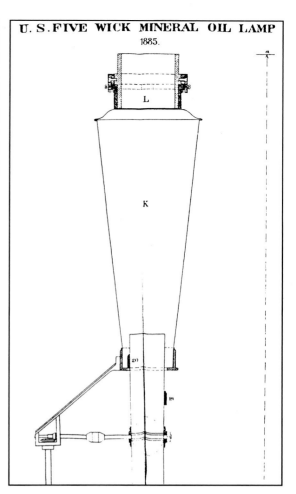

U.S. FIVE WICK MINERAL OIL LAMP
1885.

Top section of a U.S. five-wick mineral oil lamp showing (L) the crown piece and (K) connecting tube. Numbers 19 and 20 are the damper tube locks. Instructions to Lightkeepers, *1885, U.S. Lighthouse Service.*

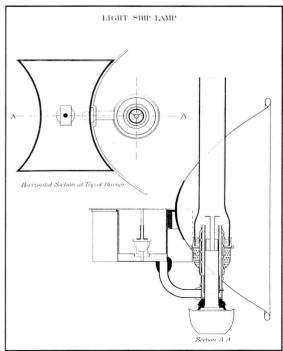

LIGHT SHIP LAMP

Types of lamps used in the lenses of lightships before the advent of electricity. U.S. Lighthouse Service, Instructions to Lightkeepers, *1889.*

Aids to Navigation Terms

An Aid to Navigation is any signal device external to a vessel or aircraft specifically intended to assist a navigator to determine his or her position or safe course, or to warn him or her of dangers or obstructions to navigation. Aids to Navigation Team Coos Bay maintains the following types of aids.

Minor Light: A fixed structure placed either on shore or in the water that is equipped with daymark and an automatic unwatched light showing a specific characteristic.

Daybeacon: An unlighted fixed structure, either on shore or in the water, that is equipped with a standard daymark for daytime identification.

Daymark: The daytime identifier of an aid to navigation presenting one of several standard shapes or colors. Examples: square, triangle, or rectangle with colors green, red, orange or white.

Unlighted buoy: A floating object not equipped with an automatic unwatched light, moored (anchored) to the bottom of a body of water to indicate a position on the water.

Fog signal: An aid to navigation that generates a loud horn-like or bell-like sound for the purpose of guiding or warning mariners in periods of reduced visibility.

Lighthouse: A fixed structure or building providing a light of high candle-power and reliability; may also provide a fog signal and radiobeacon.

Candlepower: Luminous intensity of a light measured in candelas.

Explanation of the various types of navigation aids presently in use.

Hains mineral oil lamp for fourth, fifth and sixth order lenses as of the 1880s. Instructions to Lightkeepers, U.S. Lighthouse Service publication sketch.

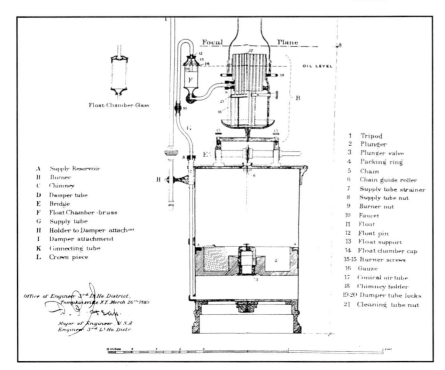

A Supply Reservoir
B Burner
C Chimney
D Damper tube
E Bridge
F Float Chamber-brass
G Supply tube
H Holder to Damper attachmᵗ
I Damper attachment
K Connecting tube
L Crown piece

1   Tripod
2   Plunger
3   Plunger valve
4   Packing ring
5   Chain
6   Chain guide roller
7   Supply tube strainer
8   Supply tube nut
9   Burner nut
10 Faucet
11 Float
12 Float pin
13 Float support
14 Float chamber cap
15-15 Burner screws
16 Gauze
17 Conical air tube
18 Chimney holder
19-20 Damper tube locks
21 Cleaning tube nut

Sketch of a lamp and its components for a five-wick mineral oil unit for a first order light as shown in the 1885 Instructions to Light-keepers, (U.S. Lighthouse Service) Government Printing Office.

The new Point Loma Lighthouse at Pelican Point near San Diego, California, built in 1890.

Types of lenses formerly used in lighthouses. Upper left is the lens-lantern frequently used in secondary lighthouses in the day of oil lamps. Note the large storage reservoir for oil over the lens. Upper right: the 375 mm lens inside the lantern housing was used on lightships, breakwaters and as an auxiliary light. It is often referred to as a drum lens. Lower photo: the original first order lens used first at Cape Disappointment and later at North Head lighthouse. The upper lenses are on display at the Columbia River Maritime Museum, and the large lens at the Lewis and Clark Interpretive Center at Cape Disappointment.

Lighthouse artist Bev Schreiber created the book mark shown here depicting the various shapes of Pacific Coast Lighthouses, one of her many creations that comes from her studio in Mukilteo, Washington.

Excellent marine artist Ronald Dean of England depicted the busy San Francisco waterfront around the turn of the century in this fine painting. In the foreground is the French ship Biarritz, *a bounty vessel.*

Carmanah Lighthouse on the ocean side of Vancouver Island's shores, north of the entrance to the Strait of Juan de Fuca. Established 1891, rebuilt 1961.

A closer view of the islet on which Race Rocks light tower stands. Ships in the Victoria-Vancouver B.C. port area depend on the beacon as well as naval vessels at Esquimalt.

British Columbia's first lighthouse was the Fisgard tower established in 1861, just a few months ahead of Race Rocks. The 56 foot tower of masonry construction is now a tourist attraction, minor aids replacing it on the searoad to Victoria B.C.

Steel steam schooner SS Melville Dollar *of the Dollar fleet, was a typical lumber vessel operating out of San Francisco and a familiar sight at the lighthouses on coastal voyages.*

A familiar site in times past—deckloads of lumber shifting on the wooden steam schooners. On occasion, when a lumber-laden wooden steam schooner was in danger of sinking, her cargo of lumber kept her afloat. In the above, the steam schooner Davenport *was towed back to port and her deck cargo reloaded. Most of these cases occurred in storm-tossed seas along the Pacific Coast.*

Opposite page, top:
Talk about a pincushion of rocks—Destruction Island has them. This lonely place off the northwestern Washington coast has been crowned by a lighthouse since 1891.

Opposite page, bottom:
With nearly all the out buildings torn down, the lighthouse, fog signal structure, and a few tanks are all that is left on Tatoosh Island (Cape Flattery). It was once the haunt of the Makah Indians who based their fishing and mammal hunting activities there.

A close-up of the Destruction Island tower and its huge optic. Note the standby light protruding from the vent at top of the dome.

In September 1990, a joint Coast Guard—Army rehab program got underway on Cape Flattery Lighthouse. It was given a general overhaul after many years of neglect. Photos courtesy Ed Peterson

The tallest, most graceful light tower in the Pacific Northwest is Grays Harbor Lighthouse, referred to by the locals at Westport Light. It tapers skyward for 107 feet and has been a star maritime attraction since 1898.

Keith Kammerzell's artistic eye framed the Browns Point Lighthouse between two evergreen trees in his camera's view. The surrounding park grounds are popular with the public.

A beautiful subject for a camera, North Head Lighthouse, a factor in safe navigation since 1898. Note the double-drum rotating beacon which many years ago replaced the Fresnel lens. The tower has been featured in many advertisements and was also the backdrop for a major Hollywood movie.

As the sun slowly sinks in the west the North Head beacon is silhouetted against a golden sky.

An eagle eye view of Cape Disappointment Lighthouse and the rugged rampart on which it stands.

As the sea mist rolls in, the venerable Cape Disappointment Light keeps its vigil around the clock, overlooking a graveyard of ships.

A structure resembling a lighthouse (non working) is located in a cove just off Fox Island, in a place called Tanglewood Island, at the south end of Puget Sound. It has served as a Boy Scout camp and a tourist center. Call it Tanglewood (Lighthouse), unofficial.

Dofflemyer Point Lighthouse, on the end of the point, east side of Budd Inlet on lower Puget Sound has been there since 1936 when it replaced the earlier navigation aid established in 1887, marking the channel to the Port of Olympia. Courtesy lighthouse artist Beverly Schreiber

The latest member of the family of lighthouses on Puget Sound is the Gig Harbor Lighthouse on the west shores of the sound. It was built by public subscription with the cooperation of the Coast Guard in recent years. Photo courtesy Beverly Schreiber (Bev's Studio)

Keith Kammerzell catches the personality of Robinson Point Lighthouse in this photo. The tower is located on Maury Island on the waters of Puget Sound.

Above:
Spit and polish is the Alki Point Lighthouse located near where the first settlers of Seattle landed in 1851. At the south entrance to Seattle's Elliott Bay the former keepers' dwelling is the residence of the commandant of the 13th Coast Guard District. The present lighthouse was built in 1918, but an aid to navigation marked the point from 1887.

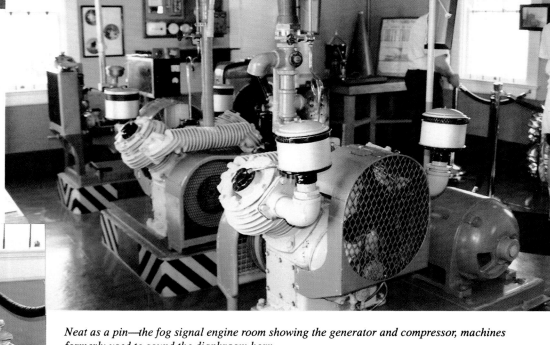

Neat as a pin—the fog signal engine room showing the generator and compressor, machines formerly used to sound the diaphragm horn.

This fourth order fixed lens displayed in the fog signal house at Alki Lighthouse is typical of those used in Puget Sound lighthouses.

Fourth Order Fresnel lens at West Point showing its red sector. The typical iron lantern house is surrounded by the lighthouse gallery, and the lightning rod protrudes from the ventilator ball.

Situated below the former Fort Lawton, now a public park (Discovery Park), is the quaint West Point Lighthouse, which passed its centennial some years back with flying colors.

It was offshore from Point No Point Lighthouse in a heavy fog that the SS Admiral Sampson *plunged to the bottom in 320 feet of water after colliding with the SS* Princess Victoria *August 26, 1914. The passengerliner went down in seven minutes taking 11 lives, including Captain Zimro Moore. Kent Barnard of Argonaut Resources located the wreck in his two-man submarine in recent years and managed to salvage several articles with the submarine's arm claw.*

City life encroaches on the Mukilteo Lighthouse.

A foggy area, a light and fog signal was placed at Marrowstone Point at the east point of the entrance to Port Townsend in 1888. The present stubby light fixture was placed there in 1918 when the first World War was flaring. The former buildings of the once large Fort Flagler abutting the light facility, are now part of the Washington State Parks system. The original keepers' dwelling is still in place.

The author had the Skunk Bay lighthouse built in 1965, utilizing the lantern house from the 1858 Smith Island Lighthouse. It was sold to a group of professional businessmen seven years later.

1. Reflections: Early Navigational Aids

*Where there is much light
the shadows are deepest.*

—*Goethe*

The curtain is falling. The final act is nearly over. It is indeed twilight time for the lighthouses. Those halcyon days have long vanished and a new era has set in. The stalwart sentinels once so important to Pacific Coast shipping are now for the most part historical symbols of the past in this age of satellite navigation and hi-technology.

Ironically the aging towers are more popular today than in the past, not as aids to navigation, but as intriguing tourist attractions. Once considered an absolute necessity for commerce on the offshore trade routes, the survivors now attract photographers, artists, and the general public which stands in awe of such remarkable works of man. Those edifices were constructed by skilled architects, engineers and rugged laborers who fashioned such creations under the most adverse conditions. The completed projects were done without sophisticated power tools. Tall timber was felled and cut to size as artisans went to work with rock, brick, cement, iron, lime and mortar. Masterpieces of majestic beauty rose skyward from virgin capes, plateaus, and basaltic outcrops. The good Lord provided the fantastic settings and the ingredients to build with, and then with picks, shovels, and beasts of burden, men with pride performed admirably.

Before 1850, only feeble consideration was given by the United States governmental bodies to construct lighthouses on the Pacific Coast. It was the California goldrush and Northwest timber that gave the greater incentive to get lighthouses funded and built. As coastal shipping flourished to a greater extent it became ever more apparent that there was an urgent need for aids to navigation.

Hugging the shore as the early coastal sailing vessels and steam schooners did, their mostly Scandinavian crewmen found it a dangerous occupation. Wrecks became legion, lighthouses and buoyage lacking. Even with guiding beacons and fog signals there were limitations, for lights were not visible in pea-soup fogs and deadspots could sometimes muzzle the raspy foghorns, or the sound might be carried in the wrong direction in high velocity winds. In howling gales, with driving rain, sleet or snow, weary seafarers craned their eyes and turned their ears for sight or sound of the navigation aids. When all marks were blotted out the frequent result was a wooden hull grinding over rocky, inundated ramparts in a gut-wrenching episode. Timbers torn asunder and panic-stricken seafarers and passengers fending for themselves were often times unable to get a boat over the side. Chilling saltwater without mercy would swirl along crumbling decks swelling up to peaks with tremendous force. Cargo would spew out through the splintered hatches, and rigging would come crashing down like broken spider webs. On many occasions there remained no hope for souls but to call out to God to save them. Some made the shore, some didn't, and the Pacific Coast become the graveyard for thousands of mariners who had gone down to the sea in ships.

Except for the many lighthouses, lightships, and properly positioned buoyage the toll would have been far greater. Most of the disasters occurred on or near the coastline, not in blue water. As Lord Byron once wrote:

*Roll on, thou deep and dark blue ocean, roll'
Ten thousand fleets sweep over thee in vain;
Man marks the earth with ruin,—his control
Stops with the shore.
He sinks into thy depths with bubbling groan,
Without a grave, unknell'd, uncoffin'd, and unknown.*

At old Fort Ross, in northern California, 70 miles north of San Francisco, Russia made a bid for trade and occupation in the early 1800s. Today the restored fortress is a notable tourist attraction and it was there that reputedly the first water-powered sawmill was erected. Though the foreigners failed to take advantage of the mighty redwoods, a door had been opened to a tremendous bonanza in timber. It took Captain Stephen Smith of the bark *George Henry* to envisage the possibilities when he scoped out the land in the early 1840s. So impressed was he that he purchased sawmill machinery in Baltimore and shipped it around the Horn. With help from the early settlers he set up his pioneer mill amid the redwoods at Salmon Creek, east of Bodega. From his location northward the Pacific Coast was green with untapped forests, both in California and in Oregon territory—redwood, cedar, fir, pine, hemlock and other varieties just waiting for the takers.

Another seafarer, an Englishman named William Richardson, came to California as first mate of the whaleship *Orion* in 1822 when San Francisco was referred to as Yerba Buena. He married the daughter of the Spanish Commandante, Martinez, and also became intrigued with the timber potential. In 1853 he set up a sawmill at Albion, named for his native county in England and began a prosperous business enterprise. Other pioneers moved further north to Humboldt Harbor and Crescent City to set up mills in the early 1850s. Redwood became highly prized in far-flung markets because it was slow burning, durable, beautiful when finished and possessed limited amounts of pitch. Steam driven and water-powered mills began popping up all over northern California, some 300 by 1860. At Scotia, on the Eel River, the entire town was built of redwood, several units being faced with the bark of the mighty tree.

Anatomy of an 1890s Lighthouse

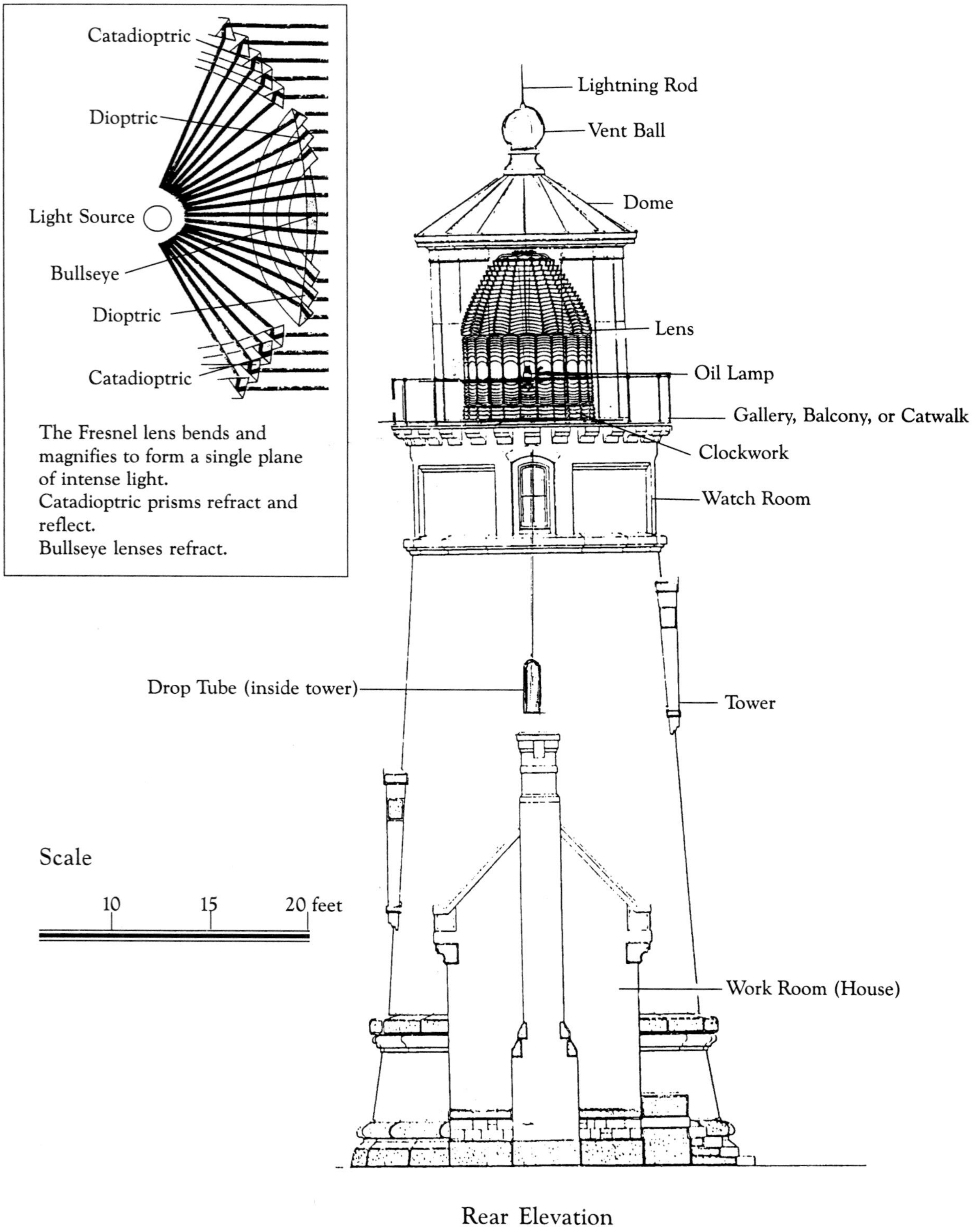

Catadioptric

Dioptric

Light Source

Bullseye

Dioptric

Catadioptric

The Fresnel lens bends and magnifies to form a single plane of intense light.
Catadioptric prisms refract and reflect.
Bullseye lenses refract.

Lightning Rod

Vent Ball

Dome

Lens

Oil Lamp

Gallery, Balcony, or Catwalk

Clockwork

Watch Room

Drop Tube (inside tower)

Tower

Work Room (House)

Scale

10   15   20 feet

Rear Elevation

The anatomy of an 1890s Pacific Coast lighthouse well before the introduction of electricity.

Other far-sighted individuals in Oregon Territory discovered the value of the Port Orford cedar and the majestic fir tree, excellent for house building and ship construction. Today, the small town of Port Gamble in Puget Sound country remains alive as the oldest mill town continually operated on the Pacific Coast. Since 1853, Pope and Talbot interests have kept the mill operating, and its port from the early days has sent billions of feet of Northwest lumber to ports the world over. It was in July of 1853 that the little 50-ton schooner *Julius Pringle* sailed north from San Francisco. Captain Talbot of Maine, part of the wealthy New England Talbots with wide-reaching shipping and lumber interests, was searching virgin country for a mill site. After skirting the shores of Admiralty Inlet and Hood Canal he found his desired haven in a deep Bay, a place that had been named Port Gamble by the Wilkes Expedition in 1841. There it was that Pope & Talbot sired its new enterprise, gaining huge acreages of timber. There a bustling town was founded where scores of commercial sailing vessels of many flags loaded capacity cargoes of raw logs and lumber. The bonanza of California was duplicated in the Pacific Northwest and along the Oregon and Washington territorial lands (including the Columbia River) where trade first started in furs, and spread to timber and finally to grain. Captain Gray of the *Columbia Rediviva* discovered the Columbia River in 1792, the last great plum of discovery on the Pacific rim, though his mission was fur trading.

Another of Puget Sound's pioneer mills was at Port Orchard where William Renton and Daniel Howard started cutting in 1854, and then built the first ship in Kitsap County, the schooner *I.I. Stevens,* named for the first governor of Washington Territory.

Even as the boom time of the California goldrush began to decline somewhat, the timber industry prospered, for there was a great migration westward by sea and land which necessitated the building of housing and factories, plus an assortment of new industry and farming. Scores of shipyards were turning out vessels of many descriptions for coastal, deepsea and harbor transport. Seacoast towns sprang up wherever the harbors were deep enough to accommodate ships, for the marine highway was for decades the main form of transportation and supply. From San Diego to Puget Sound, sailing vessels were serving every port. Steamers were still in the minority. While forestry workers were cutting multi-millions of board feet of logs and lumber, inland farmers found fertile soil for growing grain and other produce. The call grew even louder and more compelling to easterners and mid-westerners to move to the Pacific Coast. And west they came as if drawn by a magnet.

San Francisco continued its lead role as a world seaport, but new portals of trade opened in southern California at places that once housed Spanish missions. Names like Humboldt, Crescent City and a host of doghole ports in northern California became household words. Bar ports opened on the Rogue, Coquille, Coos Bay, Umpqua, Yaquina, Tillamook, Columbia River system, Shoalwater Bay, Grays Harbor and on up to the Strait of Juan de Fuca, gateway to a large number of Puget Sound and Canadian ports of entry.

Lands previously belonging to the coastal and inland Indian tribes were quickly and methodically wrenched away from those true Americans, the white juggernaut pushing them back to reservations through treaties that were worthless. The natives had occupied the stolen prop-

Pope & Talbot's lumber mill at Port Gamble on Puget Sound is the oldest continuing operation of its kind on the Pacific Coast. It dates from 1853. The mill is the lifeblood of the quaint little New England-type town. In the photo, the mill is pictured in halcyon days before the turn of the century, four tall ships awaiting cargo.

erties for countless centuries, with each generation paralleling the next. Then, like a flash of lightning, time ran out for the Indians, and their traditional world collapsed before their very eyes.

While all of this history was being made, initial surveys for logical spots for aids to navigation had continued almost unnoticed, though much in demand. Shipowners and seafarers were crying for safeguards to shipping. Hardly a week went by without news of a marine tragedy. Blind navigation often called for a shipmasters' sixth sense, a kind of game of roulette, chancy at best. Mariners often scoffed at the name Pacific, (peaceful) applied by the discoverer Balboa when he first gazed on the world's greatest ocean. The title was often misleading especially when storms born in the far northern regions swept out over vast sea masses creating mountainous swells and driving winds. Until modern times navigators searched diligently for the lighthouse beacon when danger lurked. When navigating by dead reckoning, and driving winds were ripping canvas from the yards, what more pleasant relief than to discover a landfall light piercing the murk.

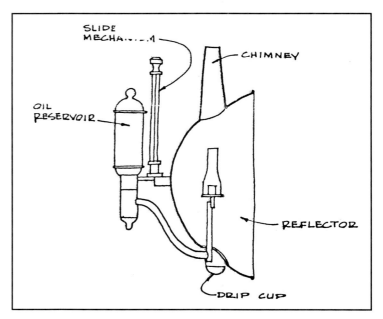

Sketch depicts the old Argand system for lighthouses. Fortunately it was replaced by the Fresnel system about the time lighthouses were being built on the Pacific Coast. It was sold to Uncle Sam in 1811 by Winslow Lewis. The parabolic reflectors and thick glass were far inferior to the new system. Sketch courtesy Jerry Hebert

It was fortunate with the advent of Pacific Coast lighthouses that a changeover from the traditional Argand lamps and reflector systems to the Fresnel lenticular system was well underway. The new mode of lighting was introduced to the world of navigation, as earlier mentioned, by French physicist Augustin Fresnel, who revolutionized the marine lighting systems on every ocean and navigable lake where aids to navigation were essential. His prismatic lenses were designed to refract and reflect the light source into one central beam of light. In other words, such creations could take a small oil flame and magnify it into a light of great intensity. Both fixed lenses and lenses rotated by clockwork mechanisms, (much like a grandfather clock) operated by a weight, made the French the world's most prominent manufacturers of the revolutionary lighting systems for several decades. The British later got on the bandwagon in the manufacture of the classic optics. Between the two countries most lighting systems the world over for major lighthouses originated either in France or England. The United States Lighthouse Service imported their Fresnel type lenses until well into the 20th century when American firms such as McBeth-Evans began producing lenses of the Fresnel type. By then, the market had begun to decline and with the advent of electricity the light source became as important as the prismatic lenses.

It was shortly after Mexico's cession of what is now the state of California to the United States that pressure fell on Uncle Sam, by shipping interests, for navigation aids. In 1848, Congress authorized (mostly in theory) several lighthouses for the Pacific Coast in the wake of surveys of prominent headlands along the coastline. The Pacific Coast had a major advantage over the east coast inasmuch that the high advantage points required in many cases shorter towers which were less expensive to build. A vexing problem however, was the difficulty of access and crude means of supply in extreme remote locations.

A bill establishing Oregon Territory provided a paltry sum for the construction of lighthouses, "out west," and two years were to pass before Congress got down to serious business. On September 28, 1850, the solons authorized funds to proceed.

Old Salt takes a sighting with his sextant. A landfall light may not be far away.

In the interim, the largest armada of commercial ships to ever enter an American port lay scattered in droves in San Francisco Bay, deserted for the most part by gold seekers, some who were to make fortunes and some who would lose everything. Business and industry had come to fruition as the new residents found that there were many opportunities in building the west. Shipping was a formidable part of the growth and the aids to navigation were vital.

Six lighthouses were to be built in California—Alcatraz Island, Fort (Battery) Point, both inside the bay of San Francisco; at isolated Farallon Islands, west of the Golden Gate; at Point Pinos near Monterey; at California's little Cape Horn, better known as Point Conception and at San Diego's Point Loma. In the Pacific Northwest, the pioneer lights were designated for Cape Disappointment at the mouth of the Columbia; at Tatoosh Island, just off Cape Flattery at the south entrance to the Strait of Juan de Fuca and at New Dungeness at the eastern end of the Strait.

The Northwest sites provided some greater difficulties than did the California sites, but the construction of each of these lighthouses presented a monumental challenge to the builders. In each case, the recommendations by the Coast Survey were accepted as the logical building sites. Prominent in that effort were A.D. Bache, superintendent; the chief topographer A.M. Harrison. Major Hartman Bache would become the Pacific Coast's first appointed Lighthouse Inspector.

All was not a dream experience. Complete dissatisfaction with the lighthouse administration led to a verbal attack in 1851 taunting Congress into appointing a board to oversee the situation. As a result, a permanent Lighthouse Board was named to administer navigational aids on all United States shorelines in 1852. The board consisted of a nine member group headed by the Secretary of the Treasury, Admiral William B. Shubrick, as chairman. The first act was to divide the country into 12 districts, with the entire Pacific Coast designated as the 12th Lighthouse District. Each district had an inspector charged with responsibility for lighthouse construction, purchase of property and major repairs as needed. The inspector was also the overseer for the installation of the lighting apparatus. Supervision of lighthouses fell to the Collector of Customs in their respective districts.

Prior to the West Coast lights coming on the scene there was much confusions among administrators. The Lighthouse Board, though not perfect, was able to accomplish considerably more than its predecessors. One of the main concerns was the type and cost of oil used in the lamps.

At first it was whale oil, but with greater demand the price gradually crept up to $1.38 a gallon. With a shortage of funds, the board looked into colza or rapeseed which came from wild cabbage. It burned well and cost less than half the price of whale oil. The problem was in acquiring sufficient amounts, which, despite the government offering an incentive to farmers to increase the yield, the effort proved unsuccessful. It was then that the Lighthouse Board returned to the use of sperm oil.

While such details were being studied, Lt. Washington A. Bartlett had been dispatched to Paris, France, to contract for lens and lighting apparatus for the Pacific Coast lighthouses.

After the initial lighthouses were completed, the delivery of oil, especially to Northwest sites, was difficult, as it had to be imported by sea. Even when whale oil was available locally, all of it had to be purchased through the Lighthouse Board which sometimes caused delays.

As to the early lighting systems, the fifth auditor of the Treasury clung tenaciously to the former inferior Argand lenses utilizing the reflector system right up until 1852, and he had suggested that the Pacific Coast lights be so equipped, but was overruled, and the Fresnel system was adopted. The controversy slowed the delivery of the equipment, but the popularity of the new system caught on so quickly that by 1859,

most of the Argands across the country were given the deep six. Though initially more costly than the old system of lighting, the savings in the amount of oil consumed more than paid for itself. The Fresnel system produced a superior light and the lamps were far more efficient as well as safer. Another oil besides whale and Colza used as an illuminant was lard oil which took over from the sperm in 1867. In the following decade came kerosene, a mineral oil refined from petroleum. By 1880 it became the principal illuminant. In that year the Lighthouse Service purchased 48,000 gallons. A decade later the total reached 330,000 gallons compared with 16,000 gallons of lard oil the same year. When the incandescent vapor oil lamps were introduced around the turn of the century the kerosene fuel produced a beam of greater intensity. The biggest innovation, however, was the later introduction of electricity, although some of the more remote lighthouses still utilized oil lamps until the early 1940s.

Undoubtedly the first contractors for the Pacific Coast lights, Francis A. Gibbons and Francis X. Kelly of Baltimore, had had second thoughts when encountering the problems involved. Eventual costs in most cases exceeded their bid to build each lighthouse for $15,000, except for Cape Disappointment, for $31,000. The total price tag for the eight lighthouses would come to $136,000. All were to be completed by November 1, 1853, but ironically none met the deadline and the government was sympathetic enough to extend the time until May 1, 1854.

In the interim, the contractors had purchased the bark *Oriole* in Baltimore to bring out the supplies and work crews. Of 1,223 tons burden, the square-rigger had her holds filled with construction materials, everything but brick and lime. Passengers included fourteen mechanics, two bricklayers, two carpenters, one painter, one blacksmith, one plasterer, two stonemasons and five laborers. William H. Hemmick was clerk and dispersing agent; Roger J. Mahon, superintendent and William J. Timanus, contractor's agent and bookkeeper.

The *Oriole* weighed anchor at Baltimore August 12, 1852, and with all sail set, commenced a rugged voyage around Cape Horn to San Francisco, entering the Golden Gate January 29, 1853. An advance party arrived the previous month and was already laying foundations at Fort Point and Alcatraz. The respective parties joined forces and construction continued with revitalized energy. The lighting apparatus, however, had yet to arrive. Moving out to the isolated and craggy Farallons, they began construction of that tower atop a steep, basaltic upheaval known as the Southeast Farallon.

Next came the lighthouse at Point Pinos near scenic Monterey. Then things began to go bad. Laden with construction materials, the *Oriole* sailed for the Columbia River with a favoring wind, the workers geared for the rigors of building a lighthouse atop Cape Disappointment. It should have been labeled "Project Disappointment," for aboard the ship were not only the building materials for Cape Disappointment but for the four remaining lighthouses as well. Within direct view of the future site of the planned lighthouse the bark was wrecked at the river entrance plunging to the bottom with her entire cargo. In perilous waters throughout the night in open boats the crew and passengers were rescued the following day, cold and miserable. Troubled, but not discouraged, the builders set about gathering replacement materials and awaited the arrival of other vessels with needed supplies.

Construction of Cape Disappointment Lighthouse and Humboldt Harbor Lighthouse was supervised by Mahon, while Timanus was named to supervise the Point Conception and Point Loma projects. Because of the setback, the Cape Disappointment job was not completed until 1856, three years behind schedule.

The rudiments of pharology were not primary in the eyes of the earlier Spanish and Russian potentates who held sway over the Pacific arena. Feeble candle type lanterns were of insignificant importance where the mission ports were located, and the Russian's best effort in Alaska was the lantern house built atop the government house at Sitka, (New Archangel) sometimes referred to as Baranof's Castle, erected in 1837. The Sandwich Islanders had a small lighthouse at Lahaina in the early 1840s.

Following in the wake of the initial eight Pacific Coast lighthouses contracted for by Gibbons & Kelly, others were put out for bid in the 1850s until all 16 originally contemplated for the Pacific Coast were completed. Beside the original eight, there were names almost unknown to the rest of America, like Umpqua River, Shoalwater (Willapa) Bay and Smith Island, (near the meeting place of the Strait of Juan de Fuca and Admiralty Inlet). Several other lighthouses were funded and built in the 1860s and 1870s, until at last mariners had a network of navigation aids all along the Pacific Coast plus improved buoyage on the harbor and river systems.

While all the effort was being promoted for safer navigation, coastal shipping was booming and new seaport towns mushroomed. Shipwreck became a household word and many early settlers built their homes and buildings from salvaged lumber drifting ashore, or filled their food cupboards with edible supplies and a variety of other items. Despite the lighthouses and buoys, sea transport grew so rapidly that the toll in ships continued, the only compensation, that it would have been much worse without the navigational aids. It also had to be remembered that human error on shipboard was the cause of many wrecks, plus the over usage of alcohol, and in extreme cases, barratry.

First departure from sail on the North Pacific was provided by the little steamer *Beaver* which was sent out from England in 1835 to be the workhorse for the Hudson's Bay Company. Arriving as a brig, she had her sidewheels and steam plant assembled at Fort Vancouver. For the most part, however, sail reigned in the following decades, due to wind conditions prevailing along the Pacific Coast, schooners proved most practical until steam finally came into its own. Ships could be found frequenting every harbor from San Diego to Tacoma. General cargo came north, lumber went south. Everything from pianos to pea-

Vintage photo of the crew of the schooner Jennie Thelin, *one of the early coastal schooners, a classic shot of the type of men who formed the so-called "Scandanavian Navy," those rugged seafarers that manned the fleet so familiar with Pacific Coast Lighthouses. Captain Edward Jensen, master of the vessel, is seated at the center of the photo which was taken in 1903. John Matson, part of the Matson Navigation family is at the left. The schooner was built near the old Santa Cruz Lighthouse in 1869. She ended her days in Mexico.* Photo courtesy of diver and historian Peter Jensen of Palos Verdes, California

Unique to the Pacific Coast were the wooden steam schooners. Here is a close-up view of the steam schooner Santa Ana, *ready to take on a large cargo of lumber on Puget Sound. Of a coastal fleet of nearly 250, only the* Wapama *survives as a museum ship in San Francisco.*

nuts traveled in the holds of the coasters, and passengers were often sandwiched in with the cargo.

Though many savvy skippers of many different backgrounds ran the coasters, it was mostly the Scandinavians, and when sailing schooners became steam schooners the fleet was labeled as the "Scandinavian Navy." Such swarthy men of the sea who weren't deterred by the dangers that existed in such an occupation were often the butt of jokes by the so-called blue water sailors who referred to them as "squareheads." In all truth, the coasting trade was much more hazardous and exacting than for square-rigger hands who spent the bulk of their voyaging experiences on the open sea where disaster was not as frequent as when dodging in and out of perilous dogholes. In either case, lighthouses were essential to all mariners, the overseas ships seeking a landfall light after a long voyage, or the coasters sailing close to shore searching for each light when nightfall closed down.

Great danger faced the crew of the schooners when they loaded redwood lumber under wire chutes in open water moorages in northern California, or when trying to maneuver in tight places when the wind died and the canvas drooped. A great innovation for the trouble-plagued coasters came in 1880 when an inventive seafarer, name unknown, came up with the suggestion of supplementing the small sailing craft with steam engines. Many believe that the first of the fleet to be so equipped was the Mendocino schooner *Beda*. Others attributed the honors to the

Newport, Laguna, Surprise, or the *Alex Duncan,* but whatever vessel it was, steam had come to stay in coastwise tradelanes and a vast fleet of steam schooners would become the standard, a type of vessel exclusive to the Pacific Coast. No longer would coastal sailing vessels be forced to lie at anchor awaiting favorable winds, and no longer would small rivers and shallow bays be inaccessible for the lumber carriers.

Typical of the steam schooner skippers, was a stocky individual, square-jawed with chin whiskers, sometimes profane, sometimes jolly, a man who had come up through the hawse pipe from generations of seafarers. Some of them fought the metamorphosis from sail to steam, gently growling every inch of the way.

One thing the navigators of the coastwise vessels all agreed upon was the importance of the lighthouses. Though all commerce at sea depended on the aids to navigation, we have somewhat dwelled on the coastwise ships because they plied the dangerous coastal waters exclusively. Shipbuilding of wooden-hulled sailing vessels and later steam schooners caught on mostly where the lumber mills were located, and San Francisco became the homeport of the majority of the ships, where most of the engines and boilers were assembled. Pacific Northwest ports became increasingly more important because of the abundance of fir and other evergreen timber used in shipbuilding and house construction.

The first steam schooner launched fully equipped with her steam engine intact was the Robert Dollar-owned steamer *Newsboy,* which slid down the ways at the Boole & Beaton yard in San Francisco in 1888. She was the forerunner of a vast fleet of similar vessels owned by nearly 100 different companies and serving nearly 60 lumber ports in northern California alone. Among the fleet there was probably not a single vessel that was free of scars sustained in scraping over outcrops and obstructions during their life span. Many others left their rotting bones in maritime graveyards along the entire coast.

Many of the former lumber ports are only in memory today while other fledgling portals became world-wide ports—San Diego, Los Angeles, San Francisco, Portland, Seattle, and Tacoma to name a few. Operations such as Matson Navigation, Alaska Steamship, and the Pacific Coast Steamship companies became household words. Crack passenger liners steamed along the Pacific shores—vessels like the *Queen, Santa Rosa, State of California* and numerous others. Redondo, Port Los Angeles, Santa Barbara and Hueneme were popular ports. As some of the smaller ports declined, major passenger liners began concentrating on San Diego, Los Angeles, San Francisco, Portland and Seattle. All the while additional aids to navigation were required and provided at strategic locations to provide safer passage.

Going back in the mists of time, the earliest aids to navigation on the Pacific Coast were kept by the coastal Indian tribes, the so called "canoe Indians" of the Pacific Northwest. Though the skillful tribal paddlers seldom got out of sight of land they killed whale and seal in open waters and at times were swept offshore or curtailed by fog. When night came on, huge bonfires were kindled to guide the errant canoes home. Sometimes they were lost and never returned to their villages. Probably the most competent among the coastal Indians at small craft handling were the Clatsops at the mouth of the Columbia, and the Makahs from Cape Flattery down to Lake Ozette in what is now the northwest corner of the United States. In the early 1800s, Lewis and Clark claimed the Clatsops to be the best at handling canoes in wild surf and rough ocean waters that they had ever seen. The partners in the expedition were astounded by such exceptional skill.

When one considers that the greater part of the Pacific Coast was the land of the Indians, where they freely fished the waters and hunted the forests unmolested by intruders for nameless centuries, the white man's invasion seems almost unconscionable. To push the true Americans into subjection and privation was a travesty in its own time. Still, where time would have stood still without the caucasian intervention, progress would have been thwarted. It was inevitable that the weaker would be conquered by the stronger as history has proven over and over.

It wasn't until the era of the 1890s that most every vital part of the coastal and harbor areas of the Pacific Coast were lighted, one arc of light overlapping the next all along the Pacific Coast. At last the west was catching up with its counterparts of the eastern and gulf shorelines. Our northerly neighbors in British Columbia had also jumped on the bandwagon starting with initial lighthouses on their side of the Strait of Juan de Fuca. Fisgard and Race Rocks Lights were both established in 1861 at the south end of Vancouver Island. Some years later came Pachena, Cape Beale and Carmanah. The Territory of Alaska had been almost overlooked until the feverish goldrush of 1897. What the goldrush was to Alaska (even though the big strike was on Canadian soil) it brought a near repetition of what occurred in the 1849 California stampede. Seattle became the jumping off port, the clarion call being "north to Alaska," and the miners came in droves. Ships of every description, seaworthy or not, joined the armada and at that time in history both Canada and the United States scurried to get the Inside Passage to Alaska made safer with aids to navigation. Before that could be accomplished the toll in lives and ships became a major nightmare.

Synonymous with the lighthouses, United States Lifesaving stations were established at vital locations along the Pacific Coast and their valiant crews performed admirably. Frequently the lighthouse keepers would alert the lifesavers when a ship was in distress.

Some lighthouse keepers in the Pacific Northwest made extra cash on the side by selling salvaged goods from wrecked ships within a near radius of their respective lighthouses. The term "mooncussers" was seldom heard on the Pacific Coast. It originated on the east coast and earlier in England, referring to the nefarious scheme of villainous, malevolent culprits who would place a lantern on the horns of a beast of burden on a dark night in order to lure a ship into a hostile shore and certain destruction, after which the wreckers would storm aboard, kill the survivors, and loot the vessel of its cargo. The name mooncusser came from the fact that the vandals could not perform their violent acts on moonlit nights. There appears to be no recorded record of such behavior on the Pacific Coast. However, before the coming of the white man, such acts were not uncommon, for when a castaway ship was thrown up near an Indian settlement it was an age-old tradition that anything brought ashore by the action of the sea became the possession of the tribe. Any survivors were taken as slaves, and if resistance occurred, the victims were killed. Little time was wasted in stripping a wreck of copper, brass, iron, or any other item that might be of value to the Indian. Early history reveals that castaways, such as Japanese and Spaniards were taken as slaves. They lived and served among the natives, sometimes intermarrying and were occasionally elevated to tribal status by their skills. Such incidences were common among coastal tribes well before written history. Most common among the castaways were the Japanese, whose junks of inferior quality became disabled at sea (Japanese junks were inferior to Chinese junks inasmuch as they had no watertight compartments like the latter—they also had poor sailing qualities and were never designed to depart Japanese waters, in fact it was forbidden) and drifted toward the Northwest with the Kuro Shiro—the Japanese Current—and were then carried ashore by the prevailing offshore winds and Davidson currents.

The practice of shanghaiing was common in the years following the California goldrush era, and in later years at bustling Port Townsend and other Puget Sound ports, as well as Portland and Astoria. Most notorious was the Barbary Coast of San Francisco, so rotten that it was sometimes referred to as a corridor of Hell. Seafaring men weary from long voyages were befriended falsely by boarding house crimps, eventually drugged, clubbed, or beaten while under the influence of rot-gut whiskey, only to wake up on the rolling deck of an outbound sailing ship. The rigorous life of a seaman was demanding, underpaid, and often cruel. Master crimps like the thickset Irishman Shanghai Kelly of San Francisco was just one of the wretched individuals who made a fortune in blood money.

Even today, one can find remnants on the Port Townsend waterfront of dives where hungry square-rigger shipmasters, short of hands, paid well for unwilling replacements. On one occasion when pickings were slim a reverend was kidnapped right off the street and forced to go to sea against his will.

Can the reader imagine the terrible frustration of such a person seeing the gleam of the lighthouse fading in the distance as the ship headed for the distant horizon on a miserable voyage before the mast.

Powerful tugs were employed in the days of sail to tow the big square-riggers to and from the sea, down the Columbia River, from Puget Sound ports and San Francisco. Lumber ports like Port Blakely, Port Madison, Port Discovery, Utsaladdy, Port Ludlow and Port Gamble were filled with tall ships before and after the turn of the century. The largest lumber mill of its kind was located at Port Blakely, and its small harbor was usually lined with square-riggers. Today it's a ghost port, only a few bits and pieces of the old mill scattered about, and the flour-

Port Townsend as it appeared in the 1880s. People of this town long agitated for a lighthouse at Point Wilson to guide ships into its harbor, the waterfront, often referred to as the "Little Barbary Coast," in early times. Photo courtesy Redding Studio

Busy Port Blakely mill town in 1881, the harbor filled with tall ships. The town was founded by Captain William Renton in 1863.

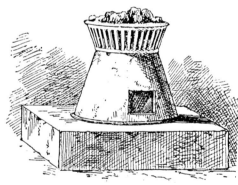

For hundreds of years, from ancient times, lighthouses featured open braziers that burned wood or coal from the crest of stone towers. It was rugged and demanding for those who kept the fires for ships, often times the smoke being sighted before the flame.

ishing shipyard where scores of wooden hulled ships were built is but a memory.

It all seems like a dream when one considers the changes that have taken place over the last century and a half. Though the lighthouses have played a major role in the maritime history of the west it is painful to see them relegated to a role of little importance in our time. Fully equipped harbor buoys are now far more important to navigation than are the lighthouses. It all started in 1939 when the United States Coast Guard took over the former United States Lighthouse Service and began a tormenting program of changes and replacements. Then came the big blow with the introduction of automation in the 1950s and 1960s. As personnel gradually faded from the scene an era of neglect and vandalism hit the historic old structures. Some lighthouses were abandoned, some razed, others vandalized. Windows were shattered, and in some cases, lenses damaged. Lower tower windows were cemented over or sealed, and high fences were placed around the towers for protection, and the one-time large reservations surrounding the beacon towers were turned over to other agencies for various uses. The old keepers residences were used for other purposes. As mentioned, the destructive era for many of the veteran watch towers was mostly ended by public pressure on the Coast Guard and the general public getting involved to save the lighthouses that had not yet been sold or abandoned. As a result, preservation societies have been organized across the country and many money raising efforts have kept that part of historic America alive.

For well over 2,000 years lighthouses have existed in the world, the first being open fire braziers atop towers in the Mediterranean. The Pacific Coast got in only on the final chapter, and the lights grow dimmer with passing decades, now that satellite navigation is able to pinpoint one's location any place in the world, even with a hand-sized computer. Indeed, we have come to twilight time for the lighthouses, a time when except for the commercial fishing vessels and small craft, ocean going vessels travel 15 to 25 miles offshore unless approaching a port. Most coastwise transit is beyond the scope of the seacoast beacons. In addition, vessels large and small are equipped with an array of navigational equipment including radio, sonar, radar, and other gadgets capable of seeing through any kind of weather.

Not all of our Pacific Coast lighthouses have a great story to tell. Some had routine, but faithful existences while others are filled with dramatic, sometimes disastrous incidents that though anomalous, capture the imagination. Still each sentinel has a personality of its own and everyone is intriguing in its own right.

No longer the keeper to set the light,
No longer the guardian to watch the night,
No longer the Fresnel to light the way,
No longer a horn by night or day.

—JAG

2. Contrasts: Cape Flattery & Point Loma Lighthouses

The landfall light where can it be?
After dreary days on timeless sea.

—JAG

We will first study the most northerly of the ocean front lighthouses in our narrative and contrast it with the most southerly. We will then commence a pictorial walk and aerial viewing of all the lighthouses in between.

✸ Cape Flattery

We begin with the lighthouse that stands proudly at the very northwest tip of the contiguous United States. The purpose of beginning here is not that Cape Flattery Lighthouse on Tatoosh Island was the very first lighthouse on the coast, but that its history best illustrates the way the white man purloined a piece of terra firma which belonged to the Makah Indians for countless centuries, an islet that had served as their center for fishing and for their whaling and seal hunting exploits. Tatoosh, less than a mile from the mainland, is a treasure trove of history. On the oldest charts Cape Flattery bore the name Punta Martinez in honor of the Portuguese navigator who logged it in 1774. The Englishman, Captain James Cook, renamed it Cape Flattery in 1778 while searching for the fabled Northwest Passage in the HMS *Resolution.* It was however, the disputed claims of the Greek, Apostolos Valerianos, who assumed the Spanish name of Juan de Fuca, that first called attention to the cape, the pillar, and what we know today as the Strait of Juan de Fuca. His avowed discovery dates from 1595 and his name remains as historical evidence that his claim was valid.

Cook first viewed the area under leaden skies, its appearance foreboding. There, up to 200 inches of rain fall annually and gales are frequent. The nasty weather thwarted the English explorer from further examination, and he lay to awaiting the new day. A furious gale then forced him to sea, and without finding the Strait he bore away to the northwest and left further discovery to the likes of Barkley, Vancouver, Gray, and others.

The entire vicinity of Cape Flattery and its offshore islet point to a prehistoric upheaval of the land mass where pounding seas have carved a myriad of strange figurations of rock, reefs, and crags that pop up here and there like rotted teeth. Beetling cliffs and weird caves abound on Tatoosh and along the mainland shores. The top of the isle has rifts as if it was rototilled by Satan's pitchfork. Names abound such as Deadman's Rock and Cave of the Winds.

Despite the punishing seas that swirl about and the unusual contour of land, the Makah Indians centered their summer activities there, going seaward with dugout canoes in search of salmon, whale, and seal, so important to a unique lifestyle.

In the Makah dialect, Tatoosh meant Thunder Bird, probably named because of the isle's resemblance to a large bird. Sitting solitary, three-quarters of a mile from shore the insular dot consists of a mere 18 acres, which erodes a little each year. Makah legend claims that when their mythical bird opened its mouth thunder bellowed, and lightning was caused by the flashing of its eye when angry. From prehistoric times the Indians had frequented Tatoosh. The rub came when the early government surveys determined that it was the only logical place to erect a lighthouse, despite any resistance the Makahs might offer. It was then that the sparks began to fly. It was only natural that the natives would object to uninvited intruders who were about to wrest away their coveted isle.

The early surveyors were part of a joint Army-Navy commission who arrived aboard the steamer *Massachusetts* to scope out the possibilities. The natives stood in awe of the smoke-blowing vessel which literally dwarfed their canoes. Immediately followed the U.S. survey schooner *Ewing* with certified surveyors of the United States Coast Survey. They were under the authority of William P. McArthur on that 1849-50 undertaking. Results of the survey were dispatched to A.D. Bache, superintendent of the Coast Survey, and accordingly approved. In the ensuing months Congress allotted $39,000 to the Lighthouse Board to construct lighthouses at Cape Flattery (Tatoosh) and the earlier mentioned New Dungeness Lighthouse. Superintendent of Construction was to be Isaac Smith.

When George Davidson arrived with the construction crew there were 150 Indians on the island and it was occupied amid threats and attempts at pilfering landed supplies. The workers moved with trepidation, fearing an outright attack. Had it occurred, the outnumbered intruders would probably have been massacred. As it was, the initial act was to issue muskets to all hands and to build a breastwork (temporary fortress) to protect themselves. Not only was there danger from the Makahs, but on occasion the much more hostile Haidas might arrive in their war canoes from northern British Columbia on one of their Viking-type raids.

It was a touch-and-go situation from the initial landings by the surveyors up to and after the lighthouse was completed. The construction crew was warned about retaliation even when supplies were stolen—anything to keep a fracas from starting. To insure their safety, the U.S. government steamer *Active* was summoned to the area to warn the Indians of reprisals in case of an attack.

The clangorous reports from shipboard cannon put fear in the hearts of the natives, and though troublesome, they gradually became somewhat passive and a few were even engaged to afford assistance with their canoes.

Suddenly a dreaded killer came among the Makahs. Smallpox broke out among the 2,000 local natives and they began dying off in droves.

It appears like a toy boat wrecked in an artificial setting. In actuality it is the troop transport General M.C. Meiggs *which was dashed on the rocks just south of Cape Flattery on January 9, 1972, after snapping the tow line from a Navy tug while being towed to layup at California's Suisun Bay. The 600-foot hull broke in two amidships when wrapped around a tall sea-stack of solid rock.* Photo courtesy E.A. Delanty

Opposite page:
In its heyday, when inhabited, both the lighthouse and the U.S. Weather Bureau station along with the families of attendants made isolated Tatoosh Island a place of activity. Photo courtesy U.S. Coast Guard

Mournful wailing was heard in the villages in the form of death knells. The white man had brought a terrible curse upon them and they had no resistance to the disease. Makahs referred to the white man as "Bostons" and the word was spoken in spiteful tones. Unable to stand against the intruders with half of their tribe already dead, they had little recourse.

How much was a treaty worth to the local Indians? The island and adjoining cape had been home to the Makah for eons of time, including Waadah Island and the village of Neah Bay, south to Lake Ozette and vicinity. It had been their earthly Valhalla, a hunk of terra firma rich in fish, game, roots, berries, and timber. In the treaty of 1855, Uncle Sam offered them $30,000 and set aside 20,000 acres for their use. It was perhaps a better deal than most of the Northwest Indian tribes were offered, but when and if that money was ever paid is unknown to this writer. Fortunately, because of the reservation, and the eventual Olympic National Park, that corner of the United States has remained, for the most part, virgin territory, with no major highways running through the bulk of the ocean coastline. In the offer, the government was to gain unrestricted useage of Tatoosh and control over the reservation.

It was a race between the individual construction crews at both Tatoosh and New Dungeness as to which lighthouse would be completed first. As it turned out, the Dungeness crew won the race by a scant 14 days, but it was a moral victory for the men on Tatoosh because of the difficult location. Smith had his work cut out for him as supervisor of the two projects both of which were completed by demanding work and devotion in the year 1857. Just getting the building supplies to the respective locations was a task in itself. Still, with completion there was no small amount of jubilation among the maritime interests of the Pacific Northwest.

Already Collector of Customs Morris H. Frost was virtually tearing his hair out over the unanticipated problems arising at Tatoosh. He had nominated George H. Gerrish of Port Townsend to be principal keeper with assistants James Berry, William Webster, and George Fitzgerald. After only three months, all except Berry resigned, citing poor pay and miserable conditions. They further complained of inferior lard oil when trimming the lamp inside the big first order Fresnel lens.

Frost then named Franklin Tucker to replace Gerrish along with assistants John Thompson and James Mutch. All of them resigned after a little more than two months complaining of paltry pay and troublesome Indians. It appeared that the brick and sandstone edifice had also developed roof leaks from the incessant rains, and drafts from the howling gales.

At times, the Indians actually occupied the lighthouse in large numbers and became defiant when ordered to leave.

F.W. James was then named as principal keeper after mariners had reported that the tower light was not showing a brilliance at sea. The revenue cutter *Jeff Davis* had to loan the keeper two of his crew as assistants. Eventually the irons were worked out and life on the little isle settled down to normal lighthouse keeping. But then by the wayside went James, and in 1860, Captain William W. Winsor of Port Angeles assumed command. That same year the roof blew off the old blockhouse and it eventually fell into ruins, the danger from the natives having subsided. By that date better fuel was being supplied for the lamp and with faithful cleaning of the lens prisms the light glowed brightly each night.

In 1878, a weather station was erected on the island, and the keepers had neighbors. Then families of attendants were allowed to live on the isle, and additional buildings appeared. For a while, there was even a small school for the children of the keepers and the weather personnel, but it closed in 1908.

Eventually, the Canadians established lighthouses at the north entrance to the Strait, (Vancouver Island) Cape Beale in 1874 and Carmanah in 1891. The set of the winter storms and current systems drove ships to destruction on the shores at both sides of the wide entrance, the general area becoming well known as a marine graveyard. While searching for the missing ship *Ivanhoe* in 1894, U.S. revenue cutters counted the remains of 34 wrecks on Vancouver Island's west shoreline. A year later the handsome square-rigger *Janet Cowan* became a total loss with seven of her crew perishing.

The three lightships that had served on Umatilla Reef since 1898 until the anchorage was terminated in 1971. Upper right is the No. 67 the first to mark the reef. She served until 1930. The No. 88 switched to the reef from the Columbia River station (upper), and lower is the WAL-196, last on duty at the lonely post, named for the SS Umatilla *which smashed into the uncharted reef in the 1880s.*

Around the turn of the century a terrible toll in lives and property occurred after grossly overloaded ships signaled the lighthouse on Tatoosh and passed out to sea, never to be seen again. Among the unfortunate victims was the HMS *Condor* which vanished with her entire complement of 104. Earlier, the steamer *Pacific* went down in 1875 after being struck by the ship *Orpheus*. More than 275 persons went to a watery grave, only two surviving, one of them later succumbing. Other ships listed as missing in the dark waters around the Strait entrance included the steamers *Montserrat* and *Keewenaw,* rung down by Lloyds as lost with all hands.

Tatoosh Island's one landing spot (before helicopters) at its north end affords the only access to the 100 foot plateau. The lantern room is about 150 feet above sea level affording a magnificent view in all directions, including the 30 mile stretch of water northwestward to Vancouver Island. Southward lie Flattery Rocks, and Umatilla Reef once guarded, (beginning in 1898) by the Umatilla Reef Lightship. It was in 1883 that the SS *Umatilla,* a staunch iron-hulled coastal vessel crashed into the then uncharted reef and almost went to Davy Jones' Locker. Except for the uncanny skill of her first officer, Captain "Dynamite" Johnny O'Brien, who managed to get on some sail, pump the bilges, and float her free of the reef after the rest of the crew had abandoned, her remains would still be there. Ironically, with assistance, the vessel made it to Esquimalt, B.C. before sinking in the harbor. Raised, repaired, and rebuilt as a coastwise passenger steamer, she enjoyed a long career.

The light continued to burn nightly at Cape Flattery Lighthouse and was later joined by a steam-operated fog whistle which was blown whenever the weather closed down. Later came a much more effective diaphragm horn that when standing near could shake one out of his boots. In later years the station was equipped with a radiobeacon and distance finding apparatus from which a ship could take its bearings. The light was later changed from a first order fixed lens to a 4th order revolving Fresnel, visible for 17 miles. In the original fixed lens of French manufacture, which ended up in pieces on the Seattle waterfront, was a red sector which fell across Duncan Rock, a ridged-back basaltic outcrop that had the potential to cut sharply into any ship in harms way. When a vessel fell under the beam in the red sector, it was time to put the helm hard over and reverse course. The lens was so arranged as to refract and reflect upon a space, scarcely a foot wide, called the focal plane.

Danger of fire was always a concern in seagirt lighthouses. On Tatoosh as well as at other early lighthouses the lamp oil was kept from exploding by a plunger which lay upon the surface of the fuel in a tank and forced it into the lamp through tubes fitted with delicate valves. The oil houses where fuel was stored were kept well away from the tower and residences for obvious reasons. Before the advent of electricity, however, the danger of fire was always a concern and one reason why so many lighthouses were built with brick and stone masonry and metal, tile, or slate roofs. With the exception of some of the early Canadian lighthouses, lantern houses were built of iron, some with copper tops.

Despite heavy construction, winter storms, which create giant waves at Tatoosh Island cause the tower to vibrate and tremble as if in a slight earthquake. Before automation, it was a lonely occupation during the long vigils by nightfall and keeper resignation was not uncommon. One such early keeper at Tatoosh who was terrified by the storm's wrath refused to stand his watch in the tower, and tendered his resignation. Given a bad time by his fellow keepers he was driven to fling himself into the ocean. Many hours later his inert body was spotted on the rocks where the keepers managed to revive him. At the first opportunity a boat picked him up and took him ashore, and he kept a wide berth from anything that resembled a lighthouse for the rest of his life.

The old Lighthouse Service dealt with many transfers, mostly petty and sometimes violent disagreements which often erupted when men in isolation were separated from the world at large over long periods of time. In days of yore duty was essential at each lighthouse and no matter how tremulous the night, the light had to be kept burning brightly at all times and that meant keeping the outer panes of the lantern house clear on the outside as well as the inside in addition to tending the lens and lamp. In many lighthouses, winding up the weight in the clockwork mechanism every four hours was necessary to keep the proper rotation of the lens. That, however, was not necessary when Cape Flattery had a fixed order lens which remained stationary.

Because of its location off the mainland, the beams from the powerful beacon on Tatoosh caused large numbers of seabirds to be temporarily blinded and crash against the outer panes. In some cases birds were known to crack the plate glass. Such incidences usually occurred on stormy nights with strong winds.

With the presence of the Weather Bureau station on the isle it was necessary to have communication with the shore in the early days, and accordingly, a vital submarine cable was laid. On many occasions the rough seas severed that link. It was usually restored shortly afterwards for at one time the weather station was one of the most important in the nation, bristling with scientific instruments located in a building held down with rods and chains against the heavy winds.

For several decades, outside of the lighthouse tenders who supplied the station, communication and transport was done by Indian canoe. When weather and sea conditions were right Indian paddlers made the seven mile trip from Neah Bay. The best known of the messengers was a native called "Old Doctor" who often delivered the mail and supplies. Skillful and experienced, he nevertheless had three dugout canoes smashed to kindling while attempting a landing at Tatoosh in rough seas. Frequently the mail bag had to be thrown ashore and retrieved by a keeper standing on the lower rocks.

Lifting containers of oil and heavy equipment brought by the lighthouse tenders necessitated the use of a derrick and a boom. Personnel could also be lifted onto the rock in an attached basket of sorts.

An island or rock station was more relaxed than shore stations, the blue uniforms seldom worn until news of the inspector's arrival when all had to be spit and polish under the old United States Lighthouse Service. Tower, residence, oil houses, storage units, grounds, and of course the lighting and fog signal equipment, had to be in topflight condition or the principal keeper was reprimanded. A log was kept daily, much as on shipboard and oil and water supplies had to be closely monitored. The general routine of the oldtime keepers (usually a head keeper and three assistants at isolated stations), was on a rotating basis of eight watch hours around the clock with each taking his trick at cooking and standby. There was constant housekeeping, painting, and the polishing of glass and brass, as well as keeping the lamp trimmed and all machinery operating properly. Spare time involved various hobbies, and reading and writing letters. Most keepers desired stations that did not have fog signals as it was not only an irritating sound over long periods of time but required more work than tending the light. It was an advance when the steam whistles were replaced with sirens, diaphones and diaphragm fog signals, for it eliminated feeding the boiler fire box with tons of coal. Compressors and generators proved much more practical.

Under the old system, employing civil servants, service was eleven months of duty and one month vacation, not exactly a situation that would make for a happy family when a keeper was assigned to a station that made no provisions for women or children.

Just below Cape Flattery, southward, a giant sea stack, long known as Fuca Pollar, rises skyward to an elevation of 140 feet. It bears the name of its reputed discoverer, Juan de Fuca. The Makahs had an age-old legend that involved the uniquely fashioned natural phenomenon.

When last manned by Coast Guardsman this is the method used to lift supplies and personnel up to the plateau of Tatoosh Island.

island's needs. Both operated out of the 13th Lighthouse District headquarters.

There was always marine activity at the entrance to the Strait of Juan de Fuca, and from the 1880s big steam tugs hovered nearby to tow the big square-riggers to both American and Canadian ports. It was the tug *Wanderer* of the Puget Sound Tug Boat Company that saved the passenger liner *City of Puebla* from going on the rocks near Cape Flattery after her shaft broke down around the turn of the century. Sailing vessels, outbound, hoisted billowing sheets of canvas in picking up the prevailing winds and setting courses for ports the world over.

In olden days the lighthouses had their limitations, and it was always a seeming travesty when a ship was wrecked within sight of any aid to navigation—embarrassing for the navigator and frustrating to the light keeper. For instance, such was the case when the bark *Matilda* rammed into the rocks in the shadow of Tatoosh Island, in September 1897, and became a total loss. It occurred on a clear night and the light was plainly visible. The aging vessel got caught in irons, or in other words in a powerful insetting tide, strong currents and confused seas followed by a wind that failed.

It was the many shipwrecks in and around the general area that prompted the placement of the lightship *SS Umatilla,* south of Cape Flattery in 1898, and the lightship *Swiftsure* off the west entrance to the Strait of Juan de Fuca in 1909.

Today Cape Flattery Lighthouse stands in complete solitude. No longer are there the sounds of humans dashing to and fro over the isle's plateau. Service crews come out on occasion to check out the light and cater to its needs. In September of 1990, a joint Coast Guard-Army rehabilitation crew was dispatched to the island for a major overhaul of the circa 1857 edifice. Part of that crew was Ed Peterson, former mayor of Waldport, Oregon. The overall project was in charge of Commander Greg Evans, of the Coast Guard Support Center at Alameda, California. The work included sandblasting the tower inside and out including all steel surfaces on the lantern housing and dome; replacing the plate glass and window frames; thermo-sealing the lighthouse dwelling and tower and repairing the roof of the dwelling. Both Coast Guard helicopters and Army Chinook copters were utilized as well as ridged-hull inflatable craft. All work was done by Coast Guard Reserve personnel, the heavy lift materials brought in by the big Army Chinooks. Remarkably, the mobilization on and off the project, and the completed work was accomplished in only 45 days, with a basic crew of eight.

The buildings on Tatoosh, with the exception of the lighthouse and its attached dwelling, lie in ruins. The light still glows but not with the importance it once enjoyed. Gone are the majestic sailing vessels, steam schooners and coastal passenger ships once such a familiar sight from the isle. Instead, container ships, tankers, bulkers, nuclear submarines and sophisticated fishing vessels pass near the insular dot. All are equipped with radar, sonar, direction finders, ship to shore radio and many new computerized push-button gadgets. Such innovations would cause the traditional old salt to turn over in his grave.

From a distance it appears as a carved column. The legend tells of a young brave in the tribe who had somehow managed to scale the "obelisk" while hunting for duck eggs. The fear of descending from his perilous perch left him virtually paralyzed. A wrong step would have seen him hurdled to the rocks below. Instead, he elected to stay atop despite the futile efforts of his tribesmen to get him down, or to encourage his descent. According to the legend, he eventually met his death by starvation. To this day, many of the local Indians believe that his spirit stands guard over the sea stack and consider it sacred ground.

During former years, before the takeover by the Coast Guard, the faithful lighthouse tenders *Columbine* and *Manzanita* supplied the

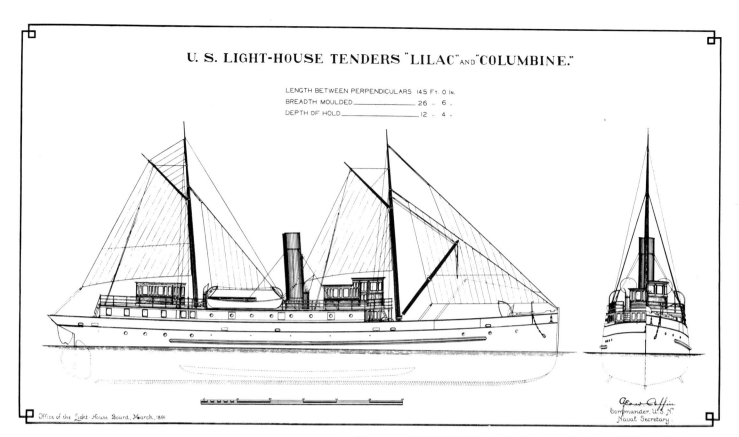

U. S. LIGHT-HOUSE TENDERS "LILAC" AND "COLUMBINE."

LENGTH BETWEEN PERPENDICULARS 145 FT. 0 IN.
BREADTH MOULDED _____ 26 " 6 "
DEPTH OF HOLD _____ 12 " 4 "

Office of the Light-House Board, March, 1891

Commander, U.S.N.
Naval Secretary.

Above:
Outline profile of the U.S. Lighthouse tenders Columbine *and* Lilac, *which performed stellar service in supplying lighthouses and tending buoys. The* Columbine *was indispensable in its service to the early Pacific Northwest lighthouses. Built in 1892, at a cost of $92,000, the vessel carried a crew of 26.*

Right:
Vintage photo of the Cape Flattery Lighthouse taken just after the turn of the century by Lighthouse keeper Thomas. Later, the government allowed families of the keepers and the weather station personnel to live on the small island. At one time some 12 families lived on the diminutive, rockbound isle. The weekly mail and supplies were lifted from the boat by an overhanging derrick crane. A school and post office was once located there as well as a temporary naval presence. The impossibility of landing or delivering supplies during heavy weather made it advisable to carry enough food for six months. On one October day in 1939 the light keepers counted as many as 436 trollers (fishing vessels) within a radius of five miles of Tatoosh.
Photo courtesy Tom Reid

The Coast Guard has a presence in Port Angeles, LaPush, and at Neah Bay where an "electronic eye" can be kept on Tatoosh, and even with revolutionary navigation aids it appears that the light on the island will not be doused in the near future, mostly because of its strategic location. The place is off limits to the general public but to the thousands of seafaring folk manning every type of sea going craft, including the Swiftsure yacht racers, it is indeed a familiar sight.

From the extreme northwest corner of the outer coastline of Washington state we go to the extreme southerly end of the California coast to offer a contrast between the histories and the future status of these two very different lighthouses. From Cape Flattery to Point Loma is a distance of several hundreds of miles but the lighthouses at each end of the line have intriguing stories to tell.

❀ Point Loma

Old Point Loma, among the first lighthouses erected on the coast, is undoubtedly one of the most visited and most photographed in the United States, sitting princely on the top of a timeless ridge of land in the middle of the Cabrillo National Monument that offers spectacular vistas in every direction.

While no longer serving its intended role as the major lighthouse in the greater San Diego area, it has been restored to its former splendor, while turning over the main duties to its offspring, the newer (as of 1891) Point Loma Lighthouse which guards the entrance to the Silver Gate at a considerably lower elevation than its aging mother. This pioneer sentinel, the highest on the coast, resides at an elevation 420 feet above sea level where it has stood through good times and bad times since 1854. When construction was started initially, the great headland on which it was to stand had only sparse population in the area. There was some fishing and whaling operations located at Ballast Point on the lee side of the harbor entrance, near the site of an old Spanish fortress, and where another lighthouse was finally placed in 1890. Most of the activities however, were centered at a little village called Roseville.

For centuries the surrounding lands were roamed by the dark Diegueno Indians who roamed through the chaparral, hunting for game. Next came the Spanish and Mexican regimes before Uncle Sam got his foot in the door. Until that latter event little consideration was given to aids to navigation. It is claimed that when a Spanish supply ship was due in olden times a feeble oil lantern was hung from a post at Ballast Point. It was not until the Mexican War and the San Francisco flurry during the goldrush era that the United States got down to business about placing a major lighthouse on Loma.

The building of the lighthouse was anything but an easy go. All materials and supplies had to be hauled to the summit of the bumpy monolith over rock-strewn roads which followed the ancient trails used by the natives for centuries. Cutting through the chaparral, beasts of burden were indispensable in the arduous and demanding task of supply and transport. In the interim, blatant arguments had exploded among the local folk as to where the lighthouse should be located. Earlier, the Coast Survey authorities had determined the desired place should be near the south end of Point Loma but the contract awarded to Gibbons & Kelly stated nothing more than "a lighthouse at San Diego." The contractors protested that the suggested site of the Coast Survey was inadequate because of the necessity of a road involving the building of temporary bridges to reach the location. It would be a cost overrun, they insisted, and in turn protested to the Lighthouse Board which offered them the option of dropping the contract. Second thoughts prompted the contractors to proceed in April 1854, and at last the structure began to take shape. The design was virtually the same as the other early lighthouses contracted for—a Cape Cod type dwelling with a tower

Old Point Loma Lighthouse as it appeared in the 1950s, fully restored.

The fine old Ballast Point Lighthouse on the ship channel into San Diego Bay. It was established in 1890 and torn down in later years. Photo (taken in the 1920s) courtesy Radford Franke, the last attendant of the station

rising from its center, thus eliminating other structures, except for the oil house and storage shed.

Editor of the local newspaper was adamant over the long delay in getting the lighthouse under construction, especially with the progress being made on the lighthouses to the north. His article read: "The appropriation was made by Congress three years ago, and as yet, there has not been a blow struck." When that article was written it was still another year before actual construction got underway.

It was on April 7, 1854, that the little schooner *Vaquero* arrived from San Francisco with materials for the lighthouse, landing lumber, brick, lime, and cement at Ballast Point from where the big haul to the summit commenced. Griping all the way, the construction crew was unhappy at having to do the hefty labor of getting building materials to the lofty summit, almost as vociferous over the problem as were Gibbons & Kelly. In the end, they would have been wise to have accepted the Lighthouse Board's offer to get out of their contract as the finished project would run them $30,000, twice the original bid. The road to the top of the ridge demanded the labor of 18 men for well over a month. Then came the bricks for the tower and sandstone for the dwelling, the latter material reputedly quarried at Ballast Point and not from the abandoned fortress as was so often claimed. It was true, however, that basement floor tiles did come from Fort Guijarros, the abandoned sanctuary of the Spaniards at Ballast Point.

Water was also a major problem and to allow for mortar mix and general usage it had to be hauled in from a well seven miles away at LaPlaya. Needless to say, the workers earned their paltry pay and sweated off pounds during the ordeal. As the hot sun beat down upon them they were glad to gain the shadows formed as the walls of the structure rose. Twenty by 30 feet with a 33 foot height, the excessive elevation of the site demanded only a relatively short tower. The Collector of Customs accepted the completed structure in August of 1854 and dispatched a letter to the Lighthouse Board. Though behind schedule and almost twice as expensive as anticipated, the Point Loma Lighthouse nevertheless became an official addition to Pacific Coast aids to navigation on August 26 of that same year.

With all the problems encountered, the workers had no fear of Indian reprisal as was the case on Tatoosh. In fact, fledgling San Diego was far removed from its counterpart at Cape Flattery and there was no newspaper anywhere near the northern site to report on the progress being made.

As earlier mentioned, it was Lt. Washington A. Bartlett, USN that the Lighthouse Board had sent to Paris to negotiate for the lighting apparatus for the new Pacific Coast lighthouses. He entered into a contract with the renowned manufacturer of optics, Sautter & Cie (Co.) for two third order Fresnel lenses and apparatus for Fort Point and Alcatraz paying slightly over 24,000 francs, or in other words $3,810 each, including lens, lamp, frame, lantern and extras. After negotiations were completed on that segment of the contract, the Lighthouse Board wired him to go full speed ahead in ordering the lighting equipment for six other lighthouses. Accordingly, first order systems costing $11,150 each were ordered for Point Loma, Southeast Farallon, Point Conception and Cape Disappointment. A second order light was ordered for Point Pinos and a third order for Humboldt Harbor. The initially purchased lenses were shipped to New York in crates and then trans-shipped around Cape Horn to San Francisco. Another year went by before four other optics reached the city by the Golden Gate and several more months until the equipment for Point Loma and Humboldt Harbor arrived.

Because of the delicate nature of the precious cargo, the responsibility of installation was placed in the hands of local artisans hired by the lighthouse inspector, Captain Henry W. Halleck. As it turned out, the first order apparatus intended for Point Loma was too big for the lantern house and was traded for the third order lens planned for the Humboldt structure. Alterations had to be made by Samuel Franklin and mason Joseph Smith. The equipment arrived on the schooner *General Pierce* August 3, 1855, along with newly assigned contractors under the guidance of Major Hartman Bache. Captain Badger, skipper of the schooner, discharged his cargo, and soon reconstruction of the tower was commenced. As overseer, Bache's report on September 5 read:

The coping course of stone had been removed, and, after raising the tower two bricks in height, to give the conical arch sufficient thickness, were replaced, and cramped with iron. The holes for the uprights of the lantern, and the channels for the brackets of the gallery, had been cut to receive them. The sleeping drum and iron manhole, to replace the one of wood, deficient in size, were also set in the conical arch—the top of

which was leveled off and well coated with cement. The lantern and lighting apparatus, which had reached the lighthouse, with slight exceptions, in perfect order, were in course of cleaning preparatory to putting up. The dwelling is of stone, and with the exception of the mortar, which is very bad, is quite a creditable piece of work. The tower is of brick, itself of such poor quality, that in places they have wasted away to a depth of a quarter of an inch to two inches. The pointing, both in the dwelling and that part of the tower exposed to the weather is entirely gone. Directed the deficient bricks in the tower cut out and replaced by good ones, and then so much of it as rises above the roof of the dwelling, as well as the brick eaves of the latter plastered or rough-cast with cement; also stone work of the dwelling pointed anew.

Bache claimed the cistern was inadequate and that its capacity of 1240 gallons was far short of the station's needs annually. He in turn raised it by placing a pavement of brick underneath and then coated the entire interior with a pavement of brick, citing bad leakage.

At exactly 15 minutes before sunset on November 15, 1855, the keeper lit the wicks and the lighthouse came to life. It would send its friendly glow seaward for the next 36 years, and the third order optic proved to be more than adequate because of its lofty perch. One sea captain reported seeing the light 25 miles at sea and another, master of the ship *Golden Gate*, claimed he picked it up 39 miles out.

Eventual improvements were made with a new road from LaPlaya to the lighthouse replacing the former zig-zag course from Ballast Point.

There was confusion over who was actually the first keeper at Point Loma. If the light had been first order instead of third order there would have been a head keeper and two assistants. With third order it became a principal keeper and one assistant. Two assistants were retained until January 1, 1856 and the second assistant tendered his resignation on that date.

The first assistant keeper, George Tolman, unhappy over pay not being retroactive to the day of his employment, tendered his resignation after a year of service. The head keeper James Keating complained about the quality of assistants he was getting. Said he: "I have been unfortunate in respect of assistants. There comes a strange one every month."

Poor calibre men were often hired for assistants, and due to poor pay, Point Loma had considerable trouble keeping personnel content at the station—11 head keepers and 22 assistants over a 36 year period. The most widely remembered keeper to serve at Loma was David R. Splaine, a naval veteran of the Civil War. Born in Ireland, he made the Lighthouse Service his career serving at Point Conception and the Farallons before his appointment to Point Loma from 1886 to 1889. In 1894 he was assigned the head keepers job at Ballast Point. He "crossed the bar" for the last time, in 1916, a phrase often used by men of the sea when one dies.

Point Loma always had water problems, and a second cistern and catch basin was installed in later years. In 1858, a severe gale lashed the San Diego area, many ships in the harbor dragging their anchors, and numerous houses were damaged. The wind was so strong at the lighthouse that keeper Keating feared it would collapse. He reluctantly abandoned the tower, but the structure remained firm. However, in 1862, the area was struck by a big earthquake at which time the lighthouse did receive considerable damage. Immediate repairs were needed.

The most beloved keeper to serve at Loma, the man who had the longest tenure of duty at the pioneer structure, was the genial Robert Israel. He was appointed assistant keeper on May 20, 1871, at an annual stipend of $600, under principal keeper Enos Wall, (at $1,000) both appointments having been made under Collector of Customs Hoffman. On June 27, 1873, Israel was appointed as head keeper and served in that post until the lighthouse was bugled out of service in 1891. When the newly built Point Loma Lighthouse took over the duties many were sad to see the historic lighthouse put out to pasture. As popular as keeper Israel had been, his wife Maria never played second fiddle. Part of the most prominent Spanish family in the San Diego area, Maria Arcadia Alipas married Israel when she was only 16, and proved to be an outstanding mother of four sons, a competent housewife, and a royal hostess. For two years she even served as an assistant keeper at the lighthouse.

Basic reasons for closing the old structure was that the light was often obscured by the frequent fogs and the fact that the station was in poor condition.

The celebrated old lighthouse keeper Robert Israel passed to his reward at Coronado in 1908.

The new lighthouse had none of the charm of its predecessor but it proved to be at a much more acceptable location for both merchant and Naval shipping. The new site was at the southern tip of Point Loma, 30 feet above the sea, almost 400 feet lower than the old tower. Inasmuch as the Army controlled the land, the Secretary of the Treasury had to apply to the Secretary of War to acquire property on which to build the new lighthouse, and also a second aid to navigation at Ballast Point. Completed in June of 1890, the beacon was mounted atop a metal skeleton tower similar to ones on the nation's southeastern coastline. It boasted a third order Fresnel lighting system which proved to be more than adequate. It was officially lighted for the first time March 23, 1891. Though it was the new Point Loma Light, it was actually situated on Pelican Point, and the dwellings were more attractive, architecturally speaking, than the tower.

The same old embarrassment that involved the bark *Matilda* being wrecked at Tatoosh also occurred at the new Loma lighthouse when the three-masted lumber schooner *Alice McDonald* ran up on the rocky outcrops directly under the red and white beams flashing from the tower on New Year's eve in the year 1909. Fortunately, her fate was not that of the *Matilda,* for after her load of lumber was discharged, a tug was able to tow her free and get her to a yard for repairs.

At this writing, the light is still very active at the Point Loma station and is a familiar sight to both seafarers and landlubbers. Her span of active service has more than doubled that of the pioneer light, and is beginning a second century.

The lighthouse at Ballast Point was also established in 1890 and was a duplicate to the sentinels constructed at both San Luis Obispo and at Table Bluff, south of Humboldt Bay, in the same time frame. All were of wood construction, dwellings attached to square-shaped towers. In the lantern room at Ballast Point was a fixed fifth order lens. The building was razed in 1961. One of the last of the keepers at Ballast Point was Radford Franke, who recalled well the situation when ordered to douse the light on news of the Pearl Harbor attack. In fact, he also shut down the buoy lights in the harbor; the entire city of San Diego was totally blacked out. A blackout was ordered for many of the aids to navigation in the Eleventh Coast Guard District, (Long Beach) for nearly six months.

Ballast Point got its name from the sailing ships, in the early days, which delivered merchandise from the east and returned with hides and tallow, a cargo that was too light to maintain stability at sea. To balance it out, ships would take on ballast rocks at the location.

The abandoned Point Loma lighthouse was the target of every kind of mistreatment for the following four decades. Little thought was given to preserving its historic value. Eventually the outbuildings disappeared and vandals went to work on the lighthouse. All the windows were smashed and everything that could be carted away was, leaving the building so desecrated that by 1913 the commanding officer at Fort Rosecrans recommended that it be razed, even though the place was the favorite viewing point of the entire San Diego population. Cool heads prevailed, however, and the Army actually made some minor repairs on the lighthouse two years later, with public pressure claiming that the "old Spanish Lighthouse" was an historic landmark. Though it was definitely not a Spanish Lighthouse, that moniker seemed to stick like glue and may have been a rumor that kept the edifice from total destruction. In 1931, the Army began an overhaul of the dilapidated structure, and in 1933 turned it over to the National Park Service. Then the Works Project Administration got on the bandwagon and completely renovated the old lighthouse, and its former splendor was returned. During those bad years the Army used it for a little while as an Army radio station. Today, the old lighthouse looks every bit as good as it did when established, and is the main attraction in the Cabrillo National Monument area, honoring Juan Rodriguez Cabrillo, who first landed near there in 1542. The National Park Service was able to secure a Fresnel lens to place in the lantern house, and as earlier mentioned, the lighthouse has become one of the most popular in the country now that it has been virtually resurrected from the dead.

3. Along the Washington Coast

*And o're them the lighthouse
looked lovely as hope,
That star of life's tremulous ocean.*

—*Paul M. James*

Now that we have seen a comparison of two diametrically different lighthouses at either end of our area of coverage we will begin an informal armchair cruise along the Washington coast and take brief glances at each lighthouse. Southward from Cape Flattery we pass Umatilla Reef, Cape Alava, Cape Johnson, the Quillayute River, and the Indian village of LaPush, opposite which lies James Island where a minor navigation light is situated. Finally we come to Destruction Island, the site of the next important lighthouse south of Cape Flattery. The lighthouse has been on the endangered list by the Coast Guard for several years as being too costly and too remote to service properly, especially with no one longer living on the island. It is flat-topped and covered with grass and shrub growth. Located three miles offshore it is a half mile long, and at its southern part 300 yards wide. Kelp languishes on the inshore side.

It was there, in 1891, that the Lighthouse Service established Destruction Island Lighthouse. It consisted of a white conical tower, black lantern and parapet, two oil houses, two dwellings, a barn, and a fog signal building. The roofs of the outbuildings were painted brown. When shipping remained close to shore the beacon was vital, but today with most vessels travelling well offshore the light has lost much of its importance, except for commercial fishermen. Originally, and hopefully in the future, its first order Fresnel will continue to shine, although by the time you read this book the lighthouse could be discontinued and its valuable classic optic removed to a museum. There has been talk of a minor light on the island. The lighthouse is monitored from the Coast Guard base at LaPush. Rich in history, both the island and the lighthouse are little known to the general public. Considerable problems were involved in the building of the station, for the landing of materials and supplies posed a major problem. All around the isle are masses of broken rock, and landings in other than the calmest seas have always been an enigma, much of which was later solved by the usage of Coast Guard helicopters.

There has always been a fog signal on the insular bit of land, it being greatly modified in later years. Originally it was a powerful first class steam siren.

Discovery of the isle is credited to Bruno Heceta, the Spanish navigator and explorer who in 1775 applied the name La Isla de los Delores, or Isle of Sorrows, because some of his crew that went ashore on the mainland for water were

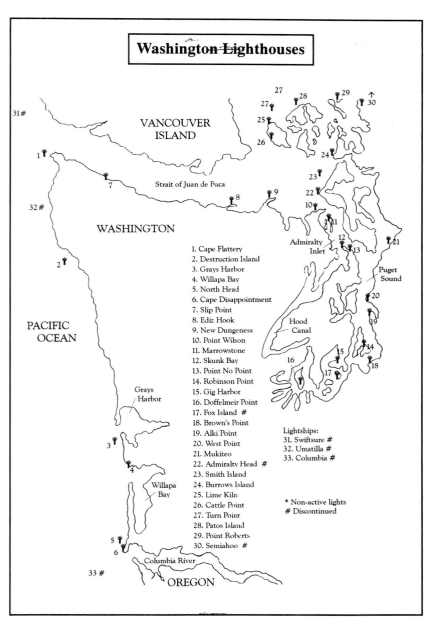

Washington Lighthouses

VANCOUVER ISLAND

Strait of Juan de Fuca

WASHINGTON

PACIFIC OCEAN

Admiralty Inlet

Puget Sound

Hood Canal

Grays Harbor

Willapa Bay

Columbia River

OREGON

1. Cape Flattery
2. Destruction Island
3. Grays Harbor
4. Willapa Bay
5. North Head
6. Cape Disappointment
7. Slip Point
8. Ediz Hook
9. New Dungeness
10. Point Wilson
11. Marrowstone
12. Skunk Bay
13. Point No Point
14. Robinson Point
15. Gig Harbor
16. Doffelmeir Point
17. Fox Island #
18. Brown's Point
19. Alki Point
20. West Point
21. Mukiteo
22. Admiralty Head #
23. Smith Island
24. Burrows Island
25. Lime Kiln
26. Cattle Point
27. Turn Point
28. Patos Island
29. Point Roberts
30. Semiahoo #

Lightships:
31. Swiftsure #
32. Umatilla #
33. Columbia #

* Non-active lights
# Discontinued

murdered by the hostile Indians. Captain Charles Barkley, of the *Imperial Eagle*, also lost several men who rowed ashore in the ship's long boat a few years later, probably by the same band of Indians. The name Destruction was given to the island and it stuck. Though the atrocities did not happen on the island itself, the name was bequeathed upon it because of its close proximity to the mainland tragedies.

Unfortunately the scintillating Fresnel lens at Destruction has not been viewed by many visitors up close. Within its cage of brass are 1176 prisms, including 24 bullseyes. From ground level to the top of the lantern house is 94 feet and there are 115 steps in the interior spiral staircase. The station was built between 1889 and 1891 and is one of the finest towers along the Washington coast.

Landing at Destruction Island Light Station in the 1920s. Note the ship's boat from the U.S. Lighthouse Tender coming through the narrow entrance. The vessel is the Manzanita, *which serviced the lighthouse for several years. A careful look will show two station keepers on the rocks ready to catch a line from the boat and then put the derrick in operation.* Photo courtesy U.S. Lighthouse Service

❀ Grays Harbor

Ninety-five miles southward from Cape Flattery lies the entrance to Grays Harbor. The bay and its tributaries furnish an outlet to an extensive timber area, and the inner ports of Aberdeen and Hoquiam have become a major lumber and log shipping arena. Entrance to the bay is about two miles in width and carries the name of the intrepid fur trader and explorer Robert Gray who also is credited with the discovery of the Columbia River.

It was only natural that commerce and the fishing industry have a major lighthouse near the harbor entrance. Point Chehalis forms the southern entrance to the harbor, and the nationally known fishing village of Westport nearby hosts a large fleet of commercial fishing vessels, and a Coast Guard station that keeps a wary eye out for distress calls. The bar has claimed a sizable number of both large and small craft down through the years.

Near Westport, the most majestic light tower from an architectural standpoint was erected in an era when engineer and architect C.W. Leick worked with sufficient funds to fashion his crowning achievement. Tallest and most outstanding of the lighthouses in the Pacific Northwest, it was commissioned in 1898 amid considerable fanfare. As the Reverend J.R. Thompson of Aberdeen dedicated the structure, scores of folk from the Grays Harbor area glanced skyward in awe of the 107 foot

giant. Next, they were allowed to climb the 135 step spiral staircase to the lantern room to view the Parisian third order lens made by Henry Lepaute. Down through the years the local population has always referred to the beacon as "Westport Light," but the official name is the Grays Harbor Lighthouse. Of masonry construction the tower has aged well, even after automation set in, perhaps due to the nearby Coast Guard presence.

Point Brown at the northern entrance to Grays Harbor is near the growing resort town of Ocean Shores, and the residents take almost as much pride in the Grays Harbor beacon as do the veteran Westporters on the opposite side.

The Coast Guard station is equipped with many radio-oriented communications, and lifesaving craft stand ready to launch out at a moments' notice.

Just west of the tower in 1916, the original fog signal house caught fire and burned to the ground. It was replaced by more modern fog signalling apparatus.

Like most harbor entrance lights, the Grays Harbor facility probably has a better chance of survival as an active aid to navigation than do some of its counterparts. Visitation privileges, at the time of this writing, are still by permission of the personnel at the Coast Guard station.

Light keepers at the Grays Harbor Light were very familiar with the four-masted schooner R.C. Slade. Captain Peder Sonerud sports a derby in this photo. Photo courtesy Wilbur E. Hespe

✤ Willapa Bay

Next on our southward voyage we find ourselves at Willapa Bay, 24 miles north of the Columbia River. At this location the most tragic story unfolds. Where ocean shipping once crossed the bar, it has not only silted over, but through the years thousands of acres of land have been eaten up by the raging Pacific seas. Once, the area was considered so important to commerce that one of the earliest lighthouses in the Pacific Northwest was placed at the north side of the entrance. At that time in history Willapa Bay was known as Shoalwater Bay. Unfortunately the government has always refused to build jetties at the entrance to stabilize the bar. That is the major reason why the entrance has gone wild and disrupted the entire area, with the exception of the thriving oyster industry unmolested inside the vast bay, which at extreme tides shows more mud than water. It is hard to believe that big freighters once crossed the bar en route to Raymond and South Bend on the Willapa River.

It was on October 1, 1858, that the first lighthouse was established at Willapa (Shoalwater) Bay with assistant keeper Daniel Wilson as the man in charge. From the beginning, the station was plagued with problems. Eleven months after the lighthouse was first lighted the tower went dark. The source of oil for the lamps had gone dry and the poor means of transporting fuel to the station presented a major problem. In fact, it wasn't until July 1861 that the government was able to supply the station on a regular basis inasmuch as all oil had to

Death of a lighthouse—Willapa (Shoalwater) Lighthouse ready to take its final plunge over the sandy bank and into the surf in 1940. The pioneer lighthouse dating from 1858, was one of the many victims of the unrelenting power of the ocean that has gobbled up much of the area. Ironically, her sister lighthouse at Smith Island was to suffer the same fate three decades later.

Long ago, erosion claimed the original 1858 stone and brick lighthouse that stood at the north entrance to Willapa (Shoalwater) Bay on the Washington coast. Hundreds of acres have been gobbled up by a demanding ocean. The light has been moved several times, two of the temporary towers seen here have also been replaced. At this writing the Willapa Bay light is on a skeleton tower with red and white horizontal boards. Beach homes, highways, farms, and former Coast Guard station and the original lighthouse have all been claimed by the forces of nature over the last several years.

be ordered through the Lighthouse Board and could not be purchased locally. It was on August 16, 1861, that Robert H. Espy was named head keeper at the station at a annual stipend of $800. He was not at all pleased with his situation and quit ten months later citing inadequate pay and the difficulty of securing supplies that had to be purchased from the local Willapa Indians.

The lighthouse was very similar to the one at Smith Island and Crescent City, the squat tower rising from the dwelling, the focal plane of the light only 32 feet above the ground.

The keeper who had the longest tenure of duty at the lighthouse was H. Peterson, who was there from 1895 until his passing in 1913. He had come out to the west coast on the lighthouse tender *Manzanita* on a voyage around Cape Horn, and before coming to Willapa he served at Tillamook Rock.

A serious blow came to the lighthouse in December 1940, not from a storm, but from erosion which had slowly eaten its way to the very doorstep of the structure. Just eight days after it was abandoned the

Coast Guard announced that it had collapsed into the ocean, a total loss. Today it lies under fathoms of water at 46 degrees 43'N. 124 degrees 04'25"W., probably a haven for creatures of the deep. Since that date the ocean has gone on a rampage chewing up farms, houses, the nearby lifesaving station, and roads, even threatening the pioneer graveyard. The Coast Guard was forced to construct a steel skeleton tower 380 yards north northeast of the original location. As the erosion continued its devastating trek, the light had to be removed again and again and again until the whole contour of the bay entrance was seriously altered and the endangered highway fortified by miles of rip-rap and heavy jetty rock. Still the erosion continues.

Will a light continue to shine at Willwapa? If so, it will only be a minor light and only because commercial fishing vessels with constantly corrected charts are still entering the bay occasionally.

This is indeed the devil's playground, not only for claiming unfortunate ships but for uncontrolled erosion.

❄ North Head

From Leadbetter Point at the southern entrance to Willapa Bay southward lies 22 miles of sand, part of a finger-like peninsula known as North Beach Peninsula. Along this barrier that protects Willapa Bay is a well known graveyard of ships which necessitated the building of North Head Lighthouse in 1898. A noble structure, the 65 foot tower is still in operation, not with its original lens but with a revolving optic of modern manufacture. The ornate keepers' dwelling and oil houses are still on the premises, credited to C.W. Leick who also built the Grays Harbor Lighthouse and several others as well. The original light at North Head was the first order fixed lens originally used at the Cape Disappointment station when it was established in 1856. When automation came to North Head in 1961, the optic in use was a Crous-Hinds beacon.

Though some neglect showed up after automation set in, the structure is now kept in apple-pie condition and is one of the more visited lighthouses in the 13th Coast Guard District, being in an advantageous position for photographers and artists.

One disadvantage to North Head are the strong winds that sweep across its extent, winds that are often above 100 mph. The rocks below have claimed the hats of many visitors, especially tourists unfamiliar with the area. Storms are frequent and rain relatively heavy. In 1932, a wild duck blinded by the light in a storm flew directly into the lantern, right through the plate glass and into the lens, chipping a prism.

A contrast in women at the station—one, a keeper's wife, committed suicide by flinging herself from the 270 foot cliff where the lighthouse stands, and the other, Mabel Bretherton became an assistant keeper at the station in the early 1900s, one of the first of her sex assigned to an oceanfront lighthouse in the Northwest.

❄ Cape Disappointment

Now we come to timeless Cape Disappointment, hardly two miles from North Head. Here, history abounds, and it was here at the entrance to the nation's second largest river that a pioneer lighthouse was established in 1856. In fact, it was to have been among the original eight lighthouses contracted for the Pacific Coast, and considered the most necessary because of the dangerous bar entrance well before the advent of jetties.

Cape Disappointment Lighthouse is like a diamond in the rough. A monarch on a throne of rock, it overlooks the meeting place of the Columbia River and the Pacific Ocean. It was built at a heavy cost inasmuch as the bark *Oriole* carrying the materials for the structure and four other lighthouses was wrecked at the Columbia River entrance, right under the shadow of the 220 foot monolith. In command of Captain Lewis Lentz, the vessel fell prey to the treacherous bar on September 10, 1853, after a 13 day voyage from San Francisco. Though the watersoaked crew was rescued from the open boat the following day, the cargo lay at the bottom of the fickle bar waters never to be retrieved, and the loss was a great blow to the newly organized U.S. Lighthouse Board. A lighthouse that was to have been lighted in 1854 awaited the lighting of its first order fixed Fresnel lens till October 15, 1856, at a cost of $38,500 not counting the loss of the *Oriole* and her cargo. As on the other cost overruns with most of the early lighthouses contracted for by Gibbons & Kelly, Cape Disappointment lived up to the name that Captain John Meares attached to it. While searching for the river entrance in 1788 he was thwarted from its discovery, sailing away in the good ship *Nootka* and leaving the name Disappointment behind. The Spaniard Don Bruno Heceta in the frigate *Santiago* was really the first to recognize the entrance to the 1,214 mile river on August 17, 1775, but was also unable to enter it, leaving the honors to Yankee fur

trader Robert Gray, master of the *Columbia Rediviva*, on May 11, 1792, who named it for his ship. Heceta had named the cape Cabo San Roque.

With considerable effort, the 53 foot tower was finally constructed along with other station buildings, and at last a great portal of commerce received its first aid to navigation.

Though one lighthouse and limited river buoyage was unable to curb the rash of shipwreck at the river entrance it certainly prevented the toll from being worse and was a great encouragement to seafarers entering the river.

Grandfather of all the lighthouses in the Pacific Northwest, it has stood fast through every howling gale the Pacific could throw its way. On only a few occasions has its light ever failed, and its strategic location is such that its light should continue to shine. The original lens and lighting apparatus with its five wick lamp consuming 170 gallons of whale oil per month, and its 1,500 pound fog bell have long since gone. The old lens is on display at the nearby Interpretive Center after having served both Cape Disappointment and North Head, and the fogbell which ended up at   rests at the Columbia County Museum (St. Helens) after being dropped and cracked when being removed from Warrior Rock station by the Coast Guard. The old lens was replaced at Disappointment by a fourth order Fresnel lens many years ago. Numerous and varying aids to navigation have been and are used at the cape, and it was also once surrounded by cannon from Fort Canby, a fortress built on the cape during the Civil War years and used up until recent times when it was turned over to the Washington State Parks. The firing of the guns sometimes shook the windows out of the light tower, and even caused the old fogbell housing to collapse.

The Coast Guard Station is located in the lee of the cape, and includes a motor lifeboat training school. For almost a quarter of a century before 1900, the old Fort Canby Lifesaving Station was located near the present station and the lightkeepers worked in conjunction with the lifesaving crew in alerting them of any vessel in distress. The old oar-propelled surfboats and the modern motor lifeboats of the Coast Guard (they took over the Lifesaving Service in 1915) have saved scores of lives and property in and around this danger area. There was also a pioneer U.S. Lifesaving Station inside Willapa Bay for many years.

It is estimated that perhaps 2,000 vessels of all descriptions have been wrecked in or around the entrance to the river since the coming of the white man to this once coveted land-sea front of the American Indians. Before the lighthouse was erected, navigators crossing the bar would set their courses by trees atop the cape or by white rags hung either by white settlers or Indians hired to keep a lookout for Hudson's Bay ships endeavoring to enter the river.

In recent times the Coast Guard painted a black stripe around the girth of the Cape Disappointment tower to differentiate it from the nearby all-white North Head tower, but for most of its years of service the Disappointment tower was all white except for its black lantern housing and dome. A lookout structure to oversee any vessels, mainly commercial and sports fishing craft, that might be in distress, is just west of the tower.

It was one of the early light keepers, Joel Munson, who became so incensed by the lack of aid for shipwrecked seamen that he organized a volunteer lifesaving crew, 1865-1877, and revamped an old ship's lifeboat to rescue souls at the Columbia River bar. The government took over that chore in 1878 after Munson had proven his point with several successful rescues.

It is believed that John Boyd was the first head keeper at Cape Disappointment though early records are lacking. In the census of 1860, Pacific County lists him in that capacity.

Visiting "Cape D," as it is affectionately referred to, is an absolute must for the lighthouse lover. Even if one doesn't care about lighthouses, the sea and landscapes found here are out of this world. Nor should one miss visiting the Interpretive Center which gives the story of the cape and its sentinels.

From the historic town of Ilwaco signs point to the many attractions on the cape, the park, Cape Disappointment and North Head Lighthouses, the Interpretive Center, the fort's remains and the fishing areas at the jetty. Its a short uphill hike to Cape Disappointment Lighthouse from the Coast Guard station and an easier hike into North Head from the parking lot. Tours are available and one should contact the Lewis and Clark Interpretive Center for information.

The Columbia River continues as one of the great portals of commerce on the Pacific Coast and a prime fishing area. Competent pilots work around the clock shepherding ocean going ships in and out across the bar. All the while the light atop the cape casts forth its friendly glow as it has done for nearly a century and a half.

> *I'd like to be a lighthouse*
> *All scrubbed and painted white.*
> *I'd like to be a lighthouse*
> *And stay awake all night.*
> *To keep my eye on everything*
> *That sails my patch of sea;*
> *I'd like to be a lighthouse*
> *With the ships all watching me.*

> —*Mary Zantow*

Cape Disappointment Lighthouse awaits a new paint job while it stands its faithful vigil over the entrance to the mighty Columbia River. Photo courtesy Larry Loudenback, 1990

4. Around Puget Sound & the Strait of Juan de Fuca

*Hast thou seen that lordly
castle by the sea?
Golden and red above it
The clouds float gorgeously.*

—Henry Wadsworth Longfellow

Certainly the exacting navigator and explorer, Captain George Vancouver, was right when he described Puget Sound, Admiralty Inlet, and the surrounding scenery as the most beautiful he had ever seen. He spoke in enduring charms about the numerous bays, inlets and passages, the fabulous snow-capped mountains and the deep navigable waterways.

He would of course be dumbfounded if he could see it as it appears today. His eyes beheld pristine wooded shores down to the water's edge and virtually unpopulated shores and islands. Though many of the glorious scenes still remain, a huge population exists along the eastern shore, and the Seattle-Tacoma area has become the largest metropolis in the Pacific Northwest.

It is no wonder that aids to navigation became ever more important as the marine traffic of every type steadily increased in this vast inland sea. Puget Sound extends about 90 miles southward from the Strait of Juan de Furca to Olympia, the Washington Sate capital. The northern boundary is formed at its entrance by a line between Point Wilson on the Olympic Peninsula and Point Partridge on Whidbey Island. There is a second entrance between the western point of Whidbey Island, Deception Pass, and Sares Head on Fidalgo Island, and a third entrance at the south end of Swinomish Channel between Fidalgo Island, and McGlinn Island.

Lieutenant Peter Puget, for whom this inland sea is named, was a member of Vancouver's crew and among those who explored these waters in May 1792. To mark these waterways are a myriad of aids to navigation. Probably the first aid, seen today at the south end of the sound, that could be termed a lighthouse is the Dofflemyer Point Light, displayed from a white pyramidal tower placed there

in 1936, replacing an earlier structure established in 1887 to guide shipping to and from Olympia. It stands on the end of the point at the east entrance to Budd Inlet and there is also a foghorn at the site. The tower stands 30 feet high.

Traveling northward to the bustling port city of Tacoma, the guiding light there is at Browns Point. There a stately little 31 foot tower, with its optic exposed, winks at the traffic that passes its door. A light was first shown there on December 12, 1887, the present tower having been erected in 1933. The importance of shipping was realized at Browns Point with the large number of square-riggers frequenting the port around the turn of the century, and it was decided that the original lantern, hung from a stake, was not a sufficient aid to navigation. Thus in 1903, a little lighthouse and a keepers' dwelling was erected on the point. The wood frame structure stood on piling just off the shore. According to Mavis Stears, who wrote the little booklet *Two Points of View*, the initial keeper and the first white residents of Brown's Point were Oscar Brown and wife Annie. In fact, he would spend the next three decades as the tender of the light and the big fog bell. He trimmed the oil lamp each night and wound the mechanism that rang the bell when fog set in. When the clockwork failed to ring the bell he and his wife worked out a deal where he would strike it with a sledge hammer while she monitored the time sequence as recorded in the *Light List*.

There was always excitement when the lighthouse tenders *Manzanita* or *Columbine* brought supplies to the station on an annual basis. Brown naturally had to don his blue uniform with brass buttons for the

The second U.S. Lighthouse tender named Manzanita *did an admirable job servicing Northwest lighthouses and buoys. Her sleek design allowed her to slide up on shallow reefs without suffering serious damage. She is seen here near the San Juan Islands in this placid scene. The vessel was built in 1908.*

U.S. L.H. Tender "Manzanita"
Borchers.
no. 91.

inspection that followed. The lighthouse supplies were brought ashore by longboat while the tender anchored offshore.

As the community grew at Browns and Dash Point, the children were drawn to Oscar and the lighthouse. He was a talented musician and music teacher, often affectionately referred to by his students as having a profile like the Indian on a buffalo nickel. The greater share of the visitors to the lighthouse came by launch or rowboat from Tacoma where rentals were made by the Foss Launch & Tug Company which in later years became the largest towing operation on Puget Sound. Visitors were often greeted by the keeper's mother, known only as Mother Brown, a lady that had a green thumb and always kept the garden full of blooming flowers.

The old lighthouse of Oscar's day has been razed and replaced by the present reinforced concrete structure surrounded by a park, open to the public. The land was taken over by the government at the turn of the century. In a judgment and decree on July 9, 1901, Joseph Swoyall, Jerry Meeker, and Frank Ross were awarded a total of $3,000 for the land by giving Uncle Sam free title, property that today would be worth a fortune.

❀ Mysteries

Southwest of Tacoma is a small bit of land just off Fox Island where a private unofficial lighthouse-like structure stands. It is opposite Tanglewood, a private resort. It has mariners scratching their heads wondering why it's there, though it fits in nicely with its surroundings.

Until 1970, another rather mysterious lighthouse-like structure stood on the tip of McDermott Point in Filucy Bay at the southern end of the Sound. Though abandoned, it added charm to the area until strangely set afire and burned to the ground.

❀ Gig Harbor

A new addition to the family of Puget Sound lighthouses stands at the entrance to Gig Harbor. It was erected in recent years in a joint effort by the people of Gig Harbor who believed that their charming little harbor rated the presence of a community lighthouse. Gig Harbor is an inlet about one mile long on the west side of the southern entrance to Colvos Passage abreast of Tacoma's Point Defiance. The structure replaced the minor light on the southern end of the sandspit at the eastern side of the entrance. The town of Gig Harbor extends along the western shore and the head of the harbor, homeport of several fishing and pleasure craft.

❀ Robinson Point

Next we come to Robinson Point Lighthouse on the eastern end of Maury Island. An aid to navigation has been at that location since 1885, but the present tower and fog signal buildings were built in 1915 and stand in an important main channel for ships, especially between Tacoma and Seattle. The white 38 foot reinforced concrete tower was one of the most favored lighthouse assignments for both Lighthouse Service, and later Coast Guard personnel and their families. When that facility was established in 1887, a lens-lantern was placed, and seven years later as ship traffic increased the light was raised to 40 feet atop a skeleton type tower. The original optic placed in the existing tower's lantern house was a beautiful little fifth order Fresnel lens, a product of L. Sautter, Lemmonier of Paris.

Maury Island is connected with Vashon Island and is a major turning point in the passage. The light is situated on a low spit projecting 140 yards from the wooded high land.

❀ Alki Point

Alki Point Lighthouse stands at the southern entrance to Seattle's Elliott Bay. Its light is shown from a 37 foot white reinforced concrete tower attached to a fog signal building. One can be sure that the lighthouse and grounds are kept in tip-top condition because the Commandant of the 13th Coast District makes his home in the former keeper's residence. And, over and above that, it was near that spot where the founders of Seattle landed in the little two-masted schooner *Exact* in 1851.

In the late 1880s the Lighthouse Service placed post lamps throughout Puget Sound; small brass lanterns which hung from posts, some of which had to be trimmed each night and some once a week, depending on the size of their reservoirs. The location of Alki Point rated a lens-lantern, larger than the post lights, and affording a better light. It was decided in 1887 that an official light should burn at the point, and Hans Martin Hanson, one of the owners of the property was named keeper. He was paid $15 a month to keep the lens-lantern fueled and cleaned, a chore he turned over to his son in later years. When the elder Hanson died in 1900 he willed the 320 acre plot to his son and six daughters. The offspring reluctantly gave up a portion of the property to Uncle Sam in 1910 for $9,000, but it was not until 1918, during World War I, that a permanent lighthouse station was constructed on the site, and that station remains today. The Fresnel lens has been replaced by a modern light, but the old fog signal house with its generators and compressors is kept more for historic purposes than for usage; a modern fog signal is in use today.

The best known of the keepers that served the light, before automation, was Albert Anderson, who put in two decades of service before retiring in 1970.

Permission for visiting the station must be gotten through the 13th Coast Guard District.

❀ West Point

Alki's senior sister light holds forth at the north entrance to Elliott Bay and the south entrance to Shilshole Bay. It is a squat, little tower rising from a fog signal house and is located below old Fort Lawton which is today part of Seattle's popular Discovery Park. If one doesn't want to hike down to the lighthouse, a park shuttle bus is frequently available. It is a beautiful scenic area except for the nearby rather extensive sewage treatment plant which unfortunately was constructed not far from the historic lighthouse.

Since 1881, the beacon has been shining at West Point and has always been known as Seattle's official maritime greeter. Good things often come in small packages and the light and fog signal at this location have witnessed a parade of ships of every kind and description for decades. Cargo vessels, passenger ships, tugs and barges, and every imaginable kind of craft have passed West Point Light, and inasmuch as Puget Sound is one of the yachting capitals of the world, that breed of craft is highly familiar with the beacon. Just north of the lighthouse, Shilshole Bay leads into the Hiram M. Chittenden Locks and the Lake Washington Ship Canal which links Puget Sound with Seattle's fresh water lakes, Union and Washington. Actually, if one has a small boat he could begin at Lake Sammamish, go down the slough to Lake Washington, through the Montlake Cut into Lake Union and then through the canal and the locks out into Puget Sound, up to the Strait of Juan de Fuca and out into the vast Pacific without ever touching dry land.

If a betting man, I would say the future of the West Point Lighthouse is well preserved as it is a favorite of locals and visitors to the Emerald City. It was obvious that there would be a small celebration when the lighthouse observed its 100th anniversary in 1981, especially when Coast Guardsman Marven Gerber, keeper at the station, climbed up on the roof and poured champagne on the structure while those below cheered.

It was a rather sad event in 1985 when the lighthouse became one of the last on Puget Sound to be automated, dismissing the keeper. Like all other stations in 1939, there was somewhat of the same kind of nostalgia when the Coast Guard took over the facility from the U.S. Lighthouse Service, many of the old-time civil servants retiring rather than taking on a ranking in the Coast Guard.

The Parisian manufactured fourth order lens has served the lighthouse well, its maximum output of 15 miles more than enough to go clear to the western shore of the Sound. The old Daboll trumpets that warned ships in the frequent fogs are gone and the holes in the fog house have been sealed over in favor of more modern fog signaling apparatus. None of the innovative electronic aids have the attractiveness of the old, though perhaps they are more efficient.

The original cost of the West Point Lighthouse was $25,000, big money in 1881.

✺ Mukilteo

The family lighthouse; that's the way people describe Mukilteo Lighthouse overlooking Possession Sound on the searoad to the Port of Everett. Ferryboats come and go right next to the lighthouse grounds and the passengers traveling between Mukilteo and Whidbey Island all get an excellent view of the sentinel. It is a 38 foot octagonal Leick-designed structure, completed in 1906.

Once the favorite spot of the natives that roamed the shores and put out into Puget Sound with their dugout canoes, Elliot Point, where the lighthouse stands, is ironically where a treaty was signed in 1855 when I.I. Stevens was governor of Washington Territory. That treaty duped the Indians into a peaceful settlement of warlike activities but was really a sham to rob them of the lands that were rightfully theirs. One of the great travesties in the history of our nation was the taking of Indian properties and pushing the tribes back to reservations. Had the Indians been able to keep ownership of their lands, they would have become wealthy beyond measure. The writer Charles Webb once said:

*Of Christian souls, more have been
wrecked on shore than were ever lost at sea.*

Today, the lighthouse has been a place of pride for the local citizenry, and the buildings and grounds are beautifully maintained just as they were in the early years. At this writing the original lens is still in the lantern house—a fourth order Fresnel, and the old equipment remains in the fog house. The station dwellings are in good condition. For many years the Coast Guard considered placing a minor light on a pole outside the tower, and though that may happen someday, the sentimentality of the old way hangs on.

As a tourist attraction, the lighthouse displays a Coast Guard photographic exhibit featuring lighthouses of the area, and members of the local Mulkilteo Historical Society tell of the first keeper assigned to the lighthouse, Peter Christianson, who trimmed the lamp until 1925 assuring that the blinking light would maintain its five second interval, and that the old Daboll would blast when necessary.

One wonders what the old Indian chiefs would think if they could come back from their graves and see this land called Mukilteo, which simply means in English, "good place for camping."

✺ Point No Point

It was indeed a sad beginning in the history of the Point No Point Lighthouse, which lies on the Western shore of Puget Sound on a low sandspit 3.5 miles southeast of Foulweather Bluff. This near sister of the West Point Light, by official decree, was to have been initially lighted on New Year's day in 1880. John Maggs, the assigned head keeper was present, but the plate glass for the lantern planes and the prisms for the lens had not yet arrived, forcing him to set up a common household kerosene lamp on the pedestal in the lantern house and try to keep the flame from blowing out in freezing temperatures with snow on the ground.

Meanwhile, carpenters were trying to rush through the finishing touches on the station. The errant glass didn't arrive until January 10, but it was only the prisms for the lens, a fourth order bullseye optic. The plate glass didn't arrive until February 1. Finally, the frustrating job of maintaining a light under the most adverse circumstances was over, and Maggs and his assistant Henry Edwards settled down to the normal lighthouse keeping chores.

Not until April 1 did the lighthouse tender *Shubrick*, with inspector Captain George Reiter and H.S. Wheeler aboard, arrive to make a final inspection before the station was at last given the stamp of approval. It was only days later that the schooner *Granger* arrived and off-loaded a cow which would provide milk for the anticipated baby of the pregnant Mrs. Maggs. The child, a girl, was born at the edifice on July 21. In October, keeper Maggs was invited to go to Seattle by boat to meet the then President of the United States, Rutherford B. Hayes.

After that highlight in his career he came home to trouble. His assistant, Edwards, was transferred and replaced by N.S. Rogers who later quit with dissatisfaction. Then in turn came a man named Manning who turned out to be a tyrant. It started with a big argument over his reprimand for not operating the fogbell properly. (Perhaps more trouble occurred with fog signals at the lighthouse than from any other cause). Manning flew into a rage, cussing out Maggs, uttering threats and flashing a knife. Later he grabbed a pistol, left the station AWOL, went to a logging camp and came back with a cohort. The two locked themselves in and Maggs out of the tower threatening him if he tried to enter. The head keeper returned a few hours later and found the tower empty and no care given to the lamp. He, in turn, took off for Port Gamble and telegraphed the Collector of Customs.

A government cutter arrived and gave the troubled assistant a dressing down and ordered him to comply with assigned duties until Inspector Reiter could arrive to investigate the charges. As a result, Manning and his family were removed from the premises and transported to Seattle while a new assistant, Neil Henley, was assigned, restoring peace to the station.

Maggs remained at his post until transfer in 1888 when a new principal keeper named Scannel took the post for the next 26 years, his assistant Carey besting him by one year, remaining till 1937. Two years later the Coast Guard took over.

The station property was acquired in 1878, a 40 acre tract, purchased for $1,800. The foghorn housing was added to the tower in 1900.

To reach the lighthouse by land it is just a hop, skip, and a jump from the sleepy little town of Hansville.

✺ Skunk Bay

Just a couple of miles north of Point No Point stands a privately-owned lighthouse, near Norwegian Point, above Skunk Bay. It is called Skunk Bay Lighthouse and was founded by this writer in 1965. The original plan was to move the historic Smith Island Lighthouse, (1858) threatened by erosion, to a safer location. Though Coast Guard permission was granted, it was determined by an engineer that the total weight of the lighthouse was about 300 tons, most of it in the sandstone and brick in its thick walls. Such an effort was not feasible. Even the location would have made it highly difficult. As a result, the iron lantern house and some of the appendages were removed piece by piece and transported by salvage vessel to the present site, reassembled, and placed atop a frame tower. By evolution, the structure was eventually accepted as a private aid to navigation by the Coast Guard and still shows a fixed light in the tower.

Some years ago it was sold to a group of professional folk who made further improvements, and share it as a retreat.

In the interim, the old structure on Smith Island has gradually slid over the cliff, with only a small portion remaining at this writing, most of it ground to bits on the beach or in the waters surrounding the small island. A part of that old lighthouse lives on at Skunk Bay.

❋ Marrowstone Point

Marrowstone Point at the eastern entrance to Port Townsend Bay was granted a light and fog signal in 1888. The fog signal was of greater importance than the light because of the frequent fog on the main shipping channel. Mariners complained that it was difficult to hear, and in turn a Scotch innovative fog signal was tried and it too failed. The importance of the waterway during World War I inspired an improved structure in 1918, with huge trumpets blasting from three sides of the structure, which became much more effective.

A traditional tower never was built above the fog signal house, but for years the station rated a keeper on the grounds who also looked after the nearby minor aids to navigation. A near neighbor across the bay entrance was at Point Hudson where a fog signal and light was established in 1887 and updated in 1916. It is located on the western shore, a low, sandy plot less than two miles southeastward from Point Wilson. Marrowstone Point is actually on an island of the same name. The growing reason for a myriad of the navigation aids in the Port Townsend area was due to the increased traffic generated there and in other sectors of Puget Sound during the busy days of World War I when several forts were active, such as Fort Worden, Fort Flagler, and Fort Casey.

❋ Point Wilson

Key to the entire list of navigation aids on Puget Sound is Point Wilson Lighthouse at the western turning point from the Strait of Juan de Fuca into Puget Sound. Though originally named Admiralty Inlet, the name Puget Sound has been applied to the entire body of water. On the official navigation charts it is still Admiralty Inlet, south to the tip of the North Kitsap Peninsula. Point Wilson Lighthouse is a 46 foot white, octagonal tower on a fog signal building on the eastern extremity of a low point where electronic communications such as radiobeacons have long been present. Heavy tide rips sweep around the point and shoal areas make it a place to give a wide berth. Major problems have always been connected with the fogs that frequent that section of the waterway. When the weather closes down and mariners can't hear the fog signal they are admonished to take immediate soundings.

Several ships have come to grief in the area, and when Vancouver surveyed and sounded there in the late 1700s he realized the problem.

It was in 1879 that Point Wilson was crowned with its sentinel. At that time it was a frame structure which was later replaced by a reinforced concrete tower and foghorn house, along with improved housing, in 1914. Still, it was on December 15, 1879, that the big celebration took place at Point Wilson, for a long and hard battle had been fought by shipping interests to get a beacon established at the front door to the then very busy Port Townsend harbor. For many years it was thought that Port Townsend would become the major shipping port on greater Puget Sound. Its location, however, favored the opposite side of this vast body of water, and eventually Seattle and Tacoma stole Port Townsend's prominence. Back in those early years, however, that port on the Olympic Peninsula was a little Barbary Coast, a rip-roaring wide open town where seafarers from the world over rubbed elbows in the waterfront dives. Many nefarious schemes were hatched, and the art of shanghaiing ran rampant. Many tall ships anchored in the harbor along with a fair share of steam powered cargo and passenger ships.

David M. Littlefield, who had distinguished himself in the Civil War, was named the first keeper of Point Wilson, and he performed well in keeping the fourth order light with its white beam varied by a red flash every 20 seconds. He and his assistant also maintained the very important steam fog signal. The place became very popular with the people of Port Townsend and visitors were frequent. In fact, Littlefield was so popular that he eventually became mayor of Port Townsend, having married a woman of social standing in the community.

An aging square-rigger, the *David Hoadley*, ground up on the outer shoals within a year of the establishment of the lighthouse, a victim of fog. Ironically, the tides gradually pushed the bark ever closer to shore within the shadow of the lighthouse. As a result, the crew was able to walk ashore on dry land as the tide ebbed. The vessel, however, had reached her port of no return.

The most remembered of the many wrecks in the area involved the beautiful British sailing vessel *Kilbrannan*, object of a long and strenuous salvage effort which eventually paid off in the months before the turn of the century. Then there was the tragic collision between the passenger liner *Governor* and the freighter *West Hartland* in 1921, which resulted in the sinking of the passenger ship and the loss of eight souls. In recent times, a salvage effort was made to dive on the wreck and recover its safe and other items but the swift currents thwarted the effort and doomed the operation.

William Thomas, who was keeper at Point Wilson when the *Governor* went to the bottom, sent out the first news of the tragedy, hearing only the distress sounds of the ships' whistles and the grinding of metal in the thick fog that blanketed the waters of Admiralty Inlet on that tragic day. He aided with rescue efforts.

Some 1,500 tons of rip-rap and rock had to be placed near the lighthouse in 1904, when it was threatened by erosion due to strong currents and extreme tidal action. Since automation came to the light station, its light and fog signal have been monitored by the Coast Guard Station at Port Angeles. The lighthouse is easily accessible, being bordered by Fort Worden State Park. Tours of the lighthouse are given by special permission of the Coast Guard.

A defense unit at Point Wilson was set up by the white settlers as early as 1855 where Battery Kinzie was established. It was for a possible defense against the raiding Haida Indians that occasionally canoed down from British Columbia waters. It was also a place once frequented by the local Clallam and Chimacum Indians.

❋ Admiralty Inlet

Though the seafaring people of Port Townsend didn't agree, the surveyors for the Lighthouse Board perhaps made the right decision, for the times, when they established a major lighthouse on Admiralty Inlet at Whidbey Island's Admiralty Head, well before the sentinel at Point Wilson. The reason was that sailing ships making the turn from the Strait of Juan de Fuca and heading southward needed much deeper water than was afforded close in to Point Wilson. Though Point Wilson later became the primary light as powered vessels became more frequent, it was Admiralty Head that was the right choice when a beacon was built there in 1860. The light was first exhibited January 21, 1861, from a frame tower attached to a dwelling. The tower was 41 feet high and 108 feet above sea level, and from a distance resembled a country church. The land had been purchased in 1858 from John and Caroline Kellogg who were homesteaders.

William Robertson was named to keep the lighthouse. His appointment was made because he was a Democrat instead of a Republican, as politics played a big part in the appointment of keepers in the early years of the Lighthouse Service. His later replacement was a man named Pearson whose continuing bad health demanded that his two daughters, Flora and Georgia, take over his chores.

During the Spanish American War the government desired a better military presence in the area and the lighthouse was at a strategic defense location, and an encumbrance. As a result, a switch of properties took place, and the lighthouse was rebuilt at another site a half mile further north. The old structure was razed. Far exceeding the old lighthouse, the new masonry building was ornate, commodious and comfortable, although its years as an active aid to navigation would be numbered. From 1903 until just past the mid-1920s Admiralty Head Lighthouse was a princely edifice surrounded by the buildings of old Fort Casey. As the importance of the Point Wilson Light increased, the Lighthouse Service decided that it was no longer necessary to keep Admiralty Head aglow. In turn, it was abandoned, and when the lighthouse at New Dungeness was rebuilt in 1927, the tower at Admiralty Head was decapitated and its lantern house moved to the other tower. In turn, the abandoned building became an officers quarters at the fort and received a coat of olive green paint. After the war years it stood empty, and its future appeared dim until the Washington State Parks and the Island County Historical Society got involved. The lighthouse was eventually restored as a museum and monument to former years, and once again took on the splendor of its inception.

Today Fort Casey and the lighthouse are part of a beautiful park visited by scores of tourists. Its location on Whidbey near the Keystone-Port Townsend ferry slip is not far from the quaint town of Coupeville. Lighthouse tours are given in the summer months. The original lighthouse is but a memory. The little hunk of land where it stood is close to the ferry landing on a plot of ground once known as Red Bluff. The existing structure, though not an active aid to navigation, had a new lantern house installed atop the tower to resemble the one that was removed years earlier. A great topic for photographers, the lighthouse smacks of splendid architecture. It was honored in recent years by being chosen as one of the selected lighthouses on a U.S. Postage stamp.

✸ Smith Island

It might be termed the island with a moving experience. Smith Island, five miles westward of Whidbey Island, is irregular in shape and 0.5 miles in extent. The eastern end is low but rises abruptly to an elevation of 55 feet at its western end. Strong currents set in, and around the shoal area, and deep draft ships must keep well outside the ten fathom curve to avoid danger. Kelp beds extend from one and a half miles westward of the isle for well over a mile, with depths up to six fathoms.

Smith Island light has had a most unusual history. As mentioned, the historic lighthouse which crowned that island in 1858 has been shattered to pieces from erosion that eats away the elevated western end of the isle and builds up the eastern end where exist low, flat shoals. Oddly enough though, neighboring Minor Island lies one mile northward, which at extreme low tide is connected to Smith Island by an exposed sandy strip with sand hard enough to support a truck. In the early days it allowed the keepers to attend a minor light on the other island as well as trimming the light on the residence isle.

Replacing the destroyed lighthouse, a skeleton tower was erected on safer ground in the early 1960s and displayed its light from a height

Smith Island Lighthouse as it appeared in its heyday. Built in 1858, on Smith Island at the eastern end of the Strait of Juan de Fuca, it succumbed to erosion in recent years. The stone and masonry structure, steeped in history, was an unfortunate casualty of the tricks of nature.

of 97 feet above the sea. A radiobeacon was also on the high ground along with a white daymark on the west slopes.

Nobody dwells on this little island anymore, and since automation it has become a lonely place seldom visited by anyone but the wild rabbits and sea birds.

It was feared that Smith Island would become a battle ground between the early white settlers and the fierce Haida Indians in the spring of 1859, less than a year after the lighthouse was established. In fact, its assistant keeper, Applegate, became somewhat of a folk hero in his time. The Haidas often had visited the isle on their raids, and were enemies of the Indian tribes of the Olympic Peninsula. Word was received that the Haidas were gathering 5,000 strong in their war canoes near Victoria, B.C., and were planning raids to the south. The report caused panic in Port Townsend and when a canoe was spotted near Point Wilson it was surrounded and its occupants, an old, blind Indian chief, three young boys, and twenty-one women were rounded up and put in the local jail. Meanwhile, the settlers banded with the local Indians and worked themselves into a frenzy. When five war canoes were sighted off Smith Island, Captain J. Jones of the schooner *Caroline* confronted them and asked their mission. He was told they were only going to go to the island to hunt ducks, but Jones refused to buy their story and immediately warned John Vail, head keeper, of impending danger. As it turned out, assistant keeper Applegate, being single, offered to hold down the fort while Vail and his wife were temporarily removed until reinforcements arrived.

Immediately Jones returned to Port Townsend with his passengers and rounded up volunteers to wage possible battle with the intruders. In the interim, Indian agent Robert Fay was pleading for the release of the innocent Haidas that had been jailed. With armed volunteers hidden below deck, the *Caroline* sailed for the island to keep an eye on the war canoes. Applegate signaled that some Haidas were already on the beach, after which they returned to their canoes and in warlike manner dared the "Bostons" to fight. Diplomacy and a warning to stay off the island was rendered but received with a snarl. The schooner stood by until the canoes were out of sight.

The following day Applegate contacted and sent two Kanakas in a skiff back to the mainland to report that the Haidas had returned during the night and shot at him as he went about his duties. Fearing the worst, the bark *Mary L. Slade* put out for the island with settlers armed to the teeth, ready to do battle. The troops stormed ashore and took up their positions using an old breastwork set up on the island during the building period for protection against Indian incursions. It wasn't long afterwards that Haidas decided that any further efforts would be fruitless and soon returned to the north taking their released hostages with them.

Keeper Applegate had fought a one-man battle being fired on before reinforcements arrived. He used the lighthouse as his fortress and fired at the enemy from the lantern house gallery, wounding one of the invaders. That proved to be the only casualty.

Vail and his wife, including their grandson, returned to the island and business as usual continued.

When the lighthouse property was taken over by the government in the early years, the island was called Blunts rather than Smith, but the latter name was permanently applied. Originally, the Spaniards had labeled it Isla de Bonilla, under the Eliza exploration, a name which has a more romantic handle but is not necessarily applicable.

Nobody knows what happened to the original fourth order fixed lens used at Smith Island, but the replacement optic, a revolving Fresnel with six panels, is displayed by the Seattle Museum of History and Industry.

❀ Burrows Island

The fate of the beautiful little Burrows Island Lighthouse may hang in the balance. Since 1906 it has remained a 34 foot frame tower rising from the fog signal building, with the dwellings and out buildings still intact at this writing. This fairy-tale setting is unique inasmuch as the isle is quite pristine with forest land in abundance. The lighthouse is another C.W. Leick design. In fact, many of the lighthouses in the Pacific Northwest were designed by this man, though in his field he never received much publicity for his fine work.

Located on the east side of the south part of Rosario Strait, the lighthouse points the way to Canadian ports and the fabulous San Juan islands. Its group flashing light has a red sector warning mariners of Dennis and Lawson shoals. The currents sweep around the island with considerable force. Some years back when visiting the station the writer recalls that his 26 foot cruiser began dragging anchor while anchored just offshore. Ashore at the time, we watched the craft being carried rapidly toward the north end of the island. The Coast Guard attendants obligingly revved the outboard on the station boat and we went in hot pursuit of the errant vessel before it got hung up on a shoal.

❀ Semiamhoo Harbor

Only a minor light and fog signal exist there today, but in 1905 a pert and cozy lighthouse was established in six feet of water on the eastern part of Semiahmoo Harbor near Blaine, Washington. It was constructed on piling and was very similar to the lighthouse built atop Desdemona Sands at the mouth of the Columbia River. The lighthouse was one of the first to go under the Coast Guard austerity program after that service took over aids to navigation from the Lighthouse Service in 1939. Just five years later, the Semiahmoo lighthouse was torn down. Its French made lens, manufactured by Barbier, Benard & Turenne of Paris cost the Lighthouse Establishment a mere $370 in 1904. The lens is displayed at Cleft of the Rock Lighthouse after being retrieved from a junk yard.

The 18 foot pyramidal tower of today, built in 1971, is a far cry from the former lighthouse. When keeper Edward Durgan was ordered there by the Lighthouse Service he did everything in his power to get out of the assignment. But because of his huge family, his wife urged him to take the appointment. With a volley of cuss words, he insisted, "I don't want to go to that little birdhouse perched on stilts." But, like the old saying goes, "The woman that rocks the cradle rules the world."

Durgan stayed from 1913 until 1920 when he died of a heart attack while hauling the station boat up on the davits.

O.P. Carver, postmaster, was the instigator of a petition to get the station established as early as 1897, but with the war heating up with Spain the effort failed. Carver tried again in April 1900 in a letter signed by shipping men, cannery workers, and mill employees backed by G.A. Ellsperman, deputy collector of customs, citing the need for a lighthouse due to increased marine traffic coming into Blaine Harbor. The lighthouse became a reality on May 5, 1905, at a cost of $25,000 and Carver became its first keeper.

Drayton Harbor is a small cove formed by Semiahmoo Spit, the extension of a sandspit northward of Birch Point. It is about two miles in extent, but flats that bare at low water occupy a large area in the eastern and southern parts of the harbor. The present light and fog signal are now located there, and a buoy 700 yards to the west southwest is near the northern end of the extensive sand flats off the northwestern side of Semiahmoo Spit.

An extensive tourist resort is presently located in the nearby area.

Only a memory—Semiamhoo Lighthouse (1904-1944) on offshore piling near Blaine, Washington (Semiamhoo Bay) was similar to the Desdemona Lighthouse at the mouth of the Columbia River.

She's only a memory now, but the Semiahmoo Lighthouse had a short but colorful history. Photo courtesy Marjorie Reichardt

The keepers' dwelling at Patos Island about 1910. The keepers and family members are seen on the porch of the unique frame structure. Photo U.S. Lighthouse Service

❊ Point Roberts

Directly west as the gull flies is perhaps the only piece of land in continental United States that can only be reached by going through a foreign country. Point Roberts is unique. One must go through British Columbia by road or else by water to gain the sparsely populated peninsula. The eastern face is nearly 180 feet high and composed of white vertical bluffs. Owing to the woods and the low land behind it, Point Roberts often appears from the sea as being an island. The southwestern extremity is marked by a navigation light (since 1910) which though never classed as a lighthouse per say, displays a lantern from a skeleton tower, and it is still very much in use today.

Point Roberts, prior to the establishment of a lighted aid to navigation, was a prime spot for smuggling illegal Chinese laborers and whiskey into the states from Canada.

❊ Turn Point

Next we come to the San Juan Islands, one of the greatest hidden secrets in the United States. It is a group of 172 islands, not including some smaller bits of terra firma that rise above the surface. This smattering of islands, the haunt of scores of yachts and various pleasure craft, has numerous intricate channels, coves, and bays that are a delight to behold. The few small towns and lack of road connections to the mainland has kept the islands' population sparse even though a Washington State ferry route connects the larger islands daily.

In prohibition days the San Juans offered prime connections for bringing illegal liquor into the United States, and the Coast Guard was given headaches trying to keep track of the rum runners that could hide out so easily.

Despite the intricate nature of navigation through the Islands there have only been three major lighthouses established amid a large number of buoys and lesser lights and fog signals that mark the waterways.

One of the lighthouses is at Turn Point on the northwest end of Stuart Island at an important turn in Haro Strait. It was established there in 1893, and though the tower was short and unimpressive, the dwelling for the keepers was commodious and the weather appealing. In the Lighthouse Service years it was considered a good family station. The present white concrete tower is only 16 feet above the ground encompassing a light and fog signal, 44 feet above sea level.

As explained in *Lighthouses of the Pacific*, two of the keepers at the Turn Point Station, Edward Durgan and his assistant Peter Christianson, were awarded the Certificate of Merit for their act of bravery in saving the tug *Enterprise*, and her inebriated crew. The vessel ran aground near the station the night of February 16, 1897.

Durgan and his wife raised a large family while living on the wooded island.

❋ Patos Island

Patos Island is a favorite rendezvous for pleasure boaters. The quaint lighthouse there and its outbuildings seem to beckon visitors. It is a charming little island where Patos Island Light shines from a 38 foot wooden tower, 52 feet above the water, at Alden Point on the western side of the isle. There is also a fog signal and radiobeacon on the premises. A light and fog signal first marked that point in 1893 at the same time as the one at Turn Point. The present facility was constructed in 1908, becoming a full-fledged light station as it gained more importance to the shipping that passed its door. The original lens-lantern was replaced by a fourth order Fresnel revolving lens and a third class Daboll foghorn.

In 1792, the Spanish navigators Galiano and Valdez were impressed by the 260 acre isle and were alerted to the large number of ducks that had congregated there. They named it Patos which translated means duck, and so it became in Spanish, Duck Island and the name has remained to this day.

Before Coast Guard personnel departed from the island, the old keepers' dwelling was razed (1958) and a two-story duplex built for the attendants. The place was another of the favorite assignments for the lighthouse keepers. The only drawback in that so-called "banana belt" was lack of water, and sometimes the cistern ran very low in the summer time. Sometimes there was contamination.

Patos is very near to the Canadian border and blinks back and forth at the Saturna Island beacon on East Point. It was at Patos in the 1850s (at Alden Point) that a temporary survey station was set up in a border dispute with the Canadians. The government survey steamer *Active* landed James Lawson and his assistants to carry on the work. In fact, the point where the lighthouse stands was named Alden in honor of the Commander of the *Active*.

The Canadian lighthouse keepers from Saturna and the Patos keepers often traveled back and forth to visit one another prior to the turn of the century. It was a lonely occupation and visitors were always welcome. It was in 1905 that Edward Durgan was transferred to Patos from Turn Point and brought his huge family with him. During the earlier course of his service at Patos three of his children died because of the inability to get prompt medical attention.

Before construction of the lighthouse there was a sector on the isle known as Smugglers Cove where illegal Chinese laborers were brought across the Canadian border for distribution in the United States, a common practice in early times.

Nobody is quite sure what the future of the lighthouse will be, but if the structure is abandoned it will almost certainly be maintained as an historic site.

❋ Lime Kiln and Cattle Point

Another of the major light stations in the San Juans is Lime Kiln, located at a prime location on the west side of San Juan Island, largest of the archipelago. A superb vista of the main shipping channel spreads itself before the lighthouse and by night scores of navigation aids blink like stars along both Canadian and American waterways. The light shines from a 38 foot white octagonal tower attached to a fog building. From

sea level the light is 55 feet high and has been a factor in navigation since 1914. It was updated to its present status in 1920, and is the pride of the people who dwell on the 13 mile long island. Its remote location kept oil burning in the lamp until the end of World War II when at last a cable was laid to that part of the island, and electricity became available. In the early days there was a considerable amount of limerock mining on the island and the remnants of the kilns still remain, thus giving the lighthouse its name.

The highest elevation on San Juan is Mt. Dallas at 1,036 feet. The island is also the site of the famous 1859 "Pig War" in a boundary dispute between the United States and Canada. There was both an American camp and a British camp on the same island. Under Captain George Pickett, the Ninth Infantry was placed there because the British-American treaty of 1846 had left the International boundary so vague that both countries were claiming the isle. Settlers from both sides had taken up the land. Complications arose in 1858, when Whatcom County levied taxes on English sheep grazing there. The following year, a British pig was shot while rooting up an American potato field. The strange incident started tempers flaring and there were threats of a boundary war. Both sides were armed and ready for battle but several of the settlers had become friends and cool heads prevailed.

Hostilities were finally curtailed in 1872 when Emperor William I of Germany was named arbitrator and the present boundaries were accepted. San Juan Island in its entirety went to the United States.

At that point in history, a major lighthouse had yet to be erected on San Juan. Probably the first structure on the island that qualified as a lighthouse was at Cattle Point, established in 1888. The lighthouse that stands there today was built in 1935 and is an octagonal concrete tower, 90 feet above sea level. A foghorn sounds continuously at the site from June until November.

Cattle Point got its name from a vessel that stranded there in 1857, forcing its cargo of livestock to swim ashore. Thereafter it became the landing place for cattle being brought from Vancouver Island, well before the boundary question was settled.

Cattle Point is at the southeastern extremity of San Juan Channel.

❋ New Dungeness

No lighthouse has had a history quite like that of New Dungeness. First of all, it stands at the end of a near six mile long finger-like sandspit, which according to Guiness is the longest of its kind any place in the world. It is a place reserved as a bird sanctuary and wildlife preserve, and from the air appears like a beckoning finger. It is well away from any settlement, the nearest on the mainland being the little village of Dungeness and the town of Sequim. The local citizenry have a close affinity with the lighthouse. There is no road on the spit and the sentinel can only be reached by boat or helicopter unless one desires to make the 11 mile round trip hike by foot from the mainland. The New Dungeness chapter of the U.S. Lighthouse Society was recently denied a permit to build a 190 foot long floating dock to transport visitors to the lighthouse who would otherwise be unable to make the long hike. The reputed $10,000 project was rejected by the U.S. Fish & Wildlife Service due to the delicate nature of the area, and because it was inconsistent with the Shoreline Management Act and the general policies of Clallam County. The New Dungeness U.S. Lighthouse Chapter has been named as overseer of the Lighthouse. It was on December 14, 1857, that the light was first displayed. It shone out over the Strait of Juan de fuca and across the spit that had claimed many ships, especially during foggy periods. If just a few points off on the compass in thick weather, a ship could easily slide up on the dangerous sands.

It will be recalled that the New Dungeness Lighthouse and the one at Cape Flattery (Tatoosh) were under construction at the same time,

The head keeper and his assistants pose in front of the New Dungeness Lighthouse before the turn of the century. In 1927 the lighthouse was reduced in size from 100 feet to 63 feet. The tall masonry tower was commissioned in 1857.

and the former was completed just two weeks ahead of the other. Originally fitted with a third order fixed Fresnel lens and a 12 inch steam fog signal, the lighthouse was of great value to early day shipping. In the late 1920s the tower was decapitated due to the fact that military gunnery practice on the Canadian side of the Strait reputedly weakened the upper masonry work and necessitated reconstruction of the tower. Whether that was the basic reason, or that natural processes had weakened the tower remained a mute question, but nevertheless rebuilding was essential. As a result, a major renovation under the guidance of Clarence Sherman got underway. The tower was reduced in size from about 100 feet down to 63 feet. It was one of the few cases under the former Lighthouse Service when a major lighthouse was so drastically reduced in height. The change demanded a new lantern house and optic. To conserve money, the iron lantern housing from the abandoned Admiralty Head Lighthouse was removed and reinstalled at Dungeness. The light source and lamp was of the fourth order of the system of Fresnel which has since been replaced and is on display today at the Coast Guard Museum at Pier 36 in Seattle. At the same time a diaphone fog signal was installed at Dungeness. In later years came the radiobeacon and distance finding unit.

The lighthouse was automated in 1976, but until recent times the Coast Guard kept personnel at the station. Among the last to hold that post was J.L. Burr, his wife and child, and all three fell in love with the place. Its isolated location didn't bother them in the slightest and there was deep lament when they heard that the station was slated for even-

tual dismissal of personnel. Burr recalled that the place originally had accommodations for three keepers and their families, but when he was assigned it was down to one. His duties were to paint, mow, paint, clean the lens, paint, clean the fog detector, mow, and paint some more. He was enamored with the station despite the hard work, and always looked forward to visits from the helicopter crew from his command base which often used the spit as a stop-over during training flights. When the station jeep was out of commission (as it was most of the time) they had to be flown on and off to get groceries as there is only one so-called road, the sand at low tide.

The Burr's young daughter spent her first three months at Dungeness, and she scribbled her name in the logbook that had been kept since the early days of the station. Visitors did come, but it was often fishermen whose boats had run out of gas who would signal for a helping hand. On one occasion a television crew from PM Magazine arrived to do a story on the lighthouse.

Though at this writing the Coast Guard still oversees the light, maintenance of the dwellings and grounds is by the local branch of the United States Lighthouse Society.

The initial keepers at Dungeness were Franklin Tucker and John Tibbals of Port Townsend, who were both classified as assistants on a temporary basis until the arrival of Captain Thomas Boyling and H.H. Blake who took over the facility on February 11, 1858.

There were sometimes pitched battles fought on the spit between rival Indian tribes, mostly the Haidas from the Queen Charlottes fighting with the local tribes. On occasion, the shutters at the station had to be closed so as to protect the premises from incursions. See detailed accounts of the Indian troubles in *Lighthouses of the Pacific* (Schiffer Publishing, 1986).

In December 1871, the spit was literally cut in half leaving a 50 foot gap. The sand blew with such ferocity that it completely plastered the tower in that December gale. The swift flowing currents and changing tidal action eventually allowed the spit to heal itself and it has remained in tact ever since.

❀Ediz Hook

The flashing green light at Ediz Hook shines from an I-beam tower in conjunction with the airport hanger. There is also a foghorn and radiobeacon on the premises. Ediz Hook is actually a junior addition of the New Dungeness Spit, only it acts as protection for Port Angeles Harbor and accommodates several buildings, including the Coast Guard air station which plays an important role in servicing the area. The spit itself is three miles long.

Though the glamour of the lighthouse at Ediz Hook is long gone, with the present aid to navigation, its glory days are still remembered by a few oldtimers. Two regular lighthouses had formerly been located on the hook to guide shipping. The first was built in 1865. In fact, President Abe Lincoln signed the first papers in 1863 to grant purchase of the land for a lighthouse. The station was opened two years later on a grant of $5,000. The edifice had a short tower rising from the dwelling and displayed a fifth order Fresnel lens. Initial keeper was George K. Smith who was a genial host to many of the visitors that came from fledgling Port Angeles.

The station also had a pyramid-shaped fog bell house where clockwork machinery tolled the bell automatically until the weights wound down at which time they had to be cranked back up.

Franklin Tucker who helped open up New Dungeness Lighthouse eventually became principal keeper at Ediz Hook.

Erosion began eating at the original lighthouse, and by 1908 it had to be replaced by a new facility. It was another frame edifice but larger and more commodious than the former. Its days were also numbered,

First and second lighthouses to serve at Port Angeles' Ediz Hook. Lower photo shows the original 1866 lighthouse, and the station that replaced it in 1908. Both were frame buildings. The present light is seen atop a structure at the Coast Guard air base in Port Angeles.

for in 1945 the Coast Guard decided that they would incorporate the navigation light and foghorn with the airport. So, once again, one of the fine little lighthouses of yesteryear bit the dust in the progress of time.

✵ Slip Point

Slip Point Lighthouse had a hard time coming into its own, for even though Uncle Sam appropriated $12,500 for its construction in June of 1900, the landowners refused to turn over the land. After threatening condemnation, they were forced to settle for $2,562.

After encountering labor problems, the lighthouse finally became operative on April 1, 1905, located on the outer fringe of Clallam Bay. From the keepers residence it was a long walk along the cliffside on a wood trestle walkway to reach the lighthouse. The Coast Guard decided that the neat, little frame lighthouse would have to go in 1951, due to maintenance costs. It was replaced by a rather strange looking unattended square, white tower on piling that was almost eradicated in 1962 when Canadian naval vessels practicing gunnery in the Strait of Juan de Fuca accidently lobbed some shells into Clallam Bay and took a hunk out of the lighthouse.

The original keepers' dwelling is still utilized and rented out to county officials today, and the light and fog signal still are operating at this writing.

Below:
A survivor. The original lighthouse keepers residence at Slip Point is still being lived in today. It stands on the shores of Clallam Bay on the Strait of Juan de Fuca. It has long outlived the old lighthouse, replaced many years back by an ugly substitute. Photo courtesy U.S. Coast Guard

Slip Point Lighthouse and fog signal building dating from 1905, and razed many years ago. The new tower is on the east bight of Clallam Bay, facing the Strait of Juan de Fuca.

Slip Point's original bivalve (clamshell) Fresnel lens showing the oil vapor lamp.

✸ Waadah Island

Since 1934, five years before the Coast Guard took over the Lighthouse Service, there has been a little concrete unmanned tower on Waadah Island, opposite the Makah Indian village off Neah Bay. Located at the north end of the island the light fixture is a welcome sight to the fishing fleet that frequents the bay. It sports an isophase white characteristic with a red sector that covers dangerous Duncan and Duntze rocks.

And so we have come full circle around the seashore of Washington State with a brief look at each of the lighthouses. We started at Tatoosh Island, the haunt of the Makah Indians for countless years, and we end back at Waadah Island off the town of Neah Bay, center of the Makah Indian Reservation, descendants of those early Indians whose island was taken from them and where once half the tribe was wiped out by smallpox and other white mans' diseases. The U.S. Coast Guard has a base at Baadah Point, the east entrance point to Neah Bay.

5. Oregon's Lighthouses

Steadfast, serene, unmovable,
the same year after year,
Through all the silent night
Burns on forevermore that quenchless flame,
Shines on that inextinguishable light!

—Henry Wadsworth Longfellow

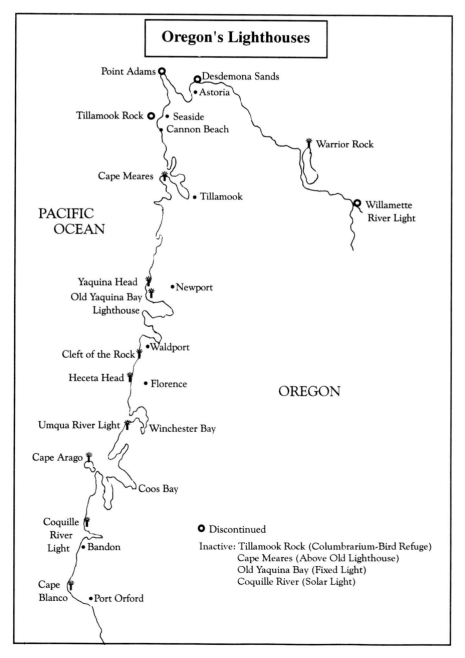

Oregon's Lighthouses

Point Adams
Desdemona Sands
Astoria
Tillamook Rock
Seaside
Cannon Beach
Warrior Rock
Cape Meares
Tillamook
PACIFIC OCEAN
Willamette River Light
Yaquina Head
Old Yaquina Bay Lighthouse
Newport
Cleft of the Rock
Waldport
Heceta Head
Florence
OREGON
Umqua River Light
Winchester Bay
Cape Arago
Coos Bay
Coquille River Light
Bandon
Cape Blanco
Port Orford

O Discontinued

Inactive: Tillamook Rock (Columbrarium-Bird Refuge)
Cape Meares (Above Old Lighthouse)
Old Yaquina Bay (Fixed Light)
Coquille River (Solar Light)

Fantastic might be one way of describing the Columbia River, that great body of water which courses for hundreds of miles gathering speed and volume as it is fed by numerous streams and rivers on its way to the mighty Pacific. It rises in British Columbia, through which it flows southerly for some 370 miles before entering the United States in northeastern Washington. At that point it flows southerly to its junction with the Snake River, from which it curves easterly and forms the boundary between the states of Washington and Oregon for the remainder of its flow to the Pacific Ocean. From source to mouth the "Great River of the West" covers more than 1,210 miles, 640 of that total in the United States. This highly important waterway is one of the greatest drainage basins in the nation, encompassing seven western states.

Discovered by Captain Gray, master of the *Columbia Rediviva*, in 1792, he bequeathed the name of his ship upon the river, the last great plum of discovery on the Pacific Coast.

Lewis and Clark reached it by land in 1805, and the Canadian, David Thompson, two years later explored it from its source down to the Astor Colony which established the Astoria settlement in 1811.

Since those early years the Columbia and Willamette rivers have become a prime seaway of commerce and industry, and though it has been abused in many ways with major dams, factory pollution, and fish reduction, it is indispensable to farmers and industrial production as well as for ocean going ships, tugs and barges, fishing vessels, pleasure craft and many other kinds of marine activity. In our present day, cruise vessels are making calls at lower river ports.

There is no way to calculate the value of the Columbia River and Snake River systems down through the years. It all started with the trading of furs, followed by timber, commercial fishing and grain, not to mention a long list of other items of export. Though much is known about the above, history has been a bit dim on the salmon canning industry which played a large role in the history of the Columbia and was responsible for garnering additional aids to navigation on the river.

For instance, at a non-existent village on the banks of the Columbia was the former locale of Eagle Cliff, below a steep cliff on the Washington side of the river. It was there that the world's first commercial salmon cannery was built in 1865. At its inception all the work was done by hand, and great losses were caused by the slowness of the process. Chinese workers were imported and hired to do the tedious work.

As innovative machinery came into vogue, canneries popped up all along the river, and the export of the commodity caught on with the appetites of foreign nations. Millions of tons of canned salmon were shipped overseas, but in our present day, it has become a major undertaking to preserve the salmon as an endangered species. Traditionally the favorite food of the Indian as well as many of the pioneers, the river was once alive with the sleek Chinook, King, and Silver salmon coming and going from their long ocean migrations. Industrial development on the river and pollution has brought the great bonanza to a screeching halt. Only the remnants of the old canneries from Astoria upriver to places like Altoona, Skamakowa, and Cathlamet remain.

Golden grain from the hinterland, however, fills the holds of many deepsea ships in contrast to the dwindling salmon population.

Lighthouse keepers at Cape Disappointment sometimes got entangled with rival fish seiners and gillnetters in arguments over rights to Sand Island inside the mouth of the Columbia. Just before and after the turn of the century Oregon and Washington fishermen argued over which state had the right to the low, flat uninhabited piece of real estate which was a good place on which to drag seine nets from the Columbia. An occasional pitched battle took place called the "Sand Island War." Nobody was ever killed or seriously wounded but temporary camps were often set up on the sandy confines. In order to keep warm, the fishermen sometimes helped themselves to the firewood and equipment on the lighthouse reservation on the nearby mainland, without permission. The keepers complained to their lighthouse inspector about the infractions and on one occasion a military presence was required until the practice was stopped once and for all.

To accommodate the great parade of marine activity on this river system down through the decades much effort has been put into buoyage, and an occasional lighthouse at strategic locations. Today navigation penetrates well into the state of Idaho, deeper draft vessels making it to Lewiston, and small craft going way beyond on the Snake River. Sternwheel steamers provided much of the traffic in early days. That type of vessel had much success on the river system before the river was tamed and controlled as it is today. Many of the rapids have disappeared by the use of locks such as those at Bonneville. Before the turn of the century and a few decades after, there were many post lanterns located at important danger points in the river. Those old kerosene lamps, which had to be trimmed each night, though some of the better river lights hung from posts, had sufficient capacity to burn for a week. Wooden markers and metal buoys were also utilized at certain locations, but the only navigation aids that might be classified as lighthouses were on the lower river, one in a strategic location at the confluence of the Columbia and Willamette rivers.

The rose city of Portland has been the hub of ocean going commerce on the two rivers from the beginning, although Vancouver predated the other under the domination of the Hudson's Bay Company. Down through the years other ports such as Longview and Kalama have become major shipping points. Grain has always been the largest commodity exported from the river ports, although lumber and logs as well as general's cargo have had a large portion of the total.

Minor lights and buoyage alone were not sufficient to mark the channel to Portland, so in 1893, the Lighthouse Board decided a lighthouse was badly needed at the confluence of the Columbia and Willamette.

Preliminaries building up to the establishment of the lighthouse took several months, but it became a reality in 1895 when the keeper lit the lens-lantern for the first time. The structure stood on piling off the northerly end of what was then called Nigger Tom Island, so-called because of a black man who had settled in the area. The lighthouse stood on the easterly side of the Willamette at the confluence with the Columbia, rising 31 feet above the water. It was a white, one-and-a-half story frame dwelling, with lead colored trimmings and red roof. The lens-lantern displayed a fixed red light, and during foggy periods a large bronze fog bell struck by machinery sounded every ten seconds.

At the time Willamette Lighthouse went into operation, there were less than 60 aids to navigation from Cape Disappointment and Point Adams on up the river to the end of navigation according to the 1896 Light List, and that included every kind of navigation light no matter how small—post lights, tubular lights, range lights, and lens-lanterns.

Down through the years the lighthouse won its way into the hearts of mariners who looked for its friendly red glow by nightfall.

The locale of the lighthouse in later years became the post for the Portland Merchants Exchange, where ship arrivals were reported to the agencies. The *Pacific Coast Pilot* described the latter day Willamette River Light in 1968 as shown from piling with a red triangular daymark on a white platform near the end of the dike extending from Kelley Point. The 1994 *Light List* mentions only Kelley Point Light, and few other minor navigation aids, as merely sitting on dolphins. The first Willamette River Light was a near sister to the early beacons at Browns Point on Puget Sound and at Warrior Rock.

✹ Warrior Rock

Warrior Rock Lighthouse still exists today. Columbia River Pilots always keep a wary eye out for its light by nightfall because of the basaltic ledge which lurks at this location where the channel makes a slight turn. Many ships have gotten hung up in this sector of the river in years past. Ironically, the lighthouse tender *Manzanita* which delivered the building materials for the lighthouse in 1888-89, grounded and sank there in 1905 and was the target of a major salvage operation, after the government wrote her off as a total loss. The firm of Kern & Kern, a marine construction company, was granted rights to the sunken vessel and performed a remarkable recovery job. After a complete refit, the steamer emerged as the tug *Daniel Kern*, bearing the name of the salvor, and she went on to a long prosperous career under private ownership.

The big fog bell that tolled at the station for many years had formerly been used at Cape Disappointment, but was eliminated there because it was often inaudible over the sounds of the surf at the entrance to the river. The bell, now housed at the Columbia County Museum (St. Helens) was cast at Philadelphia in the early 1850s and came around the Horn by ship. The maker was B.J. Bernhard & Co. The keepers at Warrior Rock labeled it the "Black Moria" because of the many times it had to be tolled by hand when the clockwork striking mechanism failed to function. It operated by a weight which had to be periodically wound. In recent years, Coast Guard personnel removed the bell for historical purposes, and while hoisting it off its base, the rope broke, the big instrument fell to the rocks and was badly cracked, never to toll again. That unfortunate incident occurred after a runaway barge crashed into the stone foundation of the lighthouse, May 27, 1969, and severely damaged the structure necessitating the placement of a buoy at the site. The

Above and right:

Warrior Rock Lighthouse was severely damaged when its base was rammed by a runaway barge that broke loose from a tug on May 27, 1969, and the Coast Guard debated whether it was worth repairing the facility. Repairs were finally made. The right photo shows the damage incurred in the accident. In the upper corner is the way the original frame lighthouse looked. A light and fog signal had been at the location on Sauvie Island from 1888-1889. The old lighthouse was similar to the former structure built at Browns Point in 1903. It was off Warrior Rock that the lighthouse tender Manzanita *sank in 1905. (Upper photo courtesy Bob DeRoy; other photo courtesy Larry Barber). The old fog bell at the location was dropped and broken when being removed from the station. It is part of the museum display at the Columbia Historical Society at nearby St. Helens. The wire cable in the upper photo was used as sort of a tram way by the keepers when the Columbia River flooded, in order to get from the dwelling to the lighthouse.*

Coast Guard debated for some time as to whether the unit should be rebuilt and finally decided it would stay at its long time position on Sauvie Island.

The station during the Lighthouse Service years had a comfortable dwelling for the keeper and his family in pleasant surroundings with the exception of the flooding periods when the river overflowed its banks. The existing light tower at the site is of reinforced concrete and rests on the same rock foundation as the original frame tower which was dismantled in its later years. A light still shines from the white pyramidal tower, 28 feet above the river and is backed by two range lights on small skeleton towers.

✸ Desdemona Sands

In the Coast Guard austerity program of the 1940s two similar lighthouses got the axe; the earlier mentioned Semiahmoo sentinel, and the Desdemona Sands Lighthouse at the mouth of the Columbia River. Both were built in the same time period and were similar in almost every respect, and both were offshore on a platform of piling. Minor lights mark both locations today, but those lighthouses are virtually forgotten in the annals of pharology.

Established in 1902, Desdemona Sands Lighthouse appeared like a fairy tale beacon. It was a white octagonal one-and-a-half story dwelling with gray-green trimmings rising from a rectangular platform on piling. It had a bronze colored pyramidal roof, surmounted by a gray-green cylindrical lantern house with a bronze colored dome. A small one-story projection for the fog signal was on the westerly side, and a one-story annex on the easterly side of the dwelling.

The structure was located in 12 feet of water, on the westerly end of the shoal making off to the westward from Desdemona Sands inside the mouth of the river. The shoal area was frequently altered down through the years and the sands shifted constantly, causing nightmares for the early day navigators crossing out to the bar or jockeying in from seaward. Several vessels got hung up on the sands and some never escaped.

The fourth order fixed lens showing a brilliant beam was shining about the river mouth from a height of 46 feet above mean high water with a range of 12 miles. The Daboll fog trumpet blasted for two seconds with alternate silent intervals of three and 23 seconds.

It was many years before Desdemona Sands rated a first-class lighthouse despite the fact that the shifting shoals took its name from the bark *Desdemona* that was wrecked there in 1857. Charts show a great difference in location of the sands over the years as the currents and tides buffet them around in constant turmoil. When Captain Frances Williams, master of the *Desdemona*, lost his vessel and its cargo at the location he insisted that the buoy marking the obstruction was out of position, but little heed was given to his plea. It was probably the shoal that had changed and not the buoy although on rare occasion buoys have broken loose from their anchor chains at the river entrance channel and been swept out to sea or up river.

The lighthouse almost burned down in 1916 when a container of alcohol exploded and set the building afire. The keepers kept their cool and bravely fought the flames as several boats at the river mouth made haste to lend a hand. The keepers had practiced for such an eventuality and managed to get the situation under control.

In later years the fixed light was replaced by a rotating lens but as time progressed the lighthouse was razed and the people of Astoria no longer looked out at the friendly glow from the lighthouse. Only the piling remained with a minor light replacing the classical structure. Its demise occurred well before the fabulous Astoria-Megler (trans Columbia) bridge was built atop the mighty Columbia, a 4.3 mile long accomplishment featuring the nation's longest continuous span, rising high enough above the river to allow the tallest ships to pass underneath.

Today, three channel lighted buoys and a channel leading light are in the general area of the pioneer lighthouse, as listed in the 1995 *Light List*. Closest to the site of the vanished lighthouse is the Sand Island range front light which gives an idea of how the sands have been altered by time and tide.

The old keepers at Desdemona would be astounded today if they could see the Astoria bridge to the east and the changes in the well marked shipping channel. They would have also witnessed a very odd incident on October 26, 1994, when the 855 foot tanker *Keystone Canyon* was ripped away from her dock in Astoria by gale-force winds careening her across the Columbia River. Despite the best of the captain and crew, the monster vessel, nearly as long as three football fields, was carried up against a buttress of the bridge's main span and held fast in the sands beneath. The wind had been strong enough to snap 19 mooring lines at dockside, as gusts nearly 70 miles-an-hour slammed against the mighty steel hull of the tanker. The entire accident took place over a 29 minute period, the ship's gangway being pulled away from the dock as she drifted into the channel from Pier 1. Breaking strength of 1 5/8 diameter wire rope is approximately 209,000 pounds, according to manufacturer's specification, and with 19 lines of nearly equal strength the tanker had been lashed dockside with almost four million pounds of holding power which gives one an idea of the winds that sometimes sweep in from the Pacific inside the river mouth.

Captain Mark Sizemore was on the bridge for a period before the lines parted and hastily reacted by alerting all hands, ordering among other precautions the ship's main turbine on line and preparations to drop both anchors. But all was vain as the vessel rammed the bridge support and held fast. The tanker grounded at low tide, hung up by the stern, her bow afloat in 50 feet of water. Ten tugs responded including the famous *Salvage Chief*, which earlier played a major role in the saving of the tanker *Exxon Valdez* after she spilled millions of gallons of oil in Alaska.

Fortunately, the *Keystone Canyon* had empty tanks and floated very high in the water. She was worked free the next day with the aid of several tugs and escorted to drydock in Portland for damage survey and repairs. The bridge suffered only minor damage.

❀ Point Adams

In our lighthouse tour of Oregon we now come to the Oregon Coast, incomparable in its beauty and accessibility. Rolling sand dunes give way to rugged cliffs of brown, black, and sometimes red basalt that rise almost perpendicular in places 500 feet above the surging Pacific surf. Two-lane Highway 101 snakes along that rockbound shore, starting with broad sand beaches. In winter, when winds howl in across the Pacific, the coast presents dramatic seascapes. Billows churn up froth and spray under clouds whipped up like a black umbrella, turning the water to a gray-blue caldron of heaving activity. One is almost mesmerized in watching the drama unfold. Big, brooding storms can erupt with a force that is thrilling and humbling. To the ones who know the coast best, the ocean is enigmatic and sometimes seemingly sorcerous, a place where winds and currents stir the ghosts of times past when the reefs, rocks, and shoals exacted a toll of sorrow from ships and their crews through calamity.

To help in preventing tragedy, the lighthouses along the Oregon coast were designed for their beacon lights to overlap at the end of their arcs of light so that no place on this 300 mile length of ocean front would be left in the dark. It took many decades to accomplish that effort. Farthest to the north was a lighthouse that no longer exists, abolished by two factors. The lighthouse in question was Point Adams, located at the south entrance to the Columbia River. The lighthouse was terminated in 1899, due to the extension of the south jetty at the entrance to the Columbia River which blocked some of the light's visibility, and the fact that the lightship placed off the river entrance in 1892 was far more effective than the Point Adams light. In addition, Tillamook Rock Light Station to the south, established in 1881, was the leading coastal light for ships inbound or outbound from the Columbia River along with the beacon at Cape Disappointment.

Point Adams Lighthouse was a frame structure somewhat similar to the Point Fermin Lighthouse in southern California. The tower rose from the dwelling to 49 feet at the focal plane of the light and was situated on the dunes, backed by the forest land and the Fort Stevens Military Reservation.

H.C. Tracy was named keeper of the lighthouse, he and his family tending the light from 1875 until 1881, when Captain J.W. "Joel" Munson took over. He was responsible for the first lifesaving operation at the river entrance when keeper at the Cape Disappointment Light. After a stint at river steamboating he came back to the Lighthouse Service and was given the family station at Point Adams. The place became the center of many social activities, and the keeper and his wife were loved by the community. He was affectionately known by some as "Fiddling Joel" for at community socials he always entertained with his fiddle. The Munsons remained at the station until the forced closure in 1899. It was a sad parting, for it had been a happy place and the chores were made easier for Munson within a year of his assignment when the Lighthouse Board, after receiving numerous complaints about the inaudibility of the fog signal, canceled it out. No longer did the boiler furnace have to be stoked up to sound the horn. Seventy-two pounds of steam consumed 130 gallons of water per hour. Further, the characteristic of the light had been changed from red flashing to fixed red after the Tillamook Light became a reality, so all and all the duties for the Munsons were somewhat minimized in comparison to other stations.

As the military might of the fort increased during the Spanish American fracas, the abandoned lighthouse was somewhat of an encumbrance and gradually deteriorated until 1912, when the War Department decided to raze the structure, deeming it a hazard to trespassers and an obvious target for any enemy operating offshore in times of hostilities. The latter reason was not too far off because with the demise of the lighthouse, Battery Russell was erected there. It will be recalled that during World War II shells whizzed over the location, fired from a Japanese submarine, the *I-25*. Little damage occurred and the big guns remained silent much to the chagrin of the Army personnel and National Guard.

The incident caused a great stir and the forts at the entrance to the river, Fort Canby, Fort Columbia, and Fort Stevens, were placed on immediate alert. The submarine moved northward and fired on the lighthouse at Estevan on Vancouver Island's west coast, after which it was back to the business of sinking ships.

It was also in the near location of the lighthouse that the wreck of the British bark *Peter Iredale* occurred in 1906, one of the scores of vessels that were victims of Clatsop Beach and the dreaded spit of the same name. The *Iredale* wreck has remained on the beach since that day and has become a major tourist attraction.

History abounds along that section of the coast. It was the haunt of the Clatsops who roamed the plains and fished the ocean for untold centuries. It is the place where ancient castaways from foreign lands remained isolated from the then known world following shipwreck. Legends of gold and treasure abound. Clatsops were canoe Indians, barrel-chested with scrawny legs, ideal for handling their dugouts. There was even Indian burial grounds there, sacred to the natives but desecrated by the white settlers in later years. Modern civilization with all of its trimmings has pretty much changed the land area, but the shoreline has remained intact and the Oregon State Parks have done a remarkable job in beautifying the landscape at places like old Fort Stevens and surroundings.

❈ Lightships

From the year 1892, a lightship was in operation off the entrance to the Columbia River. The last to serve there was the *Columbia River Lightship WAL-604*, withdrawn from service in November 1979, and now a museum ship at the Columbia River Maritime Museum in Astoria. The first was the *Columbia River No. 50*, which had no propulsion except sails that could be pulled out of the locker in case of emergency. Those sails proved inadequate in 1899, when the ship was wrenched from her moorings and driven ashore at McKenzie Head where it was believed her time would end. Union Iron Works of San Francisco had built the 123 foot vessel stout as a warship-wooden planks over steel frames. After many months and several failed salvage attempts the vessel was moved overland, in one of the most novel salvage feats of the century. Relaunched into Baker Bay, she eventually was repaired and placed back in service until replaced by a new lightship in 1908, the *No. 88*, which had steamed around the Horn in a flotilla of government vessels. She did yeoman service off the bar from 1909 until 1939 when she was transferred to another position and replaced by the *No. 93* which had been serving at Umatilla Reef station. The submarine that shelled the Oregon Coast passed by the lightship without seeing her inasmuch as she was blacked out temporarily.

Meanwhile, *No. 88* was commandeered by the military as a military recognition vessel. In all, four different lightships—several Relief lightships, and one chartered vessel, the steamer *Callender*—all stood their turns at the post. When the *604* was withdrawn and replaced by an ocean buoy in 1979, an era had ended. The *No. 50* was the first lightship on the Pacific Coast, and the *604* was the last. During the heyday of the coastal lightships, they were stationed at Swiftsure Bank, Umatilla Reef, Blunts Reef, and San Francisco, in addition to the Columbia River. All had logbooks full of dramatic incidents, being located in important shipping lanes and in dangerous posts warning of lurking obstacles to navigation. Lightships were placed where it was impossible or impractical to build lighthouses. The high cost of operation and hi-tech unmanned

buoys spelled the end for lightships which once rimmed the coastline on the east, gulf, and Pacific coasts, a sort of reverse evolution in the history of those most unusual vessels. It was a hard, demanding, and solitary life for those who manned the tethered vessels, never going anywhere but having to brave every kind of sea condition and storm sent in their direction. There was always danger of being rammed by ships underway in dirty weather and there was the nerve-wracking noise of the foghorn in protracted foggy periods which was tantamount to being inside of a metal barrel with somebody banging on the top with a hammer. Except for museum and preservation groups keeping a few lightships, all have passed from the maritime scene of America.

❈ Tillamook Rock

I remember it well, when as a keeper at Tillamook Rock Light Station in 1945 I saw one of the last of the coastal steam schooners, which I recognized as the *Bandon*, being towed up the coast, a half mile off the rock. With a sentimental attachment to that breed of vessel I wanted to signal her by flag just to see if some salty oldtimer might signal back. From its inception, Tillamook Rock's lighthouse had been equipped with a signal flag rack with a flag for each letter of the alphabet, and with messages when two were raised simultaneously. It was a practice that went well back into maritime history, and it was the early isolation of the rock that inspired the Lighthouse Board to have the flags at the lighthouse for emergencies. I pulled out the letters J and P which came out of their slots amid dust and moths, it having been so long since they were used. The two flags raised together meant, "Heavy weather coming; look sharp!" My message was for real, as storm clouds were approaching. All I really wanted was a recognition flag from the *Bandon*, but none was seen, in fact, I wondered if the aging vessel even had any signal flags aboard, and if so, if anyone really cared anymore. It put me into a reminiscent frame of mind, thinking of how the traditional things of yesteryear had passed from the scene. I watched the last of the coastal lumber steamers passing in review; I was in an obsolete lighthouse whose days were numbered and I was using a type of communication that passed with the day of the commercial sailing ship.

Tillamook Rock has been pretty much returned to the way it was before the lighthouse was completed in 1881. The U.S. Fish & Wildlife Service is the overseer, although the lonely basaltic upheaval with its abandoned lighthouse has long been owned by Eternity at Sea which had it gutted and turned into a columbarium for the ashes of the dead.

Mimi Morissette, a major stockholder in the project, has a real love for lighthouses and has done her best to keep its memory alive in making it the world's only sea-girt columbarium. The hoped for scheme of having maritime-oriented folk have their ashes placed there has thus far been a rather unsuccessful undertaking, but the sealed up crypt that was once a lighthouse has been placed on the National Register of Historic Places, which allows exterior paining so that from the sea it still looks good. All the windows have been sealed over and the lantern panes blacked out with steel plates. The interior has been gutted down to bare sandstone and brick. Nothing remains inside except the rusting spiral staircase and the racks which contain ornate urns with ashes of the dead. Unfortunately, of the 17 originally placed there, two were stolen by thieves that must have landed at night via small helicopter.

Seals and sealions sometimes occupy the lower climes of the eastern slope, and murres and gulls have whitened the rock with their droppings. Last report from the Fish & Wildlife overseer listed 6,000 murres having nested there in one year, which means the seabirds have reclaimed the rock which once was theirs exclusively before the white man invaded and decided a lighthouse should be built on its summit.

Of all the Pacific Coast lighthouses since the beginning, none, including St. George Reef, have received as much publicity as Tillamook

Rock. It's a place where considerable drama has unfolded mainly because of its exposed location, open to the fury of Mother Nature who hasn't spared 'her temper in lashing out at the timeless hunk of rock. Journalists in more recent times dubbed the place, "Terrible Tilly," but during my stint on the rock I never once heard that expression used by the oldtime keepers who had all begun their years with the Lighthouse Service. It was often referred to as "The Rock" or "Oregon's Alcatraz," but "Terrible Tilly" was pretty much adopted after the Coast Guard abandoned the lighthouse in 1957 and decreed that a light could never again be displayed at the rock.

It was no secret that near the end for the lighthouse it was the most costly to operate of any unit in the 13th Coast Guard District. Most of the machinery was old and rusty, and storm damage every year was considerable. There were wide cracks in the cement flooring and several leaks which had to be attended to constantly.

Repeating the history of the lighthouse might be somewhat counterproductive as it has been told and retold by a great number of writers including this author, in books, magazines, and newspapers down through the length of its history. It is located 20 miles south of the Columbia River and 1.2 miles off Tillamook Head. The water on the west, north, and south sides is from 25 to nearly 40 fathoms with some underwater ramparts shoaling to 16 fathoms.

First consideration for a lighthouse in the area was at Tillamook Head on the mainland where construction and supply would be much simpler. The site was ruled out however, because of the high elevation which would have frequently been shrouded by fog and cloud. A lesson had been learned from the location of the old Point Loma Lighthouse, which at more than 400 feet in elevation was often obscured in fog.

FIRST ORDER L.H., TILLAMOOK ROCK, OREGON. *Plate 8*

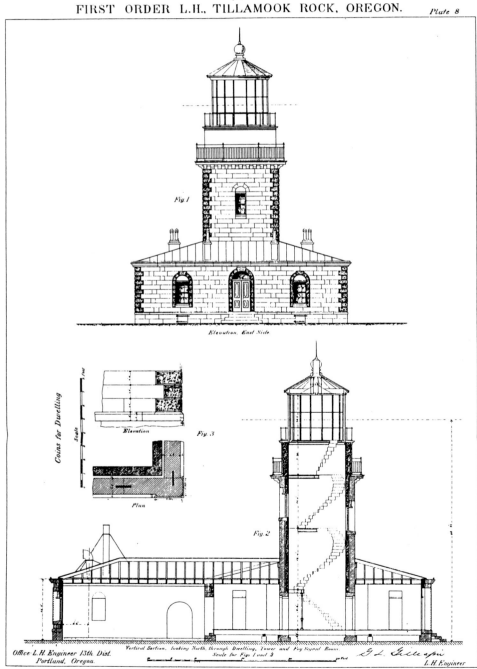

G.L. Gillespie, lighthouse engineer with the 13th Lighthouse District, Portland, Oregon, when the lighthouse was built issued this vertical sectional plan of the lighthouse structure. Damage through the years made many changes to the structure.

Construction moving along at Tillamook Rock in 1880 in this artist's rendition. The supply vessel anchored off the rock is the two-masted power schooner George Harley.

On June 20, 1878, Congress appropriated $50,000, but the hex was put on the Tillamook Head site, and Major G.I. Gillespie of the Army Engineers strongly insisted the light should go on the offshore rock despite opposition to the cone-shaped outcrop. After considerable debate the Lighthouse Board sanctioned the suggestion and eventually $75,000 more was coughed up as the growing shipwreck toll among vessels bound for the Columbia River became constant headline news.

H.S. Wheeler, district superintendent, was placed in charge, and after several futile attempts gained the rock but was unable to get his survey instruments landed. He was forced to make an immediate examination of the rock using only a hand tape, then exit before the waters made it too difficult for him to leap back into the small boat that waited for him off the rock. His recommendation was that at least 30 feet would have to be blasted off the summit in order to create a foundation.

On September 18, 1879, tragedy struck when master-mason John Trewaves was drowned while attempting to jump onto the rock. His body was never recovered and there was great public pressure to abandon the project. Despite it all, the Revenue Cutter *Corwin* secreted a crew out to the rock under the supervision of Charles A. Ballantyne. Great difficulty was experienced before four workers could be put on the rock and five more days passed before four others could be landed by improvised means, along with provisions and tools. Conquering such a beetling crag was pitting mans' ingenuity against the wrath of nature because the days that followed presented every kind of adversity. Ring bolts and temporary stagings were necessary. In January 1880, a violent storm tore the roof off the blacksmith shop and carried the storehouse and all the supplies into the sea. The fearful workers prayed for survival, the seas having flooded their shelter and the food supply all but exhausted.

It became more difficult to get additional workers because of negative publicity and the problem of conveying men to the rock, often in rough seas. It was only the courage and zeal of Ballantyne that kept the men from quitting, as he worked under the most trying of conditions,

which included the blasting of hundreds of tons of basaltic rock from the summit.

One corpulent quarryman named Gruber, who had been recruited, was brought out by the steamer *Mary Taylor*. Aboard the vessel was the derrick which was to be landed, along with additional supplies. After lines were rigged between the vessel and the rock, the construction foreman was ferried out to the ship via breeches buoy. While enroute, as was often the case, the lines dragged the man through the water and he was brought abroad dripping wet. When Gruber saw this he panicked and refused to be transported to the rock. Adding insult, it was discovered he was too fat to fit into the breeches buoy. Ballantyne then suggested lashing him to the top of the conveyance, but Gruber who was afraid of the water, balked, and nobody was willing to challenge his bulky frame. He was accordingly sent back to Astoria on the ship where he was fitted with a giant life preserver and a specially made bosn's chair. Back he went. Fortunately, the seas remained calm and he landed on the rock without getting his feet wet.

With remarkable determination the work proceeded until the cornerstone for the edifice was laid. The cut rock was sent out from a quarry at Mount Tabor, near Portland. It was a banner day on January 21, 1881, when the light sent out its friendly glow for the first time, and the accomplishment hailed as the engineering triumph of the year. Albert Roeder proudly accepted his role as the initial principal keeper of the sentinel that had taken a year and a half to build at a cost of $125,000.

In addition to the invaluable service of the USRC *Corwin*, several privately-owned vessels (chartered) that had transported equipment, supplies and personnel to and from the rock were the *Mary Taylor*, *George Harley*, and *Emily Stevens*, plus the government lighthouse tenders *Shubrick* and *Manzanita*.

As a primary seacoast light, the Tillamook beacon produced 75,000 candlepower, visible more than 20 miles at an elevation of 134 feet above sea level. Characteristic of the light was a white flash every five seconds. The station was also equipped with a first class steam siren that sounded as soon as the visibility closed down.

Unfortunately, just a few weeks before the lighting, the British sailing vessel *Lupata* fog-bound by nightfall had wandered off course and almost smashed into the rock. Workers shouted and built small fires to warn the tall ship away from danger. Their efforts might have paid off, but the next morning it was obvious the navigator was confused. The vessel had scraped over the outcroppings near Tillamook Head and had foundered with her entire crew of 16, the only survivor, the ship's mascot found whimpering on the beach.

The years that followed brought a series of storms and surging seas beating against the rock. On the south side is a narrow fissure cut deep in the basalt where seas, especially in southwesterly storms, sweep in with a vengeance. They erupt in geyser form sending great torrents as high as 160 feet and dropping the contents on the building, causing it to tremble as if in a slight earthquake. Of all the log entries kept at the lighthouse some stand out above the others. On the night of October 18, 1912, a storm of great violence struck the rock. Head keeper William Dahlgren's entry read:

I regret to state that on the evening of the 18th, or the morning of the 19th, we lost a portion of the west end of the Rock, water and rocks coming over with so much noise we could not tell, and did not know it had departed before next morning, when the sea went down, that we could go outside.

At 12:35 a.m. on the 19th the sea came up and broke one pane in the middle section of the lantern, which also put the light out and flooded the watchroom, as well as downstairs. To add to it all the soot and ashes came out of the stove in the kitchen.

At 12:50 a.m. we had the light burning and storm pane in for the rest of the night.

Siren was running until the crash came but making no regular blast on account of water filling the trumpet too fast. After getting the light burning we closed down the fog signal, as the wind hauled to westward and cleared the atmosphere somewhat. Shortly afterwards when taking the siren out to clear it, I found it filled partly full with rocks; therefore water could not get out of it.

Will also state that every one under my charge worked hard and faithfully, regardless of water and glass, everybody being drenched to the skin.

It wasn't until December 9, that the tender *Manzanita* could approach the rock with provisions and mail.

Another of the violent occurrences at Tillamook was on October 21, 1934, in a storm with winds of nearly 110 miles an hour. It blew the Columbia River Lightship off station and did considerable damage along the shores of Oregon and Washington. The lighthouse was repeatedly submerged by tremendous seas. A section of the rock was torn away, great fragments being thrown over the station, some through the plate glass and into the lens prisms. Eventually 16 panels fell prey to the onslaught and the lens was smashed beyond repair. The lantern room and watch room were flooded and the keepers worked up to their necks in cold sea water until it could escape down the spiral stairs into the interior of the structure, flooding the rotunda.

Assistant keeper Hugo Hanson suffered a badly cut hand from broken glass in the lantern room. Inasmuch as the oil vapor lamp had been extinguished and the revolving mechanism destroyed, no light, not even a standby lamp could be displayed the first night. It took days to get things temporarily repaired and even longer to reach the outside, for the cable with the shoreline had been severed. Among the cleanup work was clearing the debris out of the lantern room, including seaweed, fish, and rock fragments.

Wooden shutters were placed where the lantern planes had been knocked out and a fixed white light was displayed from a 375 millimeter lens until the main light was temporarily repaired on October 27, though of little effect due to the severe damage. The four keepers, William Hill and his assistants, Henry Jenkins, Hugo Hanson, and Werner Storm worked tirelessly to restore the station. It was the savvy of Jenkins, familiar with radio components, that contrived a short-wave radio sending and receiving apparatus from spare parts, and was successful near midnight on October 23, in reaching an amateur operator who put the lighthouse in contact with the Tongue Point base with the damage report.

Exterior railings, water and fuel tanks and other fittings had been destroyed, and the derrick boom, the means of transport to and from the rock had been ripped from its fittings. Other damage included pipelines, iron balustrades, footing walls etc.

It was on the morning of October 27 that the *Manzanita* arrived and stood off the rock until the old method of running lines between ship and rock could be secured sending officials ashore for a three-hour inspection. As a result, a major overhaul of the station followed and all of the wrongs were eventually righted, including a new lens and lighting apparatus.

The age of automation never reached Tillamook Rock as the Coast Guard found that the high cost of operation, antiquated equipment, and the fact that the steamer route moved far out to sea with the use of the radiobeacons, made the historic lighthouse a white elephant. On September 1, 1957, the curtain came down for the final time. The last keeper who had spent 20 years of his life on the rock wrote the last entry. His name was Oswald Allik and as a tribute to his faithful service he was reassigned to Heceta Head Lighthouse to finish out his career there until automation hit that lighthouse.

The abandoned Tillamook lighthouse was put up for public auction and had several bidders with grandiose ideas all being totally unfamiliar with the peculiar problems connected with the rock. Of course, the day of the helicopter had come into its own, so there were ways to get people to the rock other than by the dangerous sea route. The derrick boom had been knocked out in heavy seas and dory landings were extremely hazardous.

Buyers came and went, each ending up with frustration but making a little money with each subsequent resale. Academic Coordinators of Las Vegas got it through the GSA for $5,600 in 1959; G.E. executive George Hupman bought it for $11,000, and his dreams faded; Max Shillock Jr. paid $27,000 of borrowed money from a relative and ended up losing the lighthouse and nearly his own life. It was then that Eternity at Sea, spearheaded by Mimi Morissette and a Portland funeral home, paid $50,000 and turned the place into a columbarium. At this writing there has been rumors of an impending deal with yet another funereal buyer.

The final link is broken
The former ways have passed
Of words that once were spoken
Only memory will last.

—JAG

❀ Cape Meares

What better place to watch the gray whale migration than from the lofty heights of Cape Meares. These giant denizens of the deep travel up to 10,000 miles on their round trip between the Arctic Sea and the western coast of Mexico. In November, the grays start to depart their summer feeding grounds in the Arctic Sea. Pregnant females lead the way, followed by mature adults of both sexes, then juveniles. By late December they are seen at a rate of about 30 whales per hour off the

Oregon Coast. Traveling at about five miles-an-hour the leviathans apparently move faster southbound than northbound where the rate is only three miles-an-hour. By early February they have reached their breeding and calving grounds in three major lagoons in Baja, California. The northward migration is much more spread out. Most of the migration is seen off the Oregon coast in the March-May period when they are traveling northward moving in pods of two to ten.

Ironically, the lighthouse sites have become additionally popular in our present day as tourists often flock there to spy out the great creatures. When a whale surfaces there is a blow or spout. It is a double-plumed misty jet of vapor, six to twelve feet high, that is actually a mist which condenses from the warm moist air as it is exhaled under high pressure from the lungs. Normally they make three to five short, shallow dives of less than a minute each and then a long, deep dive. When the flukes or tail come out of the water it usually signals a deep dive lasting from three to five minutes. Their most spectacular mannerism is breaching. They sometimes come three-fourths of their body length out of the water. Many feel this is to rid their bodies of barnacles and lice as they twist and come down with a giant splash. The grays reach up to 50 feet in length and sometimes weigh in excess of 40 tons. Though they can live up to 50 years, nearly half die within the first year. There are larger whales, such as the 100 foot Blues, but no species makes as long a migration as do the Grays. A growing number of whales remain off the Oregon coast the year round refusing to make the long migration.

Despite its missing bulleyes, the first order lens at the old Cape Meares Lighthouse is still a frequent target for tourist cameras. Most don't even understand that anything is missing, or that a few years back vandals broke into the lighthouse and stole the precious bits of glass. The lighthouse has been a tourist attraction in an Oregon State Park for several years and is so situated that it attracts considerable attention. Cape Meares State Park is easily reached, located ten miles west of Tillamook on the Three Capes Loop road.

Volunteers man the lighthouse and visitors are welcome to view the mini-museum in the work room and the rotunda, and to climb the iron staircase to the lantern room.

After being retired from active service in favor of an airway type DCB beacon atop a concrete utility structure at the high point on the grounds, the older tower was neglected for a few years after 1963, and its iron plates soon became red with rust. The original work room was dismantled and for a time there was talk of doing away with the tower as well. However, public outcry and the efforts of the State Parks eventually brought new life to the tower and it has since become one of the prime attractions on the coast for those who like lighthouses.

Of masonry construction overlapped with iron plates, it was established atop the cape in 1890 as both an ocean front light and a guide light for vessels seeking the entrance to Tillamook Bay. Its lofty elevation of 217 feet above the ocean necessitated a tower of only 38 feet, the Henry LePaute lens capable of being seen 21 miles at sea.

According to those in the know, the existing modern navigation aid can produce 800,000 candlepower, visible about 25 miles at sea. It, too, might be canceled in the future.

Originally, it was planned to place the lighthouse at Cape Lookout, about ten nautical miles southward. That location remained a lighthouse reserve for several decades but no aid to navigation was ever built there. Today it is the site of another beautiful Oregon State Park.

When the land was cleared at Meares and lighthouse construction got underway in 1889, it was indeed virgin land with tall trees everywhere. Many had to be felled, and much of the lumber was used to build the station dwellings and out buildings.

Credit President Benjamin Harrison for signing the papers that made the land available after considerable controversy concerning the Cape Lookout site. Charles B. Duhrkoop was general contractor for the

station under the jurisdiction of the Army Corps of Engineers, and Anthony W. Miller was named as the first head keeper. Beasts of burden were used to build the road up to the location and many of the supplies that didn't arrive by government steamer were brought from the town of Tillamook by small boat across the bay, but only when the tide was full, for at low tide that body of water often turned to mud and sand.

Families lived in peaceful harmony when the station was completed. In fact, there was even a one-room school house there at one time for the children of the keepers.

The lighthouse had its work room added in 1895. The present replica was added after the lighthouse became a tourist attraction. All of the other outbuildings have been dismantled, including the oil houses.

At the foot of the cape, on the north side, the ocean resort town of Bayocean once stood, but it was claimed by the ocean through erosion.

In fact, the spit protecting Tillamook Bay was often breached or split, and millions of dollars of government money has been used to heal the breach and protect the valuable oyster industry that thrives in the bay.

Going back to the reason Cape Meares Lighthouse was placed on its existing loft rather than at Cape Lookout perhaps reverts to July 6, 1788, when Captain John Meares of the *Felice Adventurer* was sailing southward along the coast of what we know today as Tillamook County. He sighted a feature which he named Cape Lookout and made an illustration of it. Decades later, the U.S. Coast Survey somehow mistakenly placed the name Cape Lookout on its charts of 1850 and 1853 at another prominent cape some ten miles to the south of Meares' original location. This error was later realized, but George Davidson of the Coast Survey decided in 1857 that the mistake could not be corrected because the name Cape Lookout had already become too widely associated with the position given on the previous government nautical charts.

Still the confusion continued. Cape Lookout appeared the most prominent location for a beacon from the navigational need of those early years and the land was duly surveyed and recorded. Next came the inexplicable blunder after the U.S. Lighthouse Establishment was ready to begin actual construction. Though some may argue today that such an error could never have happened, apparently it did. The approach to the cape was so difficult to reach in 1889 that it was determined that many of the materials would have to be obtained at the site. Accordingly, a blacksmith shop was set up to produce necessary iron work and timbers were cut, in addition to bricks made from clay found nearby. It wasn't realized that a mistake had been made until the project got started which shows the lack of communication in that then isolated sector of the Oregon Coast. The government later rectified the wrong and the lighthouse was officially sanctioned.

❀ Auxiliary Lights

One may notice when checking out the lighthouses along the Pacific Coast that auxiliary lights are mounted on the galleries or catwalks of many of the lighthouses. Such lights are usually put in automatic operation once the main optic goes out for some reason. In some cases the auxiliary lights are being used on a regular basis as they are much more economical to operate and maintain than the larger light fixtures. Many of the old Fresnel optics, now referred to as "classical lenses," may soon be obsolete and maintained as museum pieces only. It has already occurred at many of the stations across the country.

With the LAMP program, the Coast Guard has introduced a new "acrylic optic" which has become a standard method of lighting in many lighthouses. The largest of these is 300mm tall. The lens is molded on the Fresnel lens design. Some optics have a belt which holds a circle of six to eight bulbs. When one burns out the other moves into place. Others have a rotating lamp holder which serves the same purpose. The globes themselves are miniature in size compared to the huge quartz iodine bulbs of 1000 watts used in the larger lighting units.

Batteries and solar panels are also being used extensively to provide power, a method that requires less tending except on an annual basis.

The new acrylic 155 and 250 mm lenses, when lighted, are not as powerful as the larger traditional Fresnels, but they are as bright as those of the small sizes utilized in harbors and bays, and with the steamer lanes farther out to sea than the range of most beacons the smaller acrylic lights in most cases are adequate. With every vessel today equipped with hi-tech electronic equipment the role of the lighthouse, as earlier mentioned, has been greatly reduced. The radiobeacon, radar, LORAN, and satellite (Global Positioning System) navigation have become the unseen lighthouses of our days and are of great value to navigators.

Will the day ever come when lighthouses are totally unnecessary? It may well happen, but for sentimental and historic reasons the aging towers should be around well into the future even though their importance to maritime commerce is almost negligible. It is doubtful that the lesser lights on buoys and minor navigation aids that mark charted routes into ports or on river bars and bays will vanish, as such units are low cost and often radio-controlled.

❈ Yaquina Head

In July of 1868, A. W. Chase of the U.S. Coast Survey wrote the following description of Cape Foulweather and Yaquina Heads:

Three and one-half miles north of Yaquina Bay is a remarkable cape, known as Cape Foulweather. It is perfectly bare of timber, extends one mile out from the beach, and consists of two conical hills; the inner one 407 feet, the outer one 360 feet above the low water mark, and terminates in a tongue or point of rocks, with one large detached islet lying off its extreme end. This cape being a very prominent landmark and unlike any other on the coastline, will identify the position of Yaquina entrance at once, if the mountains are not visible.

He went on to say, "The north shore, or "Heads" of Yaquina entrance consists of a bluff 130 feet high of sandstone formation, showing yellow from the sea. This bluff is crowned with an isolated grove of pine or fir trees, some dead and some alive..."

It was that report which started a controversy that has gone on to this day involving whether or not the materials for the lighthouse were put in the wrong place. The confusion stemmed from the fact that two places were first called Cape Foulweather, but for a certainty the Lighthouse Board employees knew the right place to put the building materials though at least one relative of the builders claimed differently. Reputedly, in 1869-70, the Lighthouse Board had considered two sites; Cape Foulweather 12 miles north of Yaquina Bay (the real Cape Foulweather) and the present Yaquina Head, 3 1/2 nautical miles north of Yaquina Bay. Colonel Robert S. Williamson visited the area and made several attempts to go to the existing Cape Foulweather to analyze the situation but not only found it too difficult to get there through the dense underbrush but similarly difficult along the rock-strewn beach. He elected therefore to "build it on the lower cape," it being much nearer to Yaquina Bay with a usable road and a somewhat protected landing against prevailing northwest winds during the summer months. He also noted that it would cost considerably more to build a road up to the distant Cape Foulweather, which he considered a monumental task at that period in history. Thus the "lower" cape was to become known as Yaquina Head. Had the lighthouse been placed on Cape Foulweather (probably near where Otter Crest is today) the short life of the Yaquina

Bay Lighthouse might well have been extended as the two lighthouses would have been 12 miles apart instead of slightly under four. That fact ended government usage of Yaquina Bay Lighthouse in 1874 after only three years of service.

Finally in March of 1871, Congress appropriated $90,000 for the construction of the tower. Though slightly less in height, it was similar in most ways to the plans used for the Pigeon Point Lighthouse in California. Building supplies were transported to a small cove below the headland including iron and 370,000 bricks, plus lumber, all of which had to be hoisted up to the plateau. In calm seas all went relatively well but in the winter storms of 1871-72 the builders experienced considerable difficulty. Twice, lighters bringing in supplies from an offshore schooner capsized, losing much of the cargo. Two other vessels grounded on the bar. The stabilizing jetties had yet to be built and the bar could be fickle with shifting sand deposits.

The ship *Ocean Queen* was dispatched to pick up the lens and lighting apparatus and other appendages in New York after transshipment from Paris. In turn, she off-loaded the shipment at Panama which was transferred to another vessel for the voyage to its Oregon Coast destination. The lighting apparatus was manufactured by the renowned optic makers, Barbier & Fenestre of Paris, France, and unfortunately some damage occurred during the transport activities, and parts had to be replaced. The precious cargo had arrived in March 1872, and inflation must have been non-existent, for according to the report the cost of the lens was only $7,000. In the interim, work was being completed on the keepers' dwellings, the head keeper's domain being a 2 1/2 story Victorian edifice, with a smaller unit for the assistants. There was also a barn, a 3,000 gallon redwood water storage tank, a wood shed, and a storage house. The principal keeper's dwelling, often claimed to be excessively drafty, was razed in 1938 when the Coast Guard built new quarters on the premises.

For the original families at the lighthouse it was necessary that they provide much of their own food. There was a sizable garden plot and a fenced off pasture including pig pens and a chicken house.

A cistern was added in 1886, and in 1889 a new oil house was built. The original oil house was one of the two rooms attached to the tower which was somewhat of a fire hazard. There was also a tramway on the south face of the head where barrels of oil and other heavy materials were hoisted up to the plateau.

Total cost of the Yaquina Head Light Station was as follows: Tower, $44,459.08; lantern, $3,300; lens and lighting apparatus, $7,000; and dwellings and outbuildings, $14,018.42 for a total of $90,908.58.

To the citizens of the area, the 93 foot tower was a skyscraper, nothing in Oregon was as high or monumental as that creation when it was commissioned on August 20, 1873. It became so popular with the public that it was difficult for the keepers to get their work accomplished. They requested their superiors to set up official visiting hours, complaining they were only averaging five hours a night of sleep.

Initial keeper of the light was Fayette S. Crosby from August 20, 1873, till December 23, 1875. No reason was given for his transfer after such a short tenure. Surprisingly, in August of 1888, a female assistant light keeper was assigned to the station. Her name was Malinda J. Plummer, the wife of then head keeper Frank Plummer. She was probably the first to receive such an appointment in the Pacific Northwest. Other female assistants served at the Cape Blanco Lighthouse and at North Head around the turn of the century. Their names were Mabel Bretherton and Mrs. Alexander.

The severe weather made it sometimes difficult for the wives of the keepers, for the brisk winds often blew their sheets to ribbons when hung out to dry. The grandchildren were offered schooling in the office of Samuel Cases's Ocean House Lodge near Yaquina Bay from 1874 till 1886, under the tutelage of Emily Stevens and Hattie Wass.

Restored in recent times after usage as an officers' residence at Fort Casey, the Admiralty Head Lighthouse has had a peculiar history. Now a tourist attraction on Whidbey Island, it has not been a working lighthouse for many years, its original lantern house switched to the rebuilt New Dungeness tower in the late 1920s. For several years the Admiralty Head tower sat decapitated, bugled out of service, shipping utilizing the Point Wilson light to a greater degree.

Since 1914, this stately lighthouse has crowned Point Wilson, an important turning point for ships entering Admiralty Inlet (Puget Sound) from the Strait of Juan de Fuca. The first lighthouse and fog signal at the location was established in 1879 when Port Townsend was a rip-roaring, lusty seaport. It was one of those serene days when Keith Kammerzell took this shot from a place where fog is a frequent visitor.

The people of Port Townsend are historically-minded, and the place abounds in history with its many old buildings and residences. A lighthouse replica (not a working lighthouse) is pictured here. It was built in 1990, and called the Dimick Lighthouse. Vintage structures are nearby.

A disappearing gun has been placed back at abandoned Fort Casey as a tourist attraction. It was near that place, called Red Bluff, where the First Admiralty Head Lighthouse was built in 1860 with William Robertson as its initial keeper. When the Army needed the spot for armament, the lighthouse had to be razed and reestablished to the north. The restored lighthouse is open to the public.

What might be called the tragic ending of a once bright chapter in lighthouse history. The Smith Island Lighthouse, dating from 1858, in recent years became the victim of erosion, only a portion of the building teetering on the edge of the cliff, pictured here.

Point Roberts Light is the northernmost lighted aid to navigation on the coast of the United States. Commercial salmon fishing began there as early as 1853 and a cannery followed later (now closed). Smugglers and fish pirates, working from the safety of Point Roberts, the American owned tip of a Canadian peninsula located 14 miles west of the town of Blaine, Washington, levied tribute on legitimate enterprise. The smuggling of Oriental aliens, illegal booze, and other items finally came to a halt in 1910 when the Federal Government (the Lighthouse Service) erected Point Roberts Light. There have been several different aids to navigation installed through the years at Point Roberts, the photo here being the installation at this writing. Displayed is a 250mm acrylic light and a diamond shaped day mark referred to as an NR in the Light List. The structure is 25 feet high.
Photo courtesy of Bev Schreiber, Bev's Studio, Mukilteo, Washington

Left:
A neat little, sweet little light station at Turn Point, at the northwest end of Stuart Island, in the San Juans, is a dinky concrete structure built in 1936 to replace the former light structure dating from 1893. Vessels pass close to the point. Note the water depths.

Below:
Idyllic setting for a lighthouse family, Burrows Island Lighthouse since automation has seen the commodious dwelling boarded up and the landing secured, though at this writing the lens still gave forth its light in the lantern room of the 1906 vintage frame structure.

Though a light and fog signal have existed on Patos Island since 1893, the present frame lighthouse was opened for business in 1908, lighted with a fourth order Fresnel lens. The frame tower and fog signal structure were backed by commodious keepers' dwellings where though families found peace and contentment, there was much isolation in early times.

Lime Kiln Lighthouse on west side of San Juan Island, facing Vancouver Island, has lost its Fresnel in favor of a smaller fixture, but the beauty of the tower and fog signal building remain. It was one of the last lighthouses on the coast to be electrified.

New Dungeness Lighthouse, showing a light since 1857, was reduced in size in the 1920s when stress of weather and the booming of Canadian guns on the other side of the Strait of Juan de Fuca weakened the structure and demanded its reconstruction.

The little concrete structure at Cattle Point, erected in 1935, is pictured here with a solar panel to fortify the light at its crown. This San Juan Island site is where cattle were once landed in early times.

Fourth order lens with a missing bullseye, a three-flasher believed to have been used at Desdemona Sands Lighthouse for a short period. It was recently purchased by the Mukilteo Historical Society for display.

New Dungeness Spit, on which New Dungeness Lighthouse stands, is one of the longest of its kind in the world. It affords a protection for Dungeness Bay and the natural bird sanctuary. Early Indians used to fight pitched battles on the spit. Several ships grounded on the sands.

Merrie Holbert is one of Oregon's most talented artists who brings her subjects alive in a unique manner following study and research of each detail. Among her many artistic accomplishments, she has done a series of Oregon's lighthouses, past and present, in most cases depicting the way they were in the beginning, before many of the outer buildings had been razed. She affords a great contrast with the way they appear today, and her artistry has added to a piece of lighthouse history that might otherwise have been lost. The first of her series of thirteen shows the Willamette River Lighthouse as it appeared after its completion in 1895, standing on pilings at the confluence of the Columbia and Willamette rivers.

A stickler for detail, Merrie Holbert, has painted the Desdemona Sands Lighthouse in its heyday at the mouth of the Columbia River. It was established in 1902 and was well known to the great armada of ships entering and departing the river. Only a few piling remain today where the edifice once stood. A church in Seaside, Oregon recently constructed a house of worship resembling the former lighthouse.

Point Adams Lighthouse was active from 1875 until 1899 at the south entrance to the Columbia River in an area known today as Fort Stevens State Park. The frame structure was torn down in 1912. Merrie Holbert has done a superb job in depicting the lighthouse during its early years.

A captivating aerial photo of Tillamook Rock and the beetling cliffs of Tillamook Head. The lighthouse, now a columbarium, is located a mile and a quarter offshore. This photo was taken by Don Sheldon, well known Oregon photographer.

A view of Cape Meares Lighthouse few people see is this aerial photo image. Both the old and new light fixtures are clearly visible. Anthony W. Miller was the first keeper of the light. He arrived at the then isolated station in November 1889, and within a few weeks trimmed the lamp.

Silhouetted against the setting sun is Yaquina Head Lighthouse. Photo courtesy Carole Reichel

Right:
Note from this air shot, looking westward, how the forces of nature have gnawed into Yaquina Head. Mariners have claimed there are iron deposits in the strata that have had an effect on ship compasses. The lighthouse has often been a backdrop for advertisements in newspapers and magazines. It was also the setting for a Nancy Drew TV production during which the lighthouse ghost was featured.

From its inception, the short life of the Yaquina Bay Lighthouse as a functioning aid to navigation has always been open to speculation. The building of the Yaquina Head Lighthouse in 1873, only a few miles to the north, put the Yaquina Bay Lighthouse out of business in 1874. Today, state park officials have placed an acrylic light in the lantern house which is turned on at night. The edifice is illuminated in colored lights during the Christmas season.

Intricate art pattern—the 114 step spiral staircase at Yaquina Head Lighthouse. This is the iron stairs that keepers complained of phantom feet treading on certain nights.

Interesting wooden staircase at the Yaquina Bay Lighthouse, restored in recent years. Photo courtesy Craig Stilwell

Built from the plans of a British Columbia lighthouse, atop a shell mound on timeless Cape Perpetua, privately owned Cleft of the Rock Lighthouse was built in 1976. It displays a revolving power beam beacon, alternating red and white, every ten seconds. The light fixture came from Solander Island light tower off Vancouver Island's west coast.

The big English-made First Order lens is still in place in the Heceta Head lantern house, but frequently the auxiliary light on the gallery has often been the light source because the Coast Guard says it is much cheaper to operate and maintain. The Oregon State Parks are making tours available.

Above:
The rugged beauty of the Oregon coast is obvious here in this Kammerzell photo of Heceta Head and its lighthouse.

Left:
Sunset and evening views at Cleft of the Rock Lighthouse on the north spur of Cape Perpetua along the picturesque Oregon coast, south of Yachats.

The scintillating First Order lens at Umpqua Lighthouse is a jewel of about 1,000 prisms. It was manufactured by Barbier & Cie of Paris and has cast out its red and white flashes since 1894, with only a few interruptions. The Coast Guard considered replacing it with a DCB in recent years but the locals rose up in protest.

Aglow by night, the beautiful first order lens in the Umpqua River Lighthouse is silhouetted against a black velvet sky. It is a far cry from the first light at the river entrance that succumbed to erosion after only four years of service. The pioneer lighthouse built in 1857 had as its first keeper Fayette Crosby, who had previously operated the pioneer hotel at Scottsburg several miles up the Umpqua River.
Photo courtesy Craig Stillwell

Below:
No lighthouse is farther back from the ocean on the Oregon coast than Umpqua River Lighthouse. Built in 1894, it is Heceta Head's sister.

Right:
The isle on which Cape Arago Lighthouse stands is connected to the mainland by a footbridge which has often been damaged in storms. The property on the land side is the site of an old Indian burial ground. At this writing, plans have been formulated for the Indian tribes of southern Oregon to develop the area into an historic site and interpretive center. Though the lighthouse is still active its future is being pondered. The isle is off-limits to the general public.

Below:
Cape Blanco Lighthouse shows its umbrella dome, rating it as one of the senior lighthouses on the coast. The big Second Order Lens is plainly seen in the lantern house. To the right is a building built by the Coast Guard for personnel when they were in attendance.

A study in glass and brass. This is the first order lens that served at abandoned St. George Reef Lighthouse, since removed and placed on permanent display at the Del Norte County Historical Museum at Crescent City.

In these photos by Lee Forest, the rust has smeared the stone walls of the great tower and the metal lantern house of the abandoned St. George Reef Lighthouse. Future of the structure is in jeopardy, a sad chapter in the history of the nation's most costly lighthouse which took ten years to complete. These pictures were taken in 1992.

Dying a tormenting death, St. George Reef Lighthouse, the most expensive aid to navigation ever built in the United States, succumbs to the punishing pranks of nature as it sits in solitude six miles west of Crescent City.

There was also a cemetery established outside the lighthouse reservation which still exists today but on private property. Some of those once affiliated with the lighthouse are buried there. Like all lighthouses Yaquina Head has its ghosts. According to one story which can not be fully authenticated, a construction worker fell to his death falling down between the double walls during the building period. Being unable to retrieve his body he was accordingly sealed inside, and remains in a crypt. The other story is authenticated. In the 1920s principal keeper William Smith and his family had gone into Newport for the evening, leaving assistant keeper Higgins in charge. While Smith was away, Higgins became ill and asked another assistant, Frank Story, to tend to the light.

While in Newport the Smiths looked back at the lighthouse at sunset and noted the beacon had not been lit. Hastily returning to the station, Smith found Story drunk and Higgins lying dead on a tower landing. Feeling a load of guilt over the incident, Story thereafter always had his pet bulldog accompany him when he went to the tower, fearing he might encounter Higgin's ghost.

To this day, the Yaquina Head ghost story remains and many of the past keepers have complained of hearing weird footsteps on the spiral staircase by night. In fact, the lighthouse was depicted in one of the Nancy Drew TV productions as a haunted lighthouse.

Yaquina Head Lighthouse is now on the National Register of Historic Places and is the third oldest aid to navigation in the state. Standing majestically atop the promontory the lighthouse is presently surrounded by the Yaquina Head Outstanding Natural Area, where under the Bureau of Land Management the acreage is being transformed into one of the finest tourist attractions on the coast.

Jutting out into the Pacific this rugged headland is battered and scoured by the forces of nature. According to geologists, this piece of land is part of an ancient volcano whose basaltic lava flows refuse to be worn away. As quickly as the surrounding sandstone beaches recede the headland endures.

Life abounds in the harsh and unforgiving environment. Harbor seals haul out year-round on the rocky outcrops. Spring and summer, thousands of seabirds flock into the near islets and sea stacks to nest. The Gray whales are frequently sighted, some of which remain exclusively on the Oregon coast instead of making the long migration annually. Yaquina Head is a very special place, and in the beach tidal pools the marine gardens feature a colorful array of sea creatures that are of great interest.

❈ Yaquina Bay

On September 2, 1994, a group of lighthouse devotees relit the Yaquina Bay Lighthouse for the first time in 120 years. All that time, the lantern house had been dark accept for the occasional report from those who insisted they saw a ghostly light when nobody was in the tower. The light was labeled as a "mock" light made to resemble a Fresnel lens but in actuality was a cluster of stationary small globes which, though not intended as an aid to navigation, came on at dusk and extinguished at dawn.

Historically, Yaquina Bay Lighthouse as an aid to navigation was only functional for a three-year period from 1871-74, being extinguished on October 1, 1874. Charles H. Pierce (pronounced Perse) and his wife Sarah had seven of their nine children living at the lighthouse. One of the children was born there. Pierce was the first and only keeper of the sentinel, receiving a salary of $1,000 per annum.

At this writing, the parties involved with, the lighthouse including state Park ranger Mike Rivers, endeavored to have a permanent light placed in the lantern house to replace the cluster of lights. When a Fresnel was not to be found, a modern 250mm acrylic lens and light was installed, and a permit granted for a private aid to navigation, a sort of reverse lighthouse evolution.

There was great unhappiness in the family when the lighthouse was ordered closed and the lightkeeper and his family transferred. The children had learned all about the lighthouse chores and often aided their father.

In 1873, with the opening of the Yaquina Head Lighthouse, the Lighthouse Board came to the conclusion that two lighthouses only a few miles apart was a redundant act. It was never determined who should have been blamed for the costly error and misuse of the taxpayers' money, but the order stuck and the Yaquina Bay Lighthouse went dark. The authorities excused the mistake by insisting the first order light at the new station was much superior to the fifth order light at the abandoned tower. Little attention was given to the fact that the first lighthouse did double duty as both a harbor entrance light as well as a sea coast light.

The edifice stood empty for 14 years and gradually went into disrepair. Uncle Sam even tried to sell the building in 1877, but the bids were considered insufficient and the property withdrawn. There was talk of recommissioning the lighthouse in the 1880s when the Oregon Development Company, a subsidiary of the Oregon Pacific Railroad, started coastwise steamer service from the San Francisco to Yaquina City. Unfortunately both of their passenger vessels, the *Yaquina City* and the *Yaquina Bay* were wrecked at the bar entrance within a year of each other (1887-88) and lighthouse revival rumors subsided.

In the interim, Pierce and his family had taken up residence at the Cape Blanco Lighthouse on Oregon's south coast.

It was in 1888, the Army Corps of Engineers requested and received permission to use the buildings as living quarters for construction workers on the north jetty. The jetty had become necessary to control the shifting shoals at the bar entrance as marine traffic increased. The work of bar and harbor improvements continued till 1896.

After the engineers had done their thing the U.S. Lifesaving Service that had established a station at South Beach in 1896 got permission to move their activities to the north side of the bay in 1906 and used the lighthouse as living quarters and a lookout until 1915, when the U.S. Coast Guard took over that branch of government service. The edifice was continually used until 1933 when a new Coast Guard station was built inside the bay.

The following year the aging lighthouse was acquired by the Oregon State Highway Division and plans to create a public park progressed. Near-sighted members of the Highway Commission decided that the old frame structure which by now was badly in need of repair should be demolished. Local residents properly protested, necessitating the formation of the Lincoln County Historical Society. With the aid of the Oregon Historical Society a long tenacious effort was made to save the lighthouse. In 1956, the building was given the needed reprieve by being named as a significant historical landmark.

For 18 years the lighthouse was leased to the Lincoln County group as a county museum. In the early 1970s the Oregon State Parks determined the edifice should be restored as part of a developing Historic Preservation Program. The structure was then closed, and in 1974 restoration got underway. Old paint was removed; the interior was replastered; the rear wing was reconstructed and all necessary repairs made. Period furniture was acquired for the interior and the place was turned into a popular tourist attraction. Brought back from rags to riches it appeared much as it did in 1871.

At the Christmas season the entire building is outlined in lights offering a myriad of color. Friends of the Lighthouse do much volunteer work and one of the former faithful members of that group has written a delightful little history of the two Yaquina lighthouses and the personalities involved, entitled *The Yaquina Bay Lighthouses on the Oregon Coast* (Webb Research Group). Her name is Dorothy Wall, who with her husband Les, spent many months at the lighthouse in valuable service. The Friends of the Yaquina Bay Lighthouse work in cooperation with the Oregon State Parks. The building is open to the public for a nominal fee.

Said to be the oldest standing structure in the Newport area, it is on the National Register of Historic Places. The site was originally part of the homestead of Lester and Sophronia Baldwin, who were among the first white settlers at Yaquina Bay. The couple sold 36 acres in April 1871 to the government for a mere $500, and construction began on the lighthouse in May of that year. Ben Simpson was the general contractor and Joseph Bien, a lampist from San Francisco did the lantern and iron work.

The traditional ghost of Yaquina Bay Lighthouse originated in a work of fiction written in *Pacific Monthly* in 1899 by Lischen Miller, sister of Poet Laureate Joaquin Miller. It was entitled "The Haunted Lighthouse," and tells the story of a young lady who was murdered in the confines of the structure. Despite the fact that it was fiction, the tale has stuck with the lighthouse since its inception.

❁ A Letter To Yaquina Bay Lighthouse...

by Dorothy Wall, author, friend and former historian of Yaquina Bay Lighthouse

Once...a long, long time ago, your rooms were glowing with the light of your fireplaces. Your hallways rang with laughter.

A Mom and a Dad and their children lived there. There was life here! Then they were sent away and you became an empty shell.

People thought you were dead, because you looked as if you were...all alone up there on the knoll...your shutters hanging askew...your windows broken...your picket fence falling like slow-motion dominoes...your many-windowed tower staring out vacantly over the restless ocean.

Oh yes...you were used from time to time by the brawny men who built the jetties and by the brave men of the Lifesaving and the Coast Guard...but you were only a shelter for them, not a precious piece of history.

Then "they" started a rumor; that you have...ghosts... supposedly a beautiful young maiden who was killed on your graceful stairway, and a crusty old sea captain who had been set adrift by his crew on the stormy Pacific. Who loved you then? Only the "ghosts."

"It's an eyesore," they said. "A temptation to vandals...a dangerous place...someone could get hurt there...never go there at night...let's get rid of it...let's use a bulldozer!, they said.

That's when you found who really cared for you, for you began hearing, "Oh no! Not a bulldozer! Let's save it for our children and their children! It's a wonderful piece of history!"

So little by little, they began to breathe life into you. They mended your torn and broken places and made you warm and cozy once again. They used big doses of TLC, something you never heard of, but liked it. You deserved it, for you are our oldest Senior Citizen.

So, little lighthouse, hang in there! Keep your doors open to the people who love you. Even though your light no longer shines, you still have a special place here in Newport and in our hearts.

You bring back memories to our older visitors and you can show our youth how it was to live over one hundred years ago...without electric lights...or hot showers...or TV...or stereo systems...or hair dryers...none of these.

Yet...you are a survivor.

❁ Cleft of the Rock

Built on top of an Indian shell mound, the privately-owned Cleft of the Rock Lighthouse was established in 1976, on the north spur of Cape Perpetua. A latter day arrival on the coast, marking its 20th year of existence, at this writing, the light has been official since 1979. In the interim, the gradual decline of lighthouses has taken place as active aids to navigation. Ironically, the official Oregon state map shown in the book *History of Benton County, Oregon*, published at Portland in 1885, is marked by a lighthouse at Cape Perpetua. The map produced in 1876 also shows a lighthouse being located at Cape lookout and on the same map a lighthouse is listed at Cape Foulweather and not Yaquina Head which is probably another reason for the mixup in early lighthouse locations. In all my research I find no record of a government lighthouse ever being placed at Cape Perpetua until the Cleft of the Rock Lighthouse was built. Obviously there must have been some consideration for an early lighthouse at the location, for Cape Perpetua was carried on all charts and maps from the time of Captain Cook's 1778 voyage to the Pacific Coast.

Since those early years Benton County has been cut in half, part of it becoming Lincoln County which includes a large section of the central Oregon coast.

At any rate, Cleft of the Rock Lighthouse commemorated the 200th anniversary of James Cook's discovery of Cape Perpetua on March 7, 1778, when in command of the HMS *Resolution*. On a gray late winter day under a heavy canopy of cloud he attached the name Perpetua, honoring a Christian saint who was martyred for her faith at Carthage in 203 A.D. At that time, England celebrated St. Perpetua Day, and it was on this day that Cook passed the lofty cape.

Nobody knows who saw Cape Perpetua first, other than the natives who roamed its slopes for thousands of years. A Spaniard, Bartolome Ferrelo, reputedly may have gotten as far the Umpqua in March 1543. Sir Francis Drake, the first Englishman to encircle the globe, passed the latitude of the cape in the *Golden Hind* in 1578, and in 1592 Juan de Fuca did the same, but neither mentioned the bold promontory. No further known attempts at exploration in the area were made until the late 18th century, when Juan Perez was off the Oregon coast. A year later in 1775, Bruno de Heceta followed Perez, and Heceta Head, ten miles to the south of Perpetua is named for him. But it was Captain Cook who stamped the name on the mist shrouded cape, and that name has remained. The headland boasts the sharpest rise from the beach of any of the capes along the Oregon Coast. It rises to 800 feet a short distance from the beach and over 1,000 feet at a distance of 0.8 mile. Consisting mainly of basaltic texture, in some areas it has a reddish lava, the ocher within once used by the early natives to obtain the color red for decorations of various kinds.

Just north of the Yachats River was the location of a forgotten building that housed the Alsea sub-agency of the Coast Range Indian Reservation, created in 1855, embracing the territory from Cape Lookout to south of the Siuslaw River, 90 miles long and 20 miles deep. At one time there were 27 distinct tribal groups in the area, many with different dialects and customs. In 1875, the sub-agency was closed and the land thrown open to white settlement. Most of the natives were transferred to the Siletz Indian Reservation. A marker denotes the locale of the sub-agency headquarters near the Yachats cemetery.

Cleft of the Rock Lighthouse tower was built from the structural plans of the 1898 Fiddle Reef Lighthouse which sat on a little islet off Oak Bay near Victoria, B.C. That old tower was demolished in the 1970s. The revolving power beam optic at Cleft of the Rock was formerly used at isolated, sea-girt Solander Island off the west coast of Vancouver Island. To differentiate its characteristic from that of Heceta Head, Cleft of the Rock light is alternating red and white every ten seconds and is visible 16 miles at sea. Ironically, the optic was manufactured in Crawley, England by Stone-Chance Ltd., successors to the Chance Brothers who furnished all the lighting equipment for the Heceta Head Light in the early 1890s. The company in recent years closed after more than a century of supplying lighthouses of England and other maritime countries throughout the world with optics and allied lighthouse equipment.

Though closed to the public, Cleft of the Rock Lighthouse can be viewed from milepost 166 on Highway 101, a mile-and-a-half south of Yachats.

❋ Heceta Head

On March 30, 1994, Heceta Head Lighthouse marked its 100th year of continued service. The impressive appearing beacon tower is located in a picture perfect location for a camera or an artist. In fact, few lighthouses in the world have been featured more than Heceta Head.

Though certainly not the oldest lighthouse on the Oregon Coast, it is one of the most cherished. A near sister to the tower at Umpqua, both were commissioned the same year. A program to celebrate Heceta Lighthouse centennial was in early April of 1994 with a variety of activities at the old keeper's dwelling, now referred to as Heceta House. The celebration was hosted by the U.S. Forest Service, the Oregon State Parks, and the U.S. Coast Guard. Included was a rededication and licensing ceremony of Heceta House. At this writing, Heceta House is being converted to an interpretive center.

Looking back through bifocals, just a few oldtimers recall the earlier days of the lighthouse. Things were pretty primitive in the beginning. Nobody alive today was around when the five-wick coal oil lamp was first lit at Heceta Head. Keeping the lamp trimmed, prisms polished (there were 640 of them), and the brass shined was the full-time job of the keeper and his two assistants. They were civil service lifetime workers, a by-the-book, spit and polish organization that took pride in their work. Their instructions were to keep the light burning brightly through the night, to turn it on just before sunset so the light would have its full effect by the time twilight ended. The flame was to be extinguished punctually at sunrise and curtains pulled to keep sunlight that magnified the bulleyes in the first order lens from melting the burner, or starting a fire outside in the trees. Another caution was that constant exposure to the sun tended to turn the lens prisms (eight panels) a greenish color.

Andrew P.C. Hald was named as the first head keeper at Heceta Head, his salary being $800 per year, including housing and firewood. His assistants were paid $550 per month. The clockworks that rotated the lens dropped a heavy weight some 35 feet down the core of the tower and had to be rewound every four hours. Failure to do so resulted in disciplinary action.

It was in 1889 that Congress allocated $80,000 for the lighthouse at Heceta Head. But from the beginning there were complications involved in the construction and transportation of building materials between 1892 and 1894. With the construction of a hazardous wagon road, the lumber was shipped from mills in Mapleton and Florence to the mouth of the Siuslaw River, then towed by raft to Cape Cove where it was hauled up the slope to the construction site. Florence was 13 miles from the headland. On occasion bundles of lumber were carried by tug, usually the *Lillian*, thrown overboard near Cape Creek beach, and then recovered as the pieces floated ashore.

Bricks and cement were shipped from San Francisco to Florence, transferred to the *Lillian*, and freighted to the mouth of Siuslaw. From there those items were hauled to the nearby Cox ranch by team and wagon. Windows, finished lumber and other accessories arrived on the lighthouse tender *Columbine* from Tongue Point "Lighthouse" depot near Astoria. The rock that forms the base of the light tower came from the Clackmas River deposits near Oregon City.

The lighthouse tender *Manzanita* transported the lens and lighting equipment to the station where it was brought in through the surf by open boat.

All structures were officially completed in August of 1893. Originally there were two keepers' dwellings along with a barn and the usual outbuildings such as oil houses. The head keeper's residence, a large two-and-a-half story family dwelling, was unfortunately razed in 1940 and some of its components were used to build what at this writing is the Alpha-Bit store and cafe in Mapleton. The other dwelling which still stands, a duplex shared by the assistants, is now referred to as Heceta House, rented out to Lane Community College by the Forest Service.

Lighthouse keepers had more to do than just keeping the light on and working properly. Those not working the midnight to sunrise shift began their cleaning duties at 9 a.m. Lighthouse inspectors would make surprise visits at least once a year, often more. The glass and brass had to be polished and the entire interior of the lantern house was frequently repainted white and kept clean of soot and grease. The inspectors would even check the keepers' dwellings, poking their noses into cupboards and sometimes donning white gloves and running their fingers atop sills and doors.

It was a grand day when electricity came to the Heceta Head Light Station in 1934. The chores were greatly eased. It was in 1963 that automation arrived and the Coast Guard soon installed the big 1,000 watt globes and an automatic lamp changer, in case one burned out. It was a nostalgic event when the last keeper, Oswald Allik, closed down the place as a resident station. It was also a long span in lighthouse evolution from the time when 2,500 gallons of coal oil was used a year till the flipping of a switch to turn on the light, and finally complete automation.

There were a lot of happy hours for the keepers and their families at Heceta. Clifford "Cap" Hermann was one of the best liked of the many who had duty there. World War II saw up to 75 Coast Guardsmen assigned there, sending out around-the-clock beach patrols to guard against possible invasion by the Japanese.

A splendid booklet has been written by Stephanie Funicane, entitled *Heceta House, A History and Architectural Survey*, published under the auspices of the U.S. Forestry Service. It tells of the many events of keepers and the members of their families that dwelled on the premises through the years, of the building of the Cape Creek Bridge and the little schoolhouse for the children of the keepers and the nearby neighbors that resided in the sparsely populated area.

Tourists who have been unhappy at not being able to view the interior of the lighthouse can now have that opportunity. Both the tower and Heceta House are now opened to public inspection under Oregon State Parks supervision. The 56 foot tall tower will continue to shine its light from a loft 205 feet above sea level. The original first order lens, manufactured by Chance Brothers, is still in place. A caretaker recently damaged the lens while cleaning the lantern house and prisms had to be replaced by Hardin Optical of Bandon.

❋ Umpqua River

Heceta's sister lighthouse, Umpqua River, marked its 100th anniversary in 1994 only a few months after its counterpart. Amid considerable fanfare the folks of the Reedsport, Winchester Bay, and visitors who love lighthouses from far and wide came to celebrate the occasion. The ready availability of the lighthouse in one of Oregon's finest state parks makes it familiar to most every tourist travelling the coast. The biggest attraction is the jewel-like first order Fresnel lens with its white and red characteristic. When the sun shines on it during the daylight hours it sparkles like a giant diamond.

If the Coast Guard had its way the big optic would have been permanently darkened and replaced by an aero-marine or DCB light or even a 300mm acrylic lens. It wasn't because the service unit didn't like the classic fixture, but because of frequent breakdowns while the lens turned 24 hours around-the-clock on its old chariot wheels. In truth, it was the public of the area that had a love affair with the giant cage of glass and brass and demanded its continuation. At this writing it is still making its rotation and still being filmed by an increasing number of tourists. The scintillating French optic is 72 inches in diameter inside the glass. Lens parts consist of eight lower panels, 24 middle panels and eight upper panels. Before electricity arrived, the two-ton optic was turned by clockwork and weight, the source of light produced by a Funck mineral oil float lamp. Today the lens is turned by an electric motor.

Situated 165 feet above the sea, the 65 foot tower is located just south of Winchester Bay, the home of a large fleet of commercial and pleasure craft, plus a busy Coast Guard Station.

To the early pioneers, Umpqua River offered a promised land of the future. Its ready availability was obvious, but with many ships coming to grief trying to make the crossing, the danger of the bar was evident. Scottsburg upriver, along with the port of Gardiner, were hopeful signs. Some visionaries even thought a northwest San Francisco might be possible. Dreams don't always come true and many hopes were dashed with the demise of the first lighthouse built at the entrance to the river. It was established in 1857 as one of the earliest lighthouses on the Pacific Coast, but from the outset trouble brewed. It was not only difficult to build because of its remote location, but there was constant danger of Indian attack and considerable purloining of materials by the natives, some of whom objected to the intrusion. Further compounding the situation was the unwise decision to build the structure on sand. After less than five years of service, storms, currents, freshets, and shifting sands caused the structure to topple into the river.

Funds were short in the nation's capital at that time in history and insufficient pressure was brought to change the minds of those on the newly formed Lighthouse Board that a lighthouse was absolutely essential at the entrance to the Umpqua. It took almost three decades before the growing timber interests convinced the powers to be that a lighthouse must be built. As a result, funds were allocated and the faithful lighthouse tender *Manzanita*, in August of 1892, delivered the initial building materials.

This time the lighthouse would not be built on the river banks nor would it be close to the scoring action where river and ocean meet. As a result the masonry tower was built high above the water, farther back from the ocean than any lighthouse on the coast. The builders figured that an ounce of prevention was worth a pound of cure. The end result with the tower, dwellings, oil houses, storehouses, and cisterns made the station a very comfortable place to live and there was a jubilation among the keepers and their families when assigned to that family oriented domicile.

Gardiner became a thriving port with many coastal lumber schooners taking out capacity cargoes of lumber across the bar in those early years, but today ocean going vessels don't cross the bar anymore. The fishing fleet is the big factor. The jetties are maintained as well as the bar depths.

Public tours are conducted of the lighthouse and there is a whale-watching platform nearby overlooking the bar and a beautiful view of the Oregon Dunes National Recreation area.

⚓ Cape Arago

In 1992, a partnership agreement was reached by the Bureau of Land Management and the Confederated Tribes of the Coos, Lower Umpqua and Siuslaw Indians to build a multi-million dollar interpretive center on or near the Cape Arago Lighthouse, situated on tiny Lighthouse Island. The grandiose plan calls for a memorial type lighthouse structure on the mainland opposite the islet. A historical record of the Indian history and artifacts would be housed at the planned building. A part of the land has been the site of an Indian burial ground for years and that plot would be protected under the plan.

As to the future of the lighthouse, reached from the mainland by a footbridge, there is still some question. Should the light go dark, should it be turned over to Indian control, or should the Coast Guard continue to maintain the light? At this writing the "ifs" are still being mulled over. The Coast Guard has consistently kept the public from visiting the lighthouse because of the hazardous conditions that prevail—constant erosion on the islet, frequent damage to the footbridge, and dangerous winds that sometimes sweep the area.

The dangers are obvious, as the present lighthouse is the third that has existed on the islet. The first was a truncated skeleton lighthouse built at the bitter west end of the isle. It was commissioned November 1, 1866, and when endangered by erosion was abandoned and replaced by a wooden frame lighthouse near the east of the islet in 1908. The third lighthouse, which is still in operation, was constructed in 1934 of reinforced concrete. Ironically, the original structure refused to fall into the sea, and what remained of it was dynamited in 1937. At this writing, a fourth order Fresnel lens was still in use in the 44 foot tall lighthouse situated 100 feet above the sea. The island continues to be re-formed by the forces of nature and the narrow sector leading to the west end is almost cut in half at places. It's hazardous going in a strong wind for one traversing the terra firma, and it's a long drop into the ocean. At one time there were some tall trees growing on the insular dot, but the Lighthouse authorities ordered them cut down to prevent any possibility of fire.

And speaking of fire, there was considerable excitement at the Cape Arago Lighthouse in 1916 with a huge blaze at sea aboard the crack coastwise liner *Congress*. It wasn't that numerous other ships had escaped peril in and around the entrance to Coos Bay and well within range of the Cape Arago Lighthouse, but this incident was rather spectacular. Fire was reported in the steamer's after hold while abeam of Crescent City as she sped northward on her regular run between San Francisco and Seattle. Captain N.E. Cousins and his officers tried to bring the fire under control but as the vessel neared Coos Bay, flames enveloped the entire ship and the orange glow and thick black smoke could be seen for miles. The Arago keepers had a front row seat.

Ironically, the sea was calm and an orderly evacuation of passengers took place as the *Congress* took a severe list to starboard, necessitating most of the passengers having to be removed by lifeboat from that side of the ship. The SOS had been telegraphed to all ships in the vicinity and the ocean going dredge *Col. P. S. Mitchie* and the tug *Salvor* were first on the scene. Gutted from stem to stern, the liner refused to sink. Few ships have ever been so devastated in a holocaust and remained afloat. When she finally cooled down enough to get a line aboard, the ship was towed to Seattle for a $2 million refit after it was found her stout hull was still seaworthy. It took 14 months to repair the vessel. She emerged as the SS *Nanking*, and was sold by the Pacific Coast Steamship Company to the China Mail Steamship Company. Still later, she became the *Emma Alexander* and ended her days as a troop transport in World War II.

The light and fog signal prevented considerable shipwreck in the vicinity of Cape Arago and many daring sea rescues were undertaken from the old lifesaving station located on the lee side of Lighthouse Island in the early days before and after the turn of the century. The light keepers often alerted the surfmen when a ship was in trouble and they would launch their surfboats and head out to sea. Originally, one individual manned the station, and a bell would be rung to tell volunteers to come running in time of emergency. In 1915, the Coast Guard took over that branch of the service and the lifesaving station was relocated at Charleston inside Coos Bay.

❀ Coquille River

Another lighthouse saved from destruction after being abused and vandalized for more than three decades is the Coquille River Lighthouse. It was one of the first major lighthouses the Coast Guard eliminated after taking over the Lighthouse Service. The lantern house went dark in 1939 in favor of a lesser light and fog signal on the river's south jetty. When established in 1896, the lighthouse sat on a wee rocky islet and was reached from the mainland by a footbridge. Through the years the north jetty was hooked up with the piece of land on which the lighthouse stood and it all became a solitary landscape.

Coquille River Lighthouse which has long been referred to as "Bandon Light" was a harbor entrance and seacoast light in one. It was the rash of bar-oriented shipwrecks that was one great impetus for an aid to navigation at that location. Bandon and the ports up the river were important lumber and shipbuilding centers in the heyday of coastwise shipping, and the port of Bandon was often crowded with sailing schooners and steam schooners, some of which were built on the river banks.

For years, in fact right up until 1975, the people of Bandon had little compassion for their lighthouse. Graffiti and names were painted all over the building mostly by teens looking for mischief. The window glass was broken and some of the brick masonry kicked out. The iron was rusting. Fortunately, when the structure was abandoned all the lighting and fog signal equipment was removed and the spiral staircase dismantled to prevent accidents to trespassers. Today the town embraces the old lighthouse and uses it as a logo on just about everything. Strange how the attitude changed so rapidly.

Responsibility fell under the Army Engineers for doing something about the building. Bordering Bullards State Park, it was a natural for a tourist attraction. Its easy access by road, entering the park from Highway 101, just north of Bandon, brings scores of visitors. The old foghorn house contains illustrations of shipping and shipwrecks around the bar entrance and is open daily to the public. The restored staircase leading up to the tower has a locked gate. A solar light was placed in the lantern house in recent times and is lit as a fixed light. During the Christmas season the entire structure is outlined in lights which makes a beautiful spectacle from both sides of the river.

The old keepers' dwelling, barn, water tank and other outbuildings were all torn down years ago, but the seeker can still find the old cistern to the north of the lighthouse.

Two ships in the early days ran up on the rocks and sand close to the lighthouse, the schooners *C.A. Klose* and *Advance*. Both were among the few vessels that escaped the vagaries of the bar. The lifesaving station was once located on the hill at the south side of the river entrance but in later years the Coast Guard had a station at the west end of the town. In the early part of the century the river bar was considered one of the most dangerous on the coast judging from the large number of shipwrecks in percentage of bar traffic. That fact made the lighthouse more important than ever. Except for the commercial and sports fishing vessels the river traffic has greatly declined in our day. An occasional tug and barge cross the bar but ocean going cargo vessels are only a memory.

Including the South Jetty light and fog signal, there are ten minor aids to navigation, mostly buoys, that mark the channel into the Coquille River today. But all the attention is focused on the aging lighthouse which seemingly gets more attention today than in its shining hours of yesteryear.

❀ Cape Blanco

Vandals did their dastardly deed at the Cape Blanco Lighthouse on November 18, 1992, when by night they went on a rampage breaking into the tower, knocking out the windows and inflicting considerable damage to the second order classical lens. The Coast Guard had just completed a $15,000 renovation of the lighthouse, the oldest on the Oregon coast. Most people have long been under the impression that the lens, though very old, was the original at Cape Blanco, but when the lighthouse was first commissioned, its jewel was a first order Fresnel lens. The writer has been unable to find a date when the lens change was undertaken.

The damage was such that the Coast Guard considered replacing the present lens with more modern equipment but then decided to get estimates on repairs. Fearful that they would run excessively high, they hunted far and wide for somebody that could make replacement components for the lens. Lo and behold, instead of running into the hundreds of thousands of dollars they found that an optical company in nearby Bandon would take on the project on a bid of $19,250. It took several months to get the exact cut, to polish and match the glass color, but the when the job was finished and the prisms set in place it was hard to see that they weren't the originals.

"Everything was super snug," Bill Shadbolt, production manager for Hardin Optical Company said after the job was completed.

"It's a big relief" chimed in Larry Hardin, owner of the firm.

The men, superior optical craftsmen, crowded inside the lantern room lens and worked in close harmony refurbishing a bank of prisms and a bullseye in the big optic. With no blueprints to work from, Hardin Optical, consisting of Shadbolt, Hardin, and optical expert Ross Reimer, showed again what American ingenuity can do. They earned the outright praise of Chief Ken McLain, head of the Coast Guard team that maintained the lighthouse from their Coos Bay base.

The French manufactured lens stands a little over six feet tall with an inside diameter of four feet, seven inches, and consists of eight panels of prisms, 144 on top and 56 on the lower section beneath the bullseyes.

In the interim, an intense search was made for finding the culprits, as damage to a government lighthouse is a federal offense. It didn't take long to discover that two high school students from Pacific High School were responsible, David Pritchard and Mark Edwards. Both were arrested and sentenced following an FBI investigation.

Commissioned on December 20, 1870, Cape Blanco Lighthouse stands on the most westerly property in the state of Oregon. The 59 foot tower is 245 feet above the ocean, the loftiest of the Oregon coast's marine lights. Where it was once in the most isolated part of southern Oregon, today an extensive Oregon State Park abuts the lighthouse property, and tourists and campers arrive in doves during the summer season to take in the charm of the cape with its abundance of features such as wildflowers, marine life, beaches of sand and rock and timeless cliffs.

One of the earliest keepers, James Langlois, spent his entire 42-year lighthouse career at Blanco, and it was said he never set foot in any other lighthouse. One of the first women ever assigned to an Oregon ocean front lighthouse also served as an assistant keeper there at the turn of the century. Her name was Mabel Bretherton. There was also a Mrs. Alexander that once served as an assistant at Cape Blanco. Langlois' son Oscar also joined the U.S. Lighthouse Service and was assigned to Cape Arago and later Coquille River Lighthouse. The Laird family in the area produced George Laird who barged building materials to the site during the construction period.

Before Highway 101 was a reality in the 1930s the cape was difficult to reach. For many years a crude wagon washboard road was the access to the station, and visitors were limited. A drawback in the off season were the terrific winds that sweep over the cape, usually the highest velocity of any cape on the coast.

A move was presently made for the ownership of the lighthouse to be turned over the Oregon State Parks and Recreation Department. An interpretive center will eventually be built on the premises to tell of the marine history, including the many shipwrecks that have occurred on the sharp basaltic teeth surrounding the cape.

All of the station buildings that once stood on the reservation have been demolished, and except for a single residence that once housed Coast Guard personnel, the tower stands solitary as it has for well over a century and a quarter.

The lighthouse is located about six miles west of Highway 101 and the nearest town of size is Port Orford. For an in-depth study of Oregon Coast lighthouses, suggested reading is *Oregon's Seacoast Lighthouse*, Webb Research Group (1992), and *Lighthouses of the Pacific*, Schiffer Publishing Ltd. (1989).

Though technology has produced new and more efficient navigational aids in our present day, electronic wonders that provide greater insurance against disaster at sea, lighthouses still stand as symbols, though slowly fading in the shadows of time. No amount of progress, however, can dim the significance of these historical sentinels so essential in days of yore.

Lighthouse lovers are on the increase, desiring to visit both the active and inactive edifices, and to collect and cherish mementos along with the tales of storms, shipwrecks, sea rescues, loneliness, isolation, and incredible heroism, all of which have been associated with the lighthouses.

The Coast Guard, Oregon State Parks, and the U.S. Forestry Service, along with the valuable assistance of volunteers, are working together to open up the lighthouses to the public on the Oregon Coast and the interest continues to grow along the line of historical significance.

Easy accessibility to many of Oregon's lighthouses has made them prime tourist attractions. The following organizations further the interest in the historical watch towers (subject to change):

Friends of Cape Meares
P. O. 282
Oceanside, Oregon 97134

Friends of Yaquina Bay Lighthouse
846 S. W. Government
Newport, Oregon 97365

Oregon Chapter, U.S. Lighthouse Society
P. O. Box 250
Sixes, Oregon 97476

Oregon Chapter, U.S. Lighthouse Society
2211 Winchester Ave.
Reedsport, Oregon 97467
(Lighthouse Gallery)

—learn the secret of the sea?
Only those who brave its dangers
Comprehend its mystery.

—Henry Wadsworth Longfellow

Three lighthouses have been placed at Cape Arago's Lighthouse Isle. This well researched painting by Merrie Holbert shows the first of the three and the station buildings erected in 1866. In the foreground is the boathouse; up on the plateau the keepers' dwellings and at the far end of the point the truncated, skeleton light tower. For fear of erosion it was abandoned in favor of a new watchtower in 1908, followed by a third in 1934. The lighthouse is situated 2-1/2 miles northward of Cape Arago (formerly named Cape Gregory). The remains of the lighthouse, pictured here, were dynamited in 1937. Nothing remains on the isle today except the light tower and attached fog signal house. Even the trees are gone.

6. Northern California Lighthouses

*A welcome sight to the
storm-tossed soul,
is the shining light
High on a knoll.*

—JAG

On a clear day when one is traveling south along Highway 101 and crossing the border from Oregon into northern California, the proverbial question is asked, "What is that strange looking castle-like structure way out in the ocean?"

That impressive silhouette is none other than the abandoned St. George Reef Lighthouse, the most expensive lighthouse ever built in the United States.

Built on a wave-swept reef, six miles west of Crescent City, St. George Reef Lighthouse was considered an unparalleled engineering triumph when completed in October of 1892. The massive tower took ten years to build, and from its water base to the top of the tower, it was the tallest ever built on the Pacific Coast - 146 feet high. John Olsen was the first head keeper, who, along with his assistant John Lind had both served as part of the building crew. Such a tiny piece of basalt demanded barracks vessels to house the crew while construction was underway. The schooners *LaNinfa* and *Sparrow* traded off on that duty while the steam schooners *Alliance* and *Santa Maria* along with *Crescent City*, *DelNorte*, and the salvage vessel *Whitelaw* were all chartered by the Lighthouse Service to aid at one time or another during the construction period. These vessels were utilized along with government tenders during the decade of construction. Total cost of the lighthouse was $704,000, which in our day would have been in the multi-millions of dollars. So rough was the sea at times during the building period that the barracks vessels had to be moored off the reef by four 12,000 pound sinkers.

Foundation work on the reef demanded the import of more than 1,000 granite blocks some weighing as much as 7,000 pounds. By 1888, the tower had only risen 32 feet and numerous difficulties had been experienced. Conditions made it so that work hours were often cut short and speedy evacuations made when the sea grew angry. The workers knew why Captain George Vancouver had applied the name

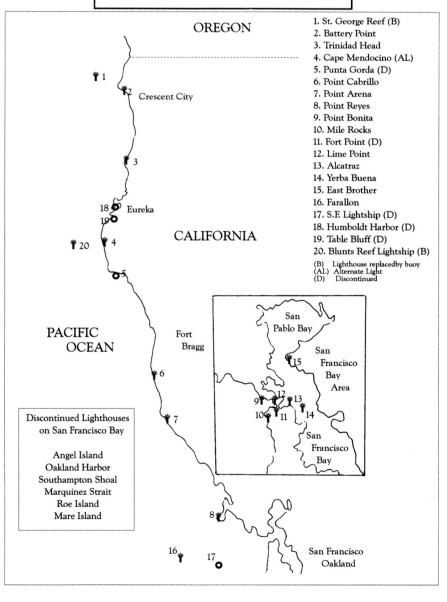

Lighthouses of Northern California

1. St. George Reef (B)
2. Battery Point
3. Trinidad Head
4. Cape Mendocino (AL)
5. Punta Gorda (D)
6. Point Cabrillo
7. Point Arena
8. Point Reyes
9. Point Bonita
10. Mile Rocks
11. Fort Point (D)
12. Lime Point
13. Alcatraz
14. Yerba Buena
15. East Brother
16. Farallon
17. S.F. Lightship (D)
18. Humboldt Harbor (D)
19. Table Bluff (D)
20. Blunts Reef Lightship (B)

(B) Lighthouse replaced by buoy
(AL) Alternate Light
(D) Discontinued

Discontinued Lighthouses on San Francisco Bay

Angel Island
Oakland Harbor
Southampton Shoal
Marquinez Strait
Roe Island
Mare Island

Dragon Rocks to that menace to navigation in the latter part of the 1700s. That title was much in the minds of the few survivors of the SS *Brother Jonathan*, torn asunder on the basaltic teeth that sent her to the bottom with nearly 200 souls in 1865. It was that tragedy that was the incentive for the lighthouse at the location.

The expertise of Charles A. Ballantyne was called on to lead the challenge against the dreaded reef, having more than proven himself in the conquering of Tillamook Rock. A cable served as an aerial tramway and allowed for the transport of workers to the barracks vessel via breeches buoy. A cage of sorts was used to get tools and supplies to the reef. The tower was built like a fortress, a total of 1,339 blocks of dressed granite all dove-tailed together sitting on a huge concrete caisson-like platform. Improved transport allowed six men at a time to ride the cage to the rock. The glycerine powder used for blasting was sometimes a problem as fragments of the rock flew in different directions when detonated. When the concrete pier was firmly attached to the rock it offered a platform on which to store the building materials. As the tower rose skyward a protrusion was placed on one side containing the spiral staircase in the 134 foot sentinel, (square, pyramidal in shape) and access to the staircase was through the boiler, coal, and laundry rooms at the base. Successive levels contained a galley, principal keepers quarters, the assistant keepers quarters, and the watch room before winding up to the lantern room which contained the big first order lens.

Though other sea-grit lighthouses were assigned four keepers, St. George rated five because of its extreme isolation, but under no circumstances were wives or children allowed to live there. It was harsh duty and only a certain type of individual could qualify for such a separated life. That point was obvious when one considered that of the service personnel serving there from 1892 till 1930, 37 of the 80 men involved resigned and 26 sought transfers to other stations. Only after the Coast Guard took over were the duty periods shortened. Some of the earlier keepers were sent ashore with injures and some with mental breakdowns. Two were even fired, as the close association of men living together in a hollow cylinder often started violent arguments. Still, the first keeper, John Olsen, put in 22 years at the station and Frenchman, George Roux, lasted for two decades.

What gave the lighthouse its bad reputation was the dangerous method of embarking and debarking via the derrick boom. The boom, rather than lifting individuals as at Tillamook, lifted the boat and its crew in a single hoist. On April 5, 1951, the worst single tragedy at a California Lighthouse occurred when five Coast Guardsmen were thrown from the station boat into the rough seas while being lowered. Three of them drowned. On October 14, 1893, assistant keeper Bill Erickson was drowned while trying to sail a small boat to Crescent City from the lighthouse.

After more than 80 years of service, the lighthouse heard the sound of taps when on May 13, 1975, the cutter *Cape Carter* arrived to remove the last of the attendants. The colors were lowered and the derrick was shackled after two men were lowered to the awaiting craft via the "Billy Pugh" net. Chief Sebastian and petty officer Salter then locked the massive door and climbed down the rocks to a rubber boat. An era had ended.

It was indeed a nostalgic scene as the boat pulled away and the lighthouse was left in total isolation for the first time in eight decades. Storm after storm had bathed the station through the years, some throwing giant breakers up the sides of the giant tower. Considerable damage had been done from time to time on the sentinel. As time progressed the proverbial question arose as to what could be done with the tower. All kinds of suggestions came and went, and a preservation group was organized to mark the centennial of the lighthouse which fell somewhat flat, as the locale was six miles offshore. It became essential to save the lens as the tower was leaking badly and the iron work turning red with rust. In 1983, via a very careful maneuver, the buoy tender *Blackhaw* was dispatched with a qualified crew and orders to remove the optic. The lens and lighting apparatus involved 6,000 pounds of delicate material. A four team specialized crew did a yeoman job of dismantling the equipment, and by use of a highline sent it back to the tender. It was a difficult but flawless undertaking, and as a result, the optic and its clockwork have been reassembled and restored as an attraction at the Del Norte County Historical Museum in Crescent City.

It is of interest that when the salvage crew first landed on the reef to begin the removal operation they were confronted by scores of angry California sea lions which had taken residence on the lower climes. After threading their way around them, they unlocked the rusty door and entered the lighthouse only to be confronted by a human-like figure that frightened them out of their shoes. The last occupants had mounted a mannequin hanging from a noose as their farewell gift.

To guard against the reef, St. George Reef Lighted Horn Buoy SG (ELB) was placed nearby as a precaution to shipping. The fate of the old tower hangs in the balance, and the future looks dim, but hopeful.

❀ Battery Point

Battery Point Lighthouse serves as a museum as well as a lighthouse under the auspices of the Del Norte County Historical Society, an aggressive group that has done much to preserve the marine history of that sector of northern California. The structure is one of the best examples of the earliest lighthouses on the Pacific Coast. For most of its service years it was known as Crescent City Lighthouse. The sentinel was automated in 1953, last occupied by veteran keeper Wayne Piland and his family. When the structure was leased to the Del Norte County Historical Society, museum curators and caretakers took up residence. For a time the lighthouse was darkened, the light eventually becoming a 300mm fixture, and the old fourth order lens placed on display. Inasmuch as the Coast Guard had set up minor lights at the harbor entrance, namely the Crescent City Entrance Light, on a white cylindrical structure, the old lighthouse lost its original moniker and had to settle for the name Battery Point Lighthouse, a restored historic light listed as a private aid to navigation.

On a piece of land that can only be reached at low tide, a new causeway was recently built to make it easier for visitors to gain the lighthouse on the right set of the tide. This well preserved monument to the past was originally opened December 10, 1856, and was similar to many of the earlier Pacific Coast lighthouses in architecture, including Point Loma and Smith Island. It was in May of 1855 that funds were appropriated for the lighthouse, $15,000. Theophilis Magruder, who was named the initial head keeper arrived 15 days late, on Christmas Day. A Mr. Van Court was assigned temporarily to man the edifice. Magruder's salary started at $1,000 annually but with a shortage of funds in the nation's capital, it was cut to $600 within that year, and to say the least the keeper was dissatisfied.

When principal keeper John Jeffrey took over in 1875, he and his wife Nellie liked the place so well they stayed for four decades. For a short time she even served as an assistant lightkeeper.

In 1907, the old fourth order lens was replaced by another with a different characteristic. The original was a fixed lens with a flash every 90 seconds.

On March 27, 1964, when Peggy and Roxy Coons were caretaking the lighthouse, a seismic tidal wave cascaded around the girth of the hunk of land on which the lighthouse stands. Though no damage was inflicted on the lighthouse the giant wave catapulted into the Crescent City waterfront doing a great amount of damage and claiming 11 lives.

Today, Battery Point Lighthouse looks very much like it did in the beginning and has become one of the most visited lighthouses on the

Pacific Coast—a genuine treasure of bygone days. If you visit there ask the caretakers about the station ghost.

At this writing Nadine and Jerry Tugel were ending several years as caretakers.

❋ Trinidad Head

It would never take a prize for architecture, but the squat little lighthouse that sits on the outer slopes of Trinidad Head has been sending a light seaward since 1871. It was on December 1 of that year that the fourth order lens was lit on a bench of rock 196 feet above sea level. Its purpose was dual, acting both as an ocean front navigation aid and a marker for picturesque Trinidad Harbor.

Located near Highway 101, 20 miles north of Eureka, abutting the quiet little town of Trinidad, the petite lighthouse is seldom seen by tourists, but the fishing fleet is very familiar with the beacon. So the tourists could see what it looks like, locals built a full-size replica at an ocean view point in town and placed the original lens in its lantern house.

Frequented by the Yurok Indians for countless years before the lighthouse was built, they launched their dugout canoes in the little harbor and put out to sea.

After white settlement came in the mid 1850s it was lumber that focused attention on Trinidad's harbor. Coastal sailing schooners and, later, steam schooners were frequent visitors to take on capacity cargoes of redwood, mostly for San Francisco. The coastal vessels passed close to Trinidad Head when bypassing the harbor, and the keepers became familiar with most of the coasters. By word of the grapevine they heard of an epic race coming their way in 1904. It was in November of that year that an exciting contest between two steam schooners became of great interest to shipping men along the entire coast. It involved the *Olympic* and the *Shasta*, both owned by the E.K. Wood Lumber Company of San Francisco.

The steamer *Olympic* left the Golden Gate at 2 p.m. on the afternoon of November 13, and the *Shasta* exactly one hour later, both resolving to reach Bellingham, Washington first. A small wager took place among the skippers of both vessels and their crews. They passed Trinidad Head within an hour of each other and arrived at their destination on the morning of November 16, exactly within an hour of each other, in the same order as they left the California port, in the record breaking time of 67 hours, which was two hours less than any previous voyage for that type of lumber carrier. All bets were off. It was a dead heat. Now keep in mind those peculiar little steamers were not built for speed,

but designed to carry capacity loads of lumber in an economical operation. Most of the breed were lucky to manage eight knots with their small steam engines.

Trinidad Head Lighthouse is best known not for its Spanish name, but for one of the greatest waves ever recorded in the Pacific. It occurred on December 31, 1914, and was witnessed by head keeper Fred Harrington. From the lantern room he watched a great Pacific storm brewing and the seas being whipped into a frenzy. He usually gaged the power of the seas by glancing a mile southward to Pilot Rock, and the waves were already sweeping over the 103 foot sea stack. As he continued his chores of cleaning the lens and wiping the moisture from the plate glass he kept a wary eye seaward. Suddenly he saw a massive liquid mountain charging toward Trinidad Head. A lump developed in his throat and his hair stood on edge. Watching in horror, he froze in his tracks as the seas hit the wall of rock, climbed clear to the top of the cliff and completely engulfed the lighthouse. The sentinel was 196 feet above the sea, and this wave went overtop of the structure. Windows were shattered, the revolving mechanism of the lens was damaged, and water dripped in everywhere. Miraculously the little tower held its ground, having been built strong by the builders, and it still stands today, undaunted by the sea's fury.

A foghorn still blasts near the lighthouse, an improvement over the bell placed there in 1898. It was a real vibrator, so much so that it shook loose the clockwork and weights and sent them plunging into the sea. The present occulting light is visible 14 miles seaward and there is a radiobeacon at the site.

❋ Humboldt Harbor

Several of the West coast lighthouses have succumbed to erosion. The ocean front is constantly being eaten away bit by bit each year. Only the hard basalt stands up against the forces of nature, and if the sentinels along our coasts are not on solid ground, they are potential victims. One of the more prime examples was the old Humboldt Harbor Lighthouse, one of the pioneer beacons. It was the first the Redwood coast of California would see. Located on the north spit of the harbor entrance the sentinel would serve both as a harbor entrance and ocean front light, as the bay presented one of the few good portals on the northern California coast that could handle deepsea shipping. And to be sure, there was a lumber bonanza in the hinterland with giant trees waiting to be cut and sent from the portals surrounding Humboldt Bay for shipment to San Francisco.

Humboldt Harbor Lighthouse was commissioned in 1856, but having been built on sand and subject to tidal action, it had slightly over three decades of active service before being replaced by Table Bluff Lighthouse on a plateau four miles to the south. The cracked and battered pioneer light stood in shame until the early 1930s and finally fell in a jumble of masonry. The old lighthouse is pictured here in its latter years.

The old Lighthouse. Humboldt Bay   No. 94

Before the turn of the century, a contraption (similar to the above sketch) was placed near the entrance to Humboldt Bay to sound its fog bell at the whims of the sea motion. It was called a bell boat, its iron hull shaped like a small vessel. It never proved too successful.

Some $15,000 was authorized for the erection of the structure. It was designed by Ammi B. Young, and the lamp was lit for the first time on December 20, 1856, just in time for head keeper J. Johnson and his family and assistants to celebrate the Christmas season. It was a hasty transfer for the Johnson family, as D.W. Pearce was to have taken the position of principal keeper but resigned the post before the lighting equipment arrived.

Sad to say, Johnson died three years after taking over the lighthouse, and his wife Sarah was appointed guardian of the light, a post she held faithfully for the next four years.

Initially there was no fog signal at the station, instead an experimental bell boat was anchored offshore from the beacon. The strange 30 foot iron-hulled, ship-shaped craft had a mast that supported a 300 pound fogbell activated by the motion of the sea. Its effectiveness fell short, however, and funds were allocated for a steam fog signal at the station in 1877. In 1883, after a lengthy period of fog, the exhausted whistle refused to blow and ships dependent on its sound narrowly averted stranding.

In the interim, the rash of wrecks in the area brought about creation of the Humboldt Bay Lifesaving Station in 1878 which was much in need.

Trouble struck with a capital T in 1885 when a powerful storm described as a cyclone struck the station. Before the very eyes of head keeper William C. Price, the roofs were ripped off both the station dwelling and the fog house. Drift logs were dashed into the station grounds and debris was everywhere. Fortunately there were no fatalities among the personnel, but the lighthouse was in trouble. Like others of its breed, it had been built on sand and the storms and tidal action began eating away at the foundation. Cracks formed and leaks opened up the everywhere. The Lighthouse Board was informed that the edifice was beyond salvation. It was finally determined it would have to go and its demise was a sad one. The building battled against the pounding surf in a losing battle.

❋ Table Bluff

It was decided by the Lighthouse Service to replace the Humboldt tower with a frame lighthouse on Table Bluff, four miles south of the entrance to Humboldt Bay. The replacement was a white, square, frame tower, attached to the northwest corner of a one-and-a-half story frame dwelling, with lead colored trimmings, green blinds and a red roof. The lantern was painted black. There were two dwellings and a fog signal house. The steam whistle did double duty, for it not only blew during foggy periods, but when it sounded five or six short, sharp blasts followed by a blast of 15 seconds, it was to alert the Lifesaving Station crew that a keeper had sighted a vessel in distress. The light tower was 178 feet above the sea, but the beacon was only 30 feet above its foundation and displayed a fixed fourth order light, visible for 17 miles.

The lighthouse was placed in operation in 1892, replacing a temporary lens-lantern that was set up at the harbor entrance in the interim. As to the original Humboldt Harbor lighthouse, its dwelling was temporarily repaired and used for housing for War Department engineers while building the jetties at the harbor entrance. Though cracked and tormented, the old tower remained somewhat intact until the depression days of 1933, and like the market, it finally collapsed and scattered its masonry into the surf.

Before the Table Bluff Station could be built, the government was forced to threaten condemnation proceedings when the owner refused to give up his land. Reluctantly, he finally relinquished six acres for the project, and on October 31, 1892, the lamp was lit in the Victorian type structure by keeper Tony Schmoll. For a short time the station was known as Humboldt Lighthouse, but to distinguish it from the abandoned structure, the name Table Bluff was applied.

There was great excitement at the lighthouse on January 13, 1917, when the heavy cruiser, USS *Milwaukee* ran aground off Samoa near the entrance to Humboldt Bay. Ironically, the Navy had decided to use the big warship to tow the stranded submarine *H-3* off the spit after it was wrecked there several days earlier. The U.S. Lifesaving Station crew began the rescue of the 500 men and officers aboard the *Milwaukee* and later housed them in homes and in bunkhouses. They were fed at the Hammond Lumber Company cookhouse which in later years was to become known as the Samoa Cookhouse. In fact, it has today become a popular tourist attraction, serving the general family style in the same way it did during the rip-roaring days of the lumber bonanza when workers with hefty appetites had to be satisfied.

The loss of the *Milwaukee* was especially serious because at the time the country was still deeply involved in World War I. The submarine was eventually salvaged, but the cruiser left her mighty steel bulk to die in the Humboldt sands.

For several years a government radio sending and receiving station was operative on the Table Bluff lighthouse grounds. In 1953, the lighthouse was automated but the beacon was in use until 1972, when minor lighting at the harbor entrance made its service obsolete. The attached dwelling was razed and the tower stood alone and empty. A religious commune took up the lands around the lighthouse and the tower's future hung in the balance.

For a few years the fate of the tower was debated. Lighthouse buffs were determined to save the old structure. Ray Glavich and volunteers spent many hours convincing the Humboldt Harbor District of the historic value of the tower so that land could be provided after its removal. In cooperation with the National Park Service, The County of Humboldt, and others, Glavich succeeded in getting crane service donated and additional volunteers organized. First the iron lantern house was removed and then the tower was cut in half horizontally and sent to its new home on a flatbed truck. The new location was a site on Woodley Island in Eureka where it was re-assembled as a tourist and historic attraction for the inner harbor area. The fourth order Fresnel lens that last served the tower is presently on display at the maritime museum in Eureka along with the vent assembly from the original Humboldt Harbor Lighthouse.

⚓ Blunts Reef

From 1905 until 1971, Blunts Reef Lightship played an important role in safeguarding coastal marine traffic, warning of the treacherous reef. The red-hulled vessel swung on her anchor in 186 feet of water, 1.7 miles southwest of the barrier. Lightship *No. 83* held the post from 1905 into the 1930s, leaving only when a relief lightship replaced her for repairs. In later years, in addition to her light and fog signal, she was equipped with a radiobeacon and distance finding equipment.

Though responsible for taking many troubled seamen aboard, the most dramatic episode came on June 15, 1916, when no less than 155 passengers and crewmen from the wreck of the passenger steamer *Bear* reached the lightship in lifeboats and were all taken aboard. The ill-fated liner had struck the outcrops near Sugar Loaf Rock off Cape Mendocino in the fog with the loss of five lives. She had only seen five years of service. Taxed to the limit for providing food and clothing for the survivors, Captain Henry Pierotti, in charge of *No. 83*, did his best to care for their needs. He was forced to improvise in every conceiv-

Blunts Reef Lightship No. 523, once classified as No. 100 under the U.S. Lighthouse Service. The diesel electric vessel, circa 1930, when on Blunts Reef was anchored in 186 feet of water, 1.7 miles southwesterly from the reef, held in position by a 7,000 pound anchor. She was later replaced by another lightship, WLV-605, which in turn was replaced by an ocean buoy in the 1970s. Photo courtesy U.S. Coast Guard

able way to accommodate his guests until relief could arrive. Nine lifeboats trailed astern.

The last lightship to serve the post, WLV-612, was relieved in 1971 and replaced by a large self-sufficient unmanned super buoy equipped with all the necessary aids to navigation. At this writing the reef is still guarded by Blunts Reef lighted horn buoy 2B (ELB), flashing red every 2.5 seconds.

❈ Cape Mendocino

The old Cape Mendocino Lighthouse stands abandoned, a forlorn sight to see. Its lens and lighting apparatus have been removed and the tower is red with rust. The light on the massive cape is presently shown from a light atop a pole. A replica tower has been built at the Ferndale Fairgrounds in the town of Ferndale, and it houses the giant first order Fresnel lens that was for so long in service at the abandoned lighthouse. The present light fixture is situated 515 feet above the sea, which makes it the highest of any coastal marine light.

Cape Mendocino, a mighty bastion of land which the early Spaniards in the Mexico-Philippines transpacific trade usually sought out as a landfall promontory on the voyage, is 185 miles north of San Francisco. For many decades it has served as a turning point for vessels traveling northward and southward along the coast. It is a dangerous area with an irregular sea bottom and fickle currents, and a place of great climatic changes. Numerous rocks and sunken ledges are all about.

Sugar Loaf, 326 feet high is 250 yards westward of the cape and is connected with it by a narrow neck of rocks and shingle beach at low tide. Blunts Reef is 2.9 miles west by north of Cape Mendocino Light. The cape is the highest marine headland on the California coast, reaching skyward for 1,400 feet.

It was on September 14, 1867, as the lighthouse tender *Shubrick* was headed for Cape Mendocino with construction workers and materials that she got off course 13 miles south of Punta Gorda and punched a sizeable hole in her wooden hull. To avert sinking, her skipper ran her aground. It took considerable salvage work to patch her up after she was nearly written off as a total loss. All of her cargo was lost and the hull half full of water. The tender was eventually refloated and repaired.

All new materials and supplies for the lighthouse had to be ordered. Below the massive cape the precious cargo was brought in through the surf by boat.

Though many shipwrecks occurred on that sector of the California coast, it was the wreck of the SS *Northerner* that encouraged the building of a lighthouse on the cape. While bound for the Columbia River from San Francisco, she crashed into Two Fathom Rock about a mile from the proposed light station on January 4, 1860, taking the lives of 38 passengers and crew, the survivors narrowly escaping.

There were not only perils in building the station but there were also perils for the keepers that manned the facility. Driving winds often swept the cape with such power that one had a difficult time keeping his feet. The lighthouse, at an elevation of 422 feet, was also the target of fog which closed down the world on the lonely station. Needless to say, it was not one of the more popular assignments for the keepers in the early days. It was far from civilization and difficult to reach. Many of the attendants requested transfers and others just dropped out. It was also hard on the families for considerable storm damage was done to the dwellings and other outbuildings from time to time. Keepers trimming the lamp were sometimes forced to remain in the lighthouse rather than trying to make it back to their dwelling in the strong winds. On one occasion a keeper put his family in the oil house for the night fearing the wind would blow their living quarters apart.

Though long abandoned, the 43 foot tower, pyramidal shaped and 16-sided, has remained at its position since 1868. The problems of possible removal to Ferndale were discussed and dismissed because of the difficulty that would be involved, and that's why a replica was built at Ferndale, the nearest town of size.

The old tower is well off the beaten path, but adventurous hikers climb the hill to photograph the old lighthouse and take a peak at the modern marine beacon now employed.

❈ Punta Gorda

If you wish to visit long abandoned Punta Gorda Lighthouse, park your car at the small village of Petrolia, put on your hiking boots, and plan a three mile trek through some rugged territory. The little lighthouse sits below a bold rounding promontory 11 miles south of Cape Mendocino. It has not been an active light since 1951, and in isolation for many years, the structure is located amidst a rather forlorn backdrop of rippled valley contours and scrub growth below a seaward face rising to about 900 feet, 400 yards back from the beach, which terminates in a spur almost overhanging the sea. It was a place the early Spaniards named Punta Gorda which translated means "Massive Point." The 25 foot high abandoned lighthouse is southerly of the point.

The wind, sea, and currents are said to be as swift as any point on the coast; frequent strong riptides abound and climatic conditions are sometimes unpredictable. Less than a mile southward of the point is Gorda Rock, ten feet high and conical in shape where a lighted whistle buoy stands to warn of the danger.

During the era of the hippies, who had an uncanny way of finding out-of-the-way places to set up their communes, the lonely and empty Punta Gorda station suited their needs well. Residence was taken up in the standing structures, the only real activity there since CBM Hank Mostovoy of the Coast Guard closed down the station and took "Old Bill," the working horse and mascot of the place, to greener pastures. The intruders lived primitively and garbage began to pile up. Fearing that the situation presented a problem, the Bureau of Land Management ordered the dwelling and all structures but the lighthouse and oil house burned to the ground in 1970, and the hippies were scattered.

There were many problems in building the lighthouse because of its isolation. In fact, the fog signal there was operative six months before the lighthouse was completed and fitted with a fourth order flashing lens. The official lighting took place on January 15, 1912. It was a complete station, the dwelling far more formidable than the lighthouse. A complete water and sewage system had to be installed for the occupants of the station.

During the World War II, the Coast Guard used the station for the service men who did the beach patrol work to guard against possible invasion. Those activities gave the keepers of the light considerably more company.

Again, it was shipwreck in the area that was the incentive for placing a lighthouse at Punta Gorda. There was talk of placing a beacon there as early as 1890. Much attention was drawn to the area when SS *Columbia* sank after colliding with the steam schooner *San Pedro* in thick fog 16 miles south of Punta Gorda, July 21, 1907. In that tragedy, 87 souls drowned and 150 were eventually rescued.

One can still see the rotted remains on the beach, near the lighthouse, of the steamer *St. Paul* wrecked there in 1905, and of the steamer *Humboldt* wrecked in the previous decade.

In recent years the old lighthouse has been painted and continues to stand on state property as a small memento of the past.

❈ Fog Bells

An interesting old fog bell made of bronze hangs from a redwood log atop two stone pylons on the campus of the College of the Redwoods, near Eureka, California. The bell bears the following legend cast into its outer surface "U.S.Y.M.I. Cal. 1883 for U.S.L.H.E.," along with a line of 13 stars. The inscription translates: United States Navy Yard, Mare Island, California, 1883, for the United States Lighthouse Establishment.

Inside the bell are some hand-painted legends. The words are "T", then an illegible letter, followed by "ERRY. Oct. 10, 1885," etc. It turns out that the bell was cast at the Navy Yard at Mare Island near Vallejo. The report of the Lighthouse Board for 1883 says the bell was made for Alcatraz Island. It weighs 3,340 pounds, and was cast from the old Alcatraz fog bell and other material sent to the yard for the making of this larger more effective replacement. It was the second one to be used as the Alcatraz Island fog signal, (south bell). A new structure was completed in 1885 to hang it from. The bell clanged at Alcatraz until 1914 when replaced by an air siren. From there it was sent to Los Angeles to become the Inner Harbor Fog Signal, and when it was replaced by a siren it was moved to Carquinez Lighthouse on San Pablo Bay where the lighthouse keeper etched his name "Bennett" on the inside. Oddly enough the bell was brought to Shelter Cove on the Redwood Coast in 1936 aboard the lighthouse tender *Lupine*, where it was installed at a fog signal station on the tip of Point Delgada, protected inside a bell house. After a decade it was replaced by a pair of bell buoys (in 1945) and the bell housing stood empty until it eventually collapsed. The owner of the cove, Tony and Mario Machi, gave the bell to the Humboldt County Historical Society and it finally ended up on the college campus where it remains today.

This is a typical story of how the old fog bells were moved about in the past. Several others had similar experiences. The above was researched by the late Carl Christensen.

✵ Point Cabrillo

Now we come to Point Cabrillo Lighthouse. Located 24 miles north of Point Arena and near the town of Mendocino, this classic frame lighthouse was first illuminated on June 10, 1909. The light was a third order apparatus shining seaward from a 47 foot tower attached to a fog signal building. Atop a 60 foot bluff, storms sometimes punish the lighthouse and the surrounding cliffs which are punctured by wave tunnels. Debris is sometimes thrown up to the plateau where the sentinel stands. A storm on February 8, 1960, struck with tremendous force, sending rocks and flotsam and jetsam into the building. The foghouse doors were ripped out, the wooden siding peeled off and an air compressor was knocked from its fittings and shoved across the floor. Oil spilled everywhere.

Keeper Bill Owens, who spent 11 of his 33 years of lighthouse service at Cabrillo was a witness to the devastation. He and his crew spent endless hours getting the station back in proper condition.

Owens and his family were a typical lighthouse family that adapted well to their interesting lifestyle. He retired February 28, 1963, as the last civilian keeper on the Pacific Coast and was presented with the Albert Gallatin Award, the highest award a civilian Federal employee can receive. He passed away in 1984, insisting to the end that automation had much to be desired. Said he:

"Anything automatic always goes haywire when you need it most."

The first keeper at Point Cabrillo was Wilhelm Baumgartner. On his very first night of duty he not only fired the lamp but had to set the fog machinery in operation as a blanket of white fell over the station.

The dwellings were far removed from the lighthouse on the flat plateau and didn't take quite the wind blasts as did the tower. All over the premises there were sectors of land somewhat unstable. Sometimes the livestock got too close to the edge of the cliffs and were either shoved over the side by the wind or managed to do so on their own. If they

survived it was always a major undertaking to get them topside.

Several years ago a large aero marine beacon was placed atop the foghorn house roof, replacing the Fresnel lens, and at this writing was still in operation. Volunteers now allow visitors to view the lighthouse, for the land is part of the Cabrillo National Monument under auspices of the National Park Service. Workers have spruced up the old building and have placed historic photos within depicting the history of the light and its surroundings.

The storms still blow and the fog rolls in, up to 1,000 hours a year, but the fog trumpets have been removed, and a buoy sounds offshore when the weather thickens.

Located off California State Route 1, the lighthouse is one of a kind. For many years it was especially well known to the so-called "Scandinavian Navy," those doughty seafarers that operated the steam schooners. They not only passed close to the point but also had a kinship with the tower, as redwood was used in its construction, the substance that was the main cargo of the steam schooners.

✵ Point Arena

From a distance it appears almost like a giant missile ready to be launched. In reality it is Point Arena Lighthouse, a 115 foot tower, cylindrical in shape and sporting a powerful beacon seen 25 miles at sea, from a height of 155 feet above the pulsating ocean. An important radiobeacon is located near the lighthouse.

Located in a fault area, Point Arena Lighthouse paid dearly when the great earthquake hit San Francisco on April 18, 1906. It was in the path of destruction, though a long distance from the city by the Golden Gate. The lighthouse tower was severely cracked, some of the bricks popped out and gaping holes appeared everywhere deeming the tower beyond repair. The lens was shattered and the keepers' dwelling a total loss. The occupants of the station had to improvise among the wreckage, and making things even worse, a frightened black bear terrified by the quake ran amok among the destruction and had to be exterminated.

The temporary lighthouse set up at Point Arena after the old lighthouse was destroyed in the 1906 earthquake. This skeleton tower was used until the new tower was completed in 1907. Photo courtesy The Keepers Log

With the tower out of commission, a temporary lighthouse was set up, and the lantern house lifted from its previous perch. Inside was placed a light of the second order which was dispatched to the scene by the Lighthouse Department. Fortunately the fog signal house had survived the quake.

In the interim, a type of metamorphosis took place within the highly damaged tower. It was completely reconstructed of reinforced concrete, the first of many to be built of that material. To guard against future earthquakes, buttresses were placed at the base of the tower. The dwellings were also enlarged and made much more commodious during the reconstruction, and the station emerged as a first class accomplishment. No longer would the head keeper have to share one large dwelling with his assistants and their families, nor place remarks in the station logbook which read:

"Threatening weather and fighting children." (George Kooms, keeper January 1880)

The lofty tower shared honors with Pigeon Point as being the tallest lighthouse on the Pacific Coast with the exception of St. George Reef Lighthouse, six miles offshore.

The initial lighthouse at the site was a masonry building, 50 feet above the sea, first lighted May 1, 1870, with a fixed first order lens. The first order lens placed in the newly constructed tower had its huge optic floating in a large tub of mercury, providing friction free rotation.

The increasing number of shipwrecks around Point Arena Lighthouse demanded the positioning of a U.S. Lifesaving Station in the vicinity of the lighthouse. Probably the most embarrassing shipwreck in the area was when the big British cargo vessel *Pacific Enterprise*, of Furness Line, ran aground in the fog near the lighthouse on September 9, 1949. In command of Captain Cogle, on his final voyage as a shipmaster after a flawless record of several years, it was additionally painful, for the ship became a total loss along with much of her $1 million cargo of lumber and grain. The 454 foot ship soon broke in half and went down in 60 feet of water. Her rusted hull became the haunt of sea creatures and marine growth.

During World War II, keepers Wayne Piland and Bill Owens alerted authorities that a Japanese submarine had been sighted offshore from the lighthouse, in the wake of Pearl Harbor. A naval officer who received Owens' message was skeptical. He told Owens to "go back to bed," that no submarines were in the vicinity. A few days later the oil tanker *Emidio* took a torpedo broadside off Blunts Reef and five of her crew perished.

During the prohibition days in the 1920s, "rumrunners" often came to the station and warned the keeper not to report unusual activities offshore. One of the culprits was a young boyish-looking character with cold, steel blue eyes, who went by the name of Lester J. "Gill" Gillis. Though not recognized as big time, his picture appeared in the newspaper when he was shot and killed in the 1930s, and some of the former attendants of the lighthouse recognized him under the moniker of Baby Face Nelson, one of the nation's most infamous criminals and gang boss in Chicago, feared for his trigger finger.

Point Arena can be reached on Lighthouse Road north of the town of Point Arena on Highway 1. A local volunteer lighthouse association offers tours of the lighthouse and fog signal house, and accommodations have been on the grounds for several years for American Hostels, Golden Gate council. At this writing the Coast Guard still maintains the light.

❀ Point Reyes

Point Reyes Lighthouse, sister to the ill-fated Cape Mendocino Lighthouse, is located a two hours drive northwest of San Francisco, and is unique in its setting. The little iron-plated tower is perched precariously on a rocky shelf and can be reached by walking down more than 300 steps—600 plus steps round trip. If the wind is blowing, which it often is, or the cold, wet fog sets in (it is the foggiest on the coast), the trek can be a bit trying. Whatever the effort, it's worth the trip, for it not only offers an excellent place to spot the California gray whales on their annual migrations, but under the control of the National Park Service the tower is open to the public, and if you hit it at the right hours you'll be able to view the 24-sided first order lens, which with its lighting apparatus weighs about two-and-a-half tons. The clockwork is in the pedestal. Near the tower is a small utility building and the fog signal house. The old lens has become a museum piece but remains in the tower lantern room and is turned on for one-and-a-half hours at prescribed times for the benefit of visitors. The active aid to navigation is a modern fixture on a cylindrical structure on top of a square building, and a foghorn blasts continuously.

As a tourist attraction, the lighthouse gets a lot of oohs's and ah's, but to the keepers of old it was a difficult station to man and the biggest complaints always involved the fog signal. With an average of 2,700 hours of fog annually and 638 steps to go back and forth it was not a comforting thought on a miserable night. Automation would have been welcomed with a capital A.

With the rash of shipwrecks in and around Point Reyes it became apparent to the government that a lighthouse would have to be built there. It was in Drakes Bay that the first recorded shipwreck on the Pacific Coast occurred. On her voyage back to Acapulco, the Spanish galleon *San Augustin*, out of Manila and in command of Sebastian Rodriguez Cermeno with Francisco Chavez as master, got into trouble off Point Reyes and was driven into Drakes Bay with both anchors dragging. Aboard was a cargo of 130 tons including silks, beeswax, and several other valuable pieces of freight from the Indies. Two members of the crew were drowned. After the crew managed to get the bulk of the cargo ashore a fracas broke out with the natives, who demanded a share. In the battle that followed the Spaniards lost food supplies and twelve of their men. The survivors were forced to take the ship's boat and make a rigorous passage south. They managed to reach Acapulco nearly exhausted and close to starvation.

The land desired for the lighthouse in the 1860s was privately owned and the owners demanded $25,000 if the Lighthouse Board wished to acquire it. The government authorities considered the cost prohibitive and threatened condemnation, as the asking price was far in excess of the allocated funds. An agreement was at last finalized in 1869 whereby 120 acres was acquired for $6,000, the owner realizing they had their backs to the wall.

A wharf was set up in Drakes Bay to receive building materials, and a construction superintendent Phineas Marston arrived on the job site straight from Port Angeles where he supervised the construction of Ediz Hook Lighthouse station.

Rock had to be blasted away and wagon roads hacked out. It was a difficult undertaking to carve two terraces out of the basalt. The lighthouse and fog signal house had to be bolted deep in solid rock on the lower level and the dwelling and other buildings had to be built to stand the rigors of the weather on the upper tier. Additionally, it was a tedious job assembling the huge lighting apparatus, a product of Barbier and Fenestre of Paris. With 24 flash panels it contained 1,024 prisms. The lamp was lit December 1, 1870, and the Lighthouse Board was so pleased with Marston's work that he was invited to supervise construction of the Pigeon Point Lighthouse.

Whether it was by accident or arson, the fog signal house burned down two years later and had to be replaced by a steam operated horn that consumed 140 pounds of coal per hour in the boiler furnace.

When the lens rotation got out of balance in 1875, the ingenious head keeper John C. Bull somehow managed to jack up the huge beehive of glass and brass and discovered the chariot wheels had become badly worn. He managed to fit new chariot wheels and got the lens rotating to perfection.

A year earlier a mystery involved the disappearance of assistant keeper E.K. Lincoln. It appears the British ship *Warrior Queen* had crashed ashore on the rocks below the lighthouse. She was enroute to San Francisco from New Zealand and was wrecked under strange circumstances that smacked of mutiny or barratry. Lincoln went down to check out the wreck and survey the damage. The ship was a total loss but her crew was saved and part of the cargo salvaged. The unsolved mystery was that Lincoln never returned to the station and completely vanished, never to be seen again.

After Bull was transferred, a period of real trouble broke out at the lighthouse. The keepers became argumentive and there were many sleepless nights. It all culminated when the hawser which pulled the handcart alongside the chute parted, sending the metal cart plunging down the cliff side and into the small building which had quarters for the keeper on duty at the lower level. Nobody was injured but there was considerable damage.

Lighthouse inspectors continued to find the facility in poor condition, but owing to the difficulties involved were a bit more lenient than at other stations, though many disciplinary actions, transfers, and dismissals transpired.

The closely allied lifesaving station at Bolinas Bay burned down in 1885, and arson was suspected. It was four years later that funds finally became available for another unit, this time at Point Reyes Beach.

In the misery of the lighthouse station, keeper E.G. Chamberlin wrote down the following in 1885:

Solitude where are the charms that sages have seen in thy face?

Better to dwell in the midst of alarms than reign in this horrible place.

When head keeper John C. Ryan took over the station in 1888 he stated:

"In taking charge of this station I must say it is broken, filthy and almost a total wreck from end to end."

The station log reported a year later:

"The second assistant went crazy and was handed over to the constable in Olema."

Conditions finally did improve at the station, but damage occurred due to storms from time to time, and in 1916 a gale ripped the roof of the tank house and knocked fences, chimneys, poles, and wires askew.

Fred Kreth became a hero in his own time by rescuing the crew of a fishboat hopelessly trapped on the rocks beneath the lighthouse. He lowered himself down the cliff on a lengthy coil of rope in the aftermath of an 80 mile-an-hour gale. The fishermen had been trapped on the slimy rocks for 13 hours. When Kreth got as far as he could go on his coil of rope he stood on a thin ledge and uncoiled the rope until it reached the trembling hands of the miserable men below. In a herculean effort by all involved, the fishermen were finally able to climb to the precipitous cliff and eventual safety.

When the old fog signal house was endangered by falling rock a new unit was installed with generators and compressors.

Some keepers liked the place. When Gustave Zetterquist arrived there with his family in 1930, they remained until 1951, making the best of a difficult station.

It would seem that the place got off to a bad start when the steam powered Russian warship *Norvick* was wrecked less than two miles north of Point Reyes September 25, 1865 (1863), the master of the vessel claiming his British charts showed a lighthouse located at the point. Some cannon and other munitions were salvaged, but the corvette was a total loss. In truth, the Lighthouse Board had considered a

lighthouse for Point Reyes many years before its construction, and perhaps the British chart makers had assumed that there was one at the location when the chart was made.

❋ The Farallons

Twenty-six miles off San Francisco's Golden Gate, scattered in a line seven miles long, is a smattering of ridges, sea stacks, and sharp cliffs chiseled out of basaltic substance known as the Farallons. Those jagged teeth have long presented a menace to navigation, the part that rises above all stages of the tide encompassing about 120 acres of barren rocks. It might well be said from the beginning that the string of isles was strictly "for the birds." Great numbers of sea birds not only nested there annually, but for others, it was a pit stop on their migrations.

Farallon Lighthouse atop this craggy monolith dating from 1855, was one of the early Pacific Coast sentinels, one of the toughest to man and supply, lying about 23 miles off the Golden Gate. Rich in history, it was the scene of many eggs wars in early times when the rookery was often raided. It is now part of the Point Reyes/Farallon Islands National Marine Sanctuary. The light is 358 feet above the sea.

To early Spanish mariners who manned the galleons and carracks the islets were known as Los Farallones de los Frayles. When Sir Francis Drake visited there in 1579, he applied the name St. James, but the title of "Farallones" won out.

There have been many unflattering names given to that place; one Navy chaplain stated that "God has done less for it and with it than any other place." Most of the oaths concerning the locale involved profanity.

In 1812, Alexander Baranov (Baranof) who held out at New Archangel as the ruling magistrate, dispatched a colony of Russians by ship to set up Fort Ross in California. It was not only to get a foothold in the new world, but to begin a trade serving at the Czar's request for needed supplies and food sources. As a result, a minor outpost was established on the largest of the Farallon Isles. Annually the Russians salted down 5,000 pounds of sea lion meat. Mammal oil was used to light their lamps and the hides were utilized to make boots, garments, and to cover small boats. Some of the take went to the fort, some to Russian Alaska, and occasionally to mother Russia.

Failing to follow up on their exploits in California as did the Spaniards, the flag of Russia was gone well before the Yankee invasion. Of the Farallons, K. T. Khlebnikov, Russian commander at Fort Ross, once stated; "During storms, the islands shake and one can hear a moaning against the breaking waves. Persons who stay there have difficulty sustaining themselves."

With as many as 400,000 Murres nesting there in the early days, the demand for eggs in early San Francisco was strong. Egg poachers came in droves and competition grew so hot at times that egg wars broke out, far beyond just throwing eggs at each other.

That rock-strewn menace to navigation, with the armada of ships descending on San Francisco in the gold rush days, demanded a lighthouse. In the late winter of 1853, the bark *Oriole* dropped her anchor in a small cove on the north side of Southeast Farallon Island. Aboard was the construction crew hired by contractors Gibbons and Kelly. They were met by a hostile reception from the egg hunters who wanted nobody trespassing on the egg hunting grounds nor disturbing the nesting areas. Uncle Sam threatened military action and an unsteady truce prevailed.

It was decided that only the lighthouse could be built high atop the precipitous summit because of the sharp contour of the terrain. The dwellings and outbuildings would have to be erected on the flat surface at the base of the isle which would make a long switchback climb for the keepers tending the beacon. Under the guidance of Major Hartman Bache, with somewhat modified plans, the work got underway. Though experienced in lighthouse construction work, the obstacles in building Farallon Light had Bache scratching his head more than once. The landing of supplies alone was difficult, most having to be lifted from small boats. The isle's summit was 348 feet above the sea and the accent up the bastion was between 45 and 55 degrees. Bricks had to be moved manually, the work next to exhausting. Surprisingly, the tower and dwelling were completed in November 1853, although the lighting apparatus had not yet arrived. In fact, the station buildings remained deserted for several months. Finally, in December of 1854, the French ship *St. Joseph*, out of Marseilles, arrived at San Francisco with the crates containing the first order lens and lighting apparatus. Then came the shock. After uncrating the goods, 73 crates in all, it was discovered that the lighting components were too large for the tower. Frustration began to build. Bache reluctantly ordered the lighthouse dismantled and rebuilt to house the big lens. To make life easier for the construction crew a road of sorts was hacked out of the precipitous hillside making it easier to get materials to the summit. Bache got some flack from the authorities in Washington D.C. on cost overrun. In a fit of temper he shot back that the road was essential if the work was to continue. He won out not only for authorization on the road but got his own boat and a mule in the bargain, as the wrong size of the original tower was not his fault but the fault of the Lighthouse Board, who in the interim had changed the type of lighting apparatus for the tower.

In December 1855 the station was finally completed. The original dwelling housed the keeper and his two assistants. It was the same dimensions as the Point Loma Lighthouse but without a tower poking through the roof. (It stood until 1969 and was finally dismantled.) Because the goldrush flurry was still in full swing it was difficult to get keepers on a stipend of only $500 annually (the assistants less) and the San Francisco Collector of Customs was frustrated. In the interim the egg wars continued and the keepers not involved with the egg traffic were often at swords points with the egg pickers. One keeper, in 1857, by the name of Wines, was actually a stockholder in the egg company. Amos Clift, Wines' replacement, was removed from his post by claiming eggs for himself in opposition to the Pacific Egg Company (later named Farallones Egg Company). He made the bad mistake of telling Uncle Sam "he could kiss his foot," if he didn't like it. Guess who was terminated?

In March of 1863, a Revenue cutter was sent to Southeast Farallon on information that several armed men were planning to take over the island and had built themselves a house with a stone wall to act as a fortress. Captain Charles Scammon landed with a token troop of soldiers to warn the egg pickers, but found they weren't easily discouraged. On June 3, three vessels full of armed men arrived. Eventually, a battle lasting almost a half hour broke out terminating with the wounding of some men and the death of others. Still the problem continued, this time with the taking of sea lions for their oil. When the government had lost its patience, the U.S. Marshal and 21 soldiers landed at Tower Bay in May 1881 and evicted all non-government personnel from the islands. Egg businesses were termed illegal although some of the keepers continued to secret eggs off the island for a profit, some working in conjunction with poachers.

Lighthouse keepers always complained about the loneliness and desolation of the station. Nor did shipwrecks add any cheeriness. When the ship *Lucas*, Captain Dagget, struck the rocks on November 10, 1858, 23 souls lost their lives. As the vessel began to sink, she turned broadside to the isle and crushed some of the would-be survivors. The sailing vessel was out of Victoria with 175 gold seekers aboard, most of which were saved by the government steamer *Active* which came to the rescue. It was that wreck that prompted a fog signal at the site. Inspector Bache ordered a train whistle placed over a blowhole that blew naturally every time a rush of air shot up through the opening. Its one defect was an inability to make a loud noise in foggy conditions when the sea was the calmest. The contraption was finally destroyed in a severe storm and replaced by a modern steam fog signal. Over the years the station was updated with new Victorian-style keepers' dwellings, and eventually families of keepers were allowed to live there. By 1897, there were ten children at the station, and a school was set up in the original keepers' dwelling.

Even with improvements the isolation presented drawbacks. Some of the children became desperately ill in 1901, and despite bonfire signals and the blasting of the fog apparatus, no passing ship recognized the emergency, and two sons of the keeper Cyrus Cain died. Another of their children fell to his death over a steep cliff a decade earlier. In addition, when assistant keeper William Beeman's son became ill in 1898, and no help was available, the parents set out in a small boat and tried to get their child to San Francisco. They were eventually picked up by a pilot boat but the child passed away before help could be reached. The first child born at the station was on April 8, 1898, and she was properly named "Farallone" Cain.

In a gorgeous afterglow, the Battery Point Lighthouse is silhouetted against the western sky, its light beaming from the little islet on which it stands. Only at low tide can one walk the causeway from the mainland to the lighthouse. One of the best preserved of the pioneer lighthouses on the Pacific Coast, it was known as Crescent City Lighthouse all through its service with the U.S. Lighthouse Service and the Coast Guard. When the Coast Guard closed it down, a long-term lease was arranged with the Del Norte County Historical Society, which operated it as a private aid to navigation, caretakers watching over it and affording tours for the many visitors. It is open to the public at prescribed hours.

Another view of Battery Point Lighthouse, showing the old water tank. The 375mm light is aglow in the lantern house.

Because the folks of Trinidad wanted tourists to enjoy their maritime heritage, and the fact the real lighthouse was long off limits to the public, they built a replica in town. It was given the original lens and a fog bell.

After abandonment in the 1970s, Table Bluff Lighthouse, south of Humboldt Bay, had its attached dwelling razed and only the frame tower remained. To save it from destruction, a civic effort was launched and the tower was eventually moved to Woodley Island and restored as a tourist attraction at a nearby marina in Eureka.

Below:
Looking down from the air, one gets an overall view of the old displaced Table Bluff light tower, made of redwood. A host of pleasure craft and commercial fishing vessels are nearby on Woodley Island, Eureka.

A close-up view of the gorgeous Cape Mendocino lens in its new home at the Ferndale Fairgrounds in a town steeped in history, featuring many historic homes and buildings.

Above:
The little maritime museum in Eureka has many mementos of a past era. Among the relics is the Fourth Order lens that served at Table Bluff from 1892, until the lighthouse was eliminated as an aid to navigation in 1972.

Left:
This thought-provoking picture of the abandoned Cape Mendocino Lighthouse reaches perfection. The damp fog lifts up from the Pacific, the tower running red with rust. This is one of Keith Kammerzell's best.

The Ferndale Fair Grounds hardly seems like the place for a lighthouse. Actually its a replica of the abandoned Cape Mendocino Lighthouse which sits rusting on the side of the bold headland. Its First Order lens was carefully removed and reassembled in the replica tower in the town of Ferndale.

A lighthouse without a beacon light, is like a person with no hope. The Punta Gorda lighthouse sits in sad abandon.

In recent years, Point Cabrillo has been off-limits to the public, although efforts are being made for lighthouse visitation.

A lovely panorama unfolds in this aerial shot of Point Arena and its artistic lighthouse. The original lighthouse at the location was badly ruined by the 1906 earthquake. It was first lit May 1, 1870. A temporary lighthouse was set up after the big quake, and the one pictured here became one of the nation's first reinforced concrete sentinels. It rises 115 feet, and went into service in 1907.

Opposite page, top:
Directly over the frowning cliffs of Point Reyes, one gets an almost dizzy feeling from looking at this photograph. There are 638 steps, round trip, between the lighthouse and the former dwellings on top of the point. It is the foggiest spot on the coast, 2700 hours of fog per annum. This was one of the least favored stations in the earlier days. Not only was there an abundance of fog, but the winds often reached a velocity of 100 miles an hour. The station, which dates from 1870, is 294 feet above the sea. The First Order Fresnel is in place but is maintained for an historic attraction while an auxiliary light performs. The Fresnel is turned on for special occasions, all of which is under the guidance of the National Park Service.

Opposite page, bottom:
A super air shot of Point Bonita Lighthouse and accompanying buildings. The long footbridge connects the upheaval of solid rock on which the lighthouse stands with the razor back peninsula. The first lighthouse at Point Bonita lighted up in 1855. Often fog enshrouded, it was replaced by the present watchtower in 1877, and it was the last of California's 59 lighthouses to be automated. Acting as the welcoming signal to San Francisco Bay, John Brown was the initial keeper at the Bonita station. The 1906 earthquake did considerable damage, destroying the keepers' dwelling.

It is hard to believe that this platform was once the foundation for a lighthouse. It was here that Mile Rocks Lighthouse was commissioned in 1906—a white cylindrical tiered tower, 78 feet above the water. Difficult to man and expensive to operate, the tower that was built with tedious and dangerous effort was eliminated by the Coast Guard in 1966. The platform and the one-story of the old lighthouse provided a place for a helicopter to land to bring maintenance men to service the small light and fog signal, still in use. The aid to navigation is located 700 yards northwest of the sharp projecting point off Lands End on the north face of Point Lobos.

Left:
Graceful symmetry of the present Alcatraz Lighthouse is caught in this unusual shot by Carole Reichel.

Left:
Summer club house for the St. Francis Yacht Club, on the San Joaquin River. This was the former Southampton Shoal Lighthouse on San Francisco Bay, a station established in 1905, and another of the casualties. The lighthouse was moved upriver in the 1960s to its new home.

Right:
Alcatraz Island, more famous for its prison than its lighthouse, was the site of the first American lighthouse to be lighted on the Pacific Coast. It was on June 1, 1854, that Gibbons and Kelly completed and saw lighted the Third Order lens. Time ran out for the initial lighthouse when the prison walls blocked the light's beam. A new concrete lighthouse replaced it in 1909. In this aerial photo the tower is at the far end of the island, the old prison buildings in the foreground.

The former dwelling of the Carquinez Lighthouse on Francisco Bay has been moved for private purposes. The station was a casualty of progress. It was established in 1910.

Left:
Unusual view of the Golden Gate Bridge and the historic Fort Point lighthouse sticking up above the fortress wall like a sore thumb.

Left:
Figure this one out. Part of the Fort Point Historical Site is framed beneath a section of the massive Golden Gate Bridge. In the center is the Fort Point Lighthouse atop the walls of Fort Winfield Scott. The building of the Bridge ended the use of the lighthouse as an aid to navigation in 1934. Actually it is the third lighthouse placed at the fort, the first in 1854 and the existing one since 1864.

California's proud sentinel, Pigeon Point Lighthouse, along with old Point Loma, is the most photographed tower on the coast. Though its big First Order Fresnel is still in the lantern house, it has not been used as the aid to navigation for the past few years, the auxiliary on the gallery affording the light. The 115 foot tower dating from 1872 has become highly popular with the public. The out-buildings are open to the public as a hostelry. The place is also open for tours, and is located south of Pascadero.

A most unusual view of East Brother Lighthouse, perfectly restored all buildings intact. As the last of the many frame lighthouses that once graced San Francisco Bay, East Brother was saved by an aroused public after the Coast Guard threatened its demolition. Erected in 1874, the place has been turned into a highly popular bed and breakfast unit. The light is still active, on the little rocky islet.

Point Montara Light tower seen here was erected in 1928, although a light and fog signal had graced the point from 1875, the fog signal coming before the light due to the large amount of fog annually. Most of the station buildings, including the Victorian style former keepers quarters are utilized as a part of the Youth Hostel program. The public is welcome to roam the grounds at prescribed hours.

A close-up view of the Santa Cruz Memorial Lighthouse, a splendid replica of earlier lighthouses.

Left:
A section of the spiral staircase at Pigeon Point Lighthouse.

Left:
Looking down from the air at the bitter end of Point Sur, below the sea mists, Point Sur Lighthouse and its two oil houses are visible. Situated 270 feet above the sea, the tower commands an excellent position. Located off California Highway 1 in Pfeiffer Big Sur State Park, the nearest town is Big Sur. Sunday tours are offered, with greater access planned for the future.

Below:
Point Pinos Lighthouse, one of the first on the California coast, was lit on February 1, 1855. It has had a colorful history including the many years its keepers was Emily Fish, who took over the post from her deceased husband. The original structure still remains intact along with its Fresnel lens, despite damage from the 1906 earthquake which necessitated considerable reconstruction. Robert Louis Stevenson was one of the many celebrities to visit the lighthouse, at Pacific Grove.

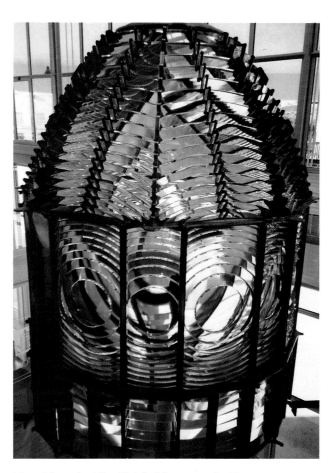

Swooping down from the air, the present Piedras Blancas beacon offers 1.4 million candlepower. The removed first order Fresnel formerly utilized is now a tourist attraction along the roadside at Cambria.

Moved from the Allen Knight Museum to the Monterey Maritime Museum, the old Point Sur Fresnel lens is seen in its permanent home. Photo courtesy Carole Reichel

San Luis Obispo Lighthouse, on Point San Luis, west side of the bay, has been a factor in navigation since 1890. The present light on a cylindrical structure is located east of the old lighthouse, 116 feet above the sea. A foghorn and radio beacon are at the site.

Above:
Point Vicente Lighthouse is located north of Marineland off Palos Verdes Drive in Los Angeles. The nearby center offers information on the lighthouse and the Palos Verdes Peninsula.

Left:
This cracked ship's bell is from the Yankee Blade, *recovered by divers in recent years. The vessel was wrecked north of Point Arguello, near The Honda in 1854, one of the earliest wrecks recorded on the southern California coast.* Photo courtesy Bob Schwemmer

Right:
The first lighthouse on Point Conception became a reality in 1856, its inception fraught with numerous problems during the construction period. The present tower was built in 1882 to replace the original. The old Spanish navigators often used the bold headland as a landfall on return from the Philippines. The lighthouse is not open to the public.

Right:
Anacapa Island from the air offers an entirely different perspective than from the sea. This lonely island is the locale of Anacapa Lighthouse, seen at the end of the point. The other station buildings are also visible. An aid to navigation was placed on the island in 1912, but the present structure was built in 1932, one of the last traditional lighthouses built under the U.S. Lighthouse Service.

Left:
It is hard to find the light in this cluster of buildings at Santa Barbara. It shines from a short 24 foot tower at the end of the point. Santa Barbara had a lighthouse from the year 1856, one of the earlier beacons on the coast. It was replaced by a new facility in 1935.

505:—Breakwater and Lighthouse,   Los Angeles Harbor, San Pedro, Calif,

Vintage post card of the Los Angeles Harbor Lighthouse.

Spectacular view of the Los Angeles Harbor Light (San Pedro Breakwater). Since 1913 this Greek-like structure has been in operation. Its flashing green light is known to mariners the world over. It is not open to the public, as waves sometimes sweep over the breakwater.

Aerial view of the Point Fermin Lighthouse and the buildings in the palm-studded park.

When the schooner *Morning Light* was wrecked on North Farallon Island January 18, 1868, the keepers rowed seven miles to aid in the rescue of the crew of the vessel. She was laden with 50,000 feet of lumber, both the ship and cargo being lost.

The German sailing vessel *Bremen* struck the rocks 1,200 yards from the station; 200 yards from a "silent" fog signal on the foggy night of October 16, 1882. The assistant keeper had failed to activate the signal and found himself in big trouble. The *Bremen* had a 2,700 ton cargo of coal in her holds. Captain Dougall and his crew were rescued but the ship and cargo were a total loss. There were several dismissals of keepers for such things as theft, negligence, and the usual clash of personalities. One keeper, Charles Bjorling, who had earlier been transferred to the Farallons from Tillamook Rock because of friction there, was belatedly charged with attempted murder for placing glass in the principal keepers food.

The Coast Guard assumed control of the station in 1939 and made considerable changes. The length of duty was shortened and more time off granted to attendants. As an economy measure in the latter 1960s, the service decided that families would no longer be housed at the station. It was Brent Franze who was the final keeper when the lighthouse was automated in 1972. The old derrick and landing machinery were battened down, and eventually the islands were placed under the jurisdiction of the U.S. Fish and Wildlife Service, naturalists being the only legal inhabitants visiting from time to time to check on the bird life and the sea lions.

In recent times the old tower was decapitated with the removal of the iron lantern housing. A DCB type beacon, exposed, was installed atop the tower. A radiobeacon is nearby. The keepers' dwellings were razed except the one built in 1878, which houses Coast Guard personnel on occasional maintenance checkups of the equipment, and also affords housing for the Fish and Wildlife visitors. The place is now considered one of the most important wildlife preserves in the country.

And finally, a word about the two mules that once rendered invaluable service to the workers and keepers on the Isle. Jerry, the one which Bache garnered for the construction crew, served faithfully until he died on Christmas night 1874. His replacement, Paddy, slightly more stubborn, worked hard on the traditional "boat day" when supplies and heavy cargo had to be hauled from the landing area.

✸ The San Francisco Lightship

Just a word about the erstwhile San Francisco Lightship. In 108 feet of water off the Golden Gate, the red-hulled San Francisco Lightship was an important aid to navigation for many years. The first of the breed was stationed there in 1898, the *No. 70*. Except for her annual overhaul when replaced by *Relief* No. 76, she held the post, swinging on

her anchor from 1898 until 1930. She ended her days in the Alaska fishery when wrecked in 1941. Her replacement was the *No. 83*, later *WAL-508*. The latter lightship served on the Blunts and San Francisco stations and later as a *Relief* Lightship. She is still afloat today as a unit of the Northwest Seaport, a museum society in Seattle, the last on the Pacific Coast with her original steam engine, installed in 1904 (Note: *Lightship No. 83*, or *Relief* as she has been known for some years, was renamed *Swiftsure* on September 17, 1995, in a ceremony which took place at Seattle's Lake Union. The *Swiftsure* is the oldest survivor of its breed on the West Coast, built in 1904. There are plans to provide for a new deck and to restore the deckhouses to their 1950-59 configuration, as they would have been when the lightship was on station at the Swiftsure Bank). The reciprocating engine, originally coal fired, was later oil fed. The three oil lanterns shown from her mainmast were later replaced by electric beacons and the steam chime whistle by a diaphone in 1934. The vessel is open to the public at her moorings at the south end of Lake Union in Seattle. When the last lightship at the San

Upper photo shows the Relief lightship No. 83, dating from 1904, still with her original steam reciprocating engine. She has been enshrined as a museum ship at the Northwest Seaport moorings on Seattle's Lake Union, oldest such vessel afloat on the Pacific Coast. Lower photo shows the Coast Guard buoy tender Fir *escorting the Swiftsure Lightship No. 113 through Shilshole Bay en route to the Coast Guard buoy station inside the Chittenden Locks at Seattle. The* Fir, *dating from 1939, is still afloat but the lightship was sold, last becoming a floating restaurant at Newport, Oregon. Sold to another firm, the lightship went down in deep water off Cape Lookout, Oregon while under tow.*

Francisco Station *WAL-100* was removed in 1971, a large LNB type ocean buoy replaced her. It was also withdrawn sometime later. In the interim, the lightship was outfitted for service in the Vietnam war area and towed across the Pacific.

❈ Point Bonita

San Francisco's official marine greeter is Point Bonita Lighthouse. The first lighthouse at that location was commissioned on April 30, 1855, one of the earliest on the California coast. The tower was separate from the residence for the keepers, unlike many of the earliest lights. It seems hard to believe today that the place was once considered isolated. The initial keeper complained; "There are no inhabitants within five miles from this point, from San Francisco to Point Bonita; there is no direct communications but by chance a sail boat may be procured at an expense of $5 and $2 for freight."

Backing up that keeper's words was the fact that seven keepers resigned their positions in the first nine months of the station's existence. The main complaint was the poor pay, the persistent fog and the loneliness.

It was the wreck of the 1,275 ton sidewheel steamer *Tennessee* off Point Bonita in a thick early morning fog on New Year's day in 1851 that earlier had added incentive for a light and fog signal. The Pacific Mail Steamship Co. executives insisted that an aid to navigation be placed on the point, because their ill-fated ship represented a loss of $300,000. Though the passengers and crew were saved, the deep water and swift currents nixed any hope of salvage. The underwriters had to pay, but far less than the value of the ship and cargo.

Even though the Coast Survey had recommended Point Bonita for a beacon as early as 1850, it would be another five years before it became a reality. The station had the distinction of having the first fog signal on the California coast in the form of a surplus army cannon which sounded with ear-shattering noise when the fog rolled in. And fog did roll in and mariners complained that the location of the lighthouse, 324 feet up on the cliff, was often shrouded in fog when the lower climes were visible.

The Lighthouse Inspector once threatened to fire a keeper because the glass chimney controlling the oil flame in the lamp kept shattering. His post was saved when it was discovered that the lens had been installed off center in the lantern room, and without proper ventilation the heat got so hot it caused the chimney glass to shatter.

After much correspondence by maritime interests with the Lighthouse Board concerning the poor location of the lighthouse, it was decided to abandon the old tower and build a new one at a much lower elevation.

It was on February 2, 1877, that keeper John Brown lit the lamps' circular wicks in the second order lens. The structure was only 33 feet in height, but stood 124 feet above the water on the west end of a split piece of land reached by a long footbridge. The location far exceeded that of the original tower. An updated fog signal building was erected in 1902. Four years later the station was severely rocked in the great San Francisco earthquake. The 50 year old keeper's dwelling was destroyed forcing him to take up residence in the fog signal house. There was debris everywhere and all the outbuildings lost their chimneys. Fortunately, the lighthouse escaped with minor damage while much of San Francisco lay in ruins.

The mounting number of shipwrecks in and around the Golden Gate inspired the use of powerful searchlights at places on the point to aid mariners in trouble.

In January of 1915, assistant keeper Alex Martin, on seeing distress flares from a wreck at Potato Patch (a series of menacing rocks north of the station), hurried to the scene. From a high cliff he lowered himself down with a coil of rope to reach the deck of the stranded steamer *Eureka*. Unfortunately his rope was not long enough and he had to pull himself back up. In turn, he took off on foot to alert the lifesaving station crew. Surfmen from both Point Bonita and Fort Point stations responded and saved all but one of the seamen in the daring rescue effort.

The National Park Service has opened the lighthouse to public visitation and it has become extremely popular with tourists and locals alike. It still acts as the marine greeter for the maritime traffic entering the Golden Gate. By nightfall, its occulting white light has become a familiar sight, the foghorn a familiar sound. Nearby is an important radiobeacon constantly broadcasting one dash and three dots.

❈ Mile Rocks

Time has nor been so kind to the former Mile Rocks Lighthouse. A light still shines and a fog signal still blares but only from the lowest deck of the former lighthouse. The caisson on which the lower deck rests has broad orange stripes painted about its girth. The light is exposed, and flashes every five seconds. There is also a helicopter pad where Coast Guard crews can land to service the equipment.

There was considerable agitation among lighthouse buffs when the unique lighthouse was razed in 1966; it having been built in 1906, the year of the San Francisco earthquake. For the Coast Guard it was a practical move, but for the San Francisco maritime scene, it left much to be desired. Actually, in the beginning it was a major disaster that was the main incentive for a lighthouse at Mile Rocks. The regrettable loss of the SS *City of Rio de Janeiro*, February 21, 1901, took the lives of 131 and sent shock waves around San Francisco and across the nation. The vessel went down in the early morning fog after slashing her hull on the sharp rocks between Point Lobos, Mile Rocks, and Fort Point. The pilot, Frederick Jordan, lost his bearings in the fog. It took only eight minutes for the liner to take her plunge. Even though Captain William Ward did his best to conduct an orderly evacuation, only 80 souls were saved. The shipmaster went down with his vessel. Ironically, the pilot was rescued.

Mile Rocks, 700 yards northwestward of Land's End on the northern face of Point Lobos, are two small 20 foot high black rocks, about 100 feet apart. Originally, Mile Rocks Lighthouse stood 49 feet above sea level. A white, cylindrical three-tier tower, it was self-contained within a single unit. It was a difficult station to man and supply, waves constantly washing over the tiny piece of rock on which it stood. It appeared like a poor man's castle rising out of the sea, but was a monumental piece of construction built under the direction of John McMahon. So difficult was the construction work that most of the original workers resigned and a new crew had to be hired. The little motor schooner *Rio Rey* was anchored off the rock to act as living quarters, but sometimes she dragged anchor, victim of the currents that frequented the area. Likewise, the buoy that had previously marked the location was often carried from its position.

After the base rock had been blasted, four foot reinforced concrete walls were erected, and as the tower rose skyward, a worker would occasionally fall from the scaffolding and have to be pulled from the churning waters below. The first level contained the oil engine for the compressed air fog signal and the second level featured a kitchen, office, day room and a half tier for bedrooms and bathroom for a four man crew. The third level acted as the watch room, including storage area. That level was topped by the lantern house. The metal tower was a masterpiece in its own right.

It was rugged and isolated duty serving there even though in full view of the lights of San Francisco. The confinement was obvious and all transfer of supplies and personnel was done by a derrick and boom. The tower was no place for a sleep walker—nothing on the outside but narrow galleries. Several transfers and resignations took place. When Alcatraz had prisoners, some of the keepers, far more confined at Mile Rocks, titled the place "San Francisco's Devils Island."

Not all of the keepers hated the place. Lyman Woodruff put in 18 years at the facility, and another, Theodore J. Sauer, did a couple of hitches, hampered by a narrow escape from death while painting the exterior of the tower. A metal plate suddenly broke loose, striking the staging he was working from. Down he went sprawling 25 feet onto the slimy rocks below. Knocked out by the impact, he slipped into the water and would have drowned except for the quick response of the assistant keepers. He later recovered, and after a long period of service, received the Gallatin award on his retirement.

❋ Alcatraz Island

History will forever record that Alcatraz Island was the site of the first American lighthouse to go into operation on the Pacific Coast. Although the island was originally the site of a fortress and later a federal prison, a lighthouse (not the original) is still in operation at this writing. Unfortunately, the scores of visitors that take the boat to the island today are far more interested in the prison than the lighthouse. The prison no longer houses felons, and the fortress is but a memory, but the lighthouse shines on. The entire island has become one of San Francisco's biggest tourist attractions, and under the control of the National Parks, its history will be forever preserved.

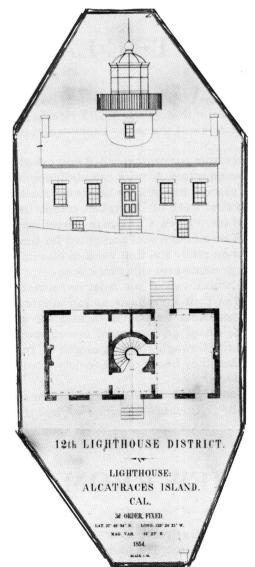

A portion of the original plans for the initial Alcatraz Lighthouse was built in 1854, when the island was used as a fortress, by the military.

By 1852, the sites for the first 16 lighthouses on the Pacific Coast were pretty well decided by the Lighthouse Board. Congressional funding was not easy to come by, and California, mostly due to the flurry of activity in the wake of the goldrush, was given priority for most of those 16 lighthouses. They included, in addition to Alcatraz and Fort Point, Point Bonita, Farallons, Point Loma, Santa Barbara, Point Pinos, Point Conceptions, Humboldt Harbor, and Crescent City in California. The remainder to go in at Pacific Northwest sites included Cape Disappointment, Umpqua River, Cape Flattery, New Dungeness, Smith Island, and Willapa (Shoalwater) Bay.

Inasmuch as Congress appropriated only $148,000 for the project, it was obvious that considerably more money would be needed if all 16 were to be built. A single contractor was hired to build the first eight, all of which would be in California except for Cape Disappointment, then in Oregon Territory. After some rather crude shuffling in the nation's capital, the firm of Gibbons & Kelly of Baltimore was given the contract. Francis Gibbons was an experienced lighthouse engineer having built some east coast lighthouses.

Today, Alcatraz Island, 2.5 miles east of the Golden Gate Bridge, has among the buildings on the property one that stands above all others—the tall, gray octagonal light tower. Fog signals still blare at either end of the island. The 84 foot sentinel, erected in 1909, was given its lofty height so as to be seen clearly above the prison walls. It is built of reinforced concrete and is a far cry from the little Cape Cod type sentinel originally lighted there on June 1, 1854. At that time, the keepers kept company with the soldiers stationed on the island. A fog bell was placed there within two years of the commissioning of the beacon. The bell had to be rung manually, and with frequent fogs blowing in from the ocean the overworked keeper sometimes was tardy in clanging the bell. Unfortunately, he got caught by a surprise visit from the lighthouse inspector and lost his job. Shortly after, clockwork mechanism was added so the bell could be rung automatically as the weight dropped on a chain.

Quarters for the keepers were enlarged in 1881, and the fixed lens was replaced by a fourth order revolving bullseye lens in 1902. Four years later, damage occurred at the station from the powerful San Francisco earthquake, and immediate repairs had to be done on the masonry work and chimneys. The hand-writing was on the wall, however, for as the prison walls rose it became obvious the lighthouse would either have to be raised in height or torn down and replaced. The latter plan won out, and keeper George W. Young said goodbye to his residence and was transferred to the world of retirement after 22 years of service.

Focal plane of the new lighthouse was 200 feet above the water and the lens was transferred from the old tower to the new. At that time in history, the structure was probably the highest in San Francisco, most of the taller buildings having been leveled in the quake three years earlier.

There was always some concern among the keepers that served Alcatraz about the possible escape of prisoners, but the penitentiary was pretty escape proof, though some attempts were made. The Marines had to be called in 1946 in one of the worst prison breakout attempts. Several of the guards were captured and there was an exchange of bullets, but the Marines won out and the guards were released.

During the flurry of excitement, Edward Schneider was in charge of the lighthouse and became more than a little concerned as the bullets were whizzing all around the island. He put in a record 28 years of service on Alcatraz. The prison was closed in 1963, and the lighthouse was automated in November of the same year. It has been monitored from the Yerba Buena Island Coast Guard base ever since. The Fresnel lens was replaced by a double-drum revolving beacon, and fog detectors were employed at either end of the island.

In 1964, a band of Sioux Indians attempted to reclaim the 20 acre island as their own under an 1868 treaty,* and were allowed to occupy the place for a while. When they refused to leave after several months following considerable damage to facilities, including a fire that did damage to the lighthouse and burned down a duplex dwelling, Uncle Sam said, "enough!" When federal agents landed they found a token of the original tribe, most of which were hungry and made no resistance to their forced departure.

*The treaty granted the Sioux the right to claim federal land "not used for a specific purpose."

❊ Fort Point

In the beginning it was a race as to which California lighthouse would be lighted first, Fort Point or Alcatraz. Fort Point, on the south shores of San Francisco Bay, east of Mile Rocks, is an historic fortress built of brick bordered by a seawall. The 33 acre plot is presently part of the Fort Point National Historic Site. Atop the fort's wall stands an abandoned lighthouse which has been restored as an historic attraction.

The original Fort Point Lighthouse had to be dismantled just after its completion when the Army decided it needed the site for fortifications. Why the problem wasn't addressed before construction began reminds us that there were government "boo-boos" back then as well as today. The lighthouse was only three months old when the order came to remove it. When the lighting equipment arrived for Fort Point it was the wrong size and was in turn dispatched to Point Pinos Lighthouse.

With the fortification changes at Fort Winfield Scott (as Fort Point was then known), it was decided to build the new Fort Point Lighthouse on a narrow ledge between the fort and the seawall, a truncated frame tower displaying a fifth order lens. That lighthouse was likewise jinxed when erosion began eating away the shoreline. So, it too got the axe, and a third tower was built in 1864, an iron skeleton tower above the fortress wall, and that's the one that's preserved today (83 feet above the bay).

When the Golden Gate Bridge was constructed, it virtually blocked out the Fort Point Lighthouse. It was actually in 1934 that keeper George Cobb closed the door on the lighthouse and was transferred to Point Arena. Many tourists now visit the site and ponder visions of the past at both the fort and the lighthouse.

In early days while serving 14 years at Fort Point Lighthouse, head keeper James Rankin rescued several people from drowning before his transfer in 1878.

❊ Lime Point

One San Francisco Lighthouse that managed to survive under the Golden Gate Bridge was Lime Point. A fog signal was first established there in 1883, followed by a lens-lantern in 1900. The structure today sits on a rock base on the north side of the bay, a place where frequent rock slides come tumbling down the cliff. Damage was done at the station from time to time but the navigation aids are still there today dwarfed by the 740 foot high bridge supports. The light is on a post, the fog signal nearby.

Even at a peaceful little station like Lime Point, unusual incidents have occurred, in addition to rock slides. Former attendants sometimes dodged bottles and debris from the high bridge above them. On another occasion two thugs held up the Coast Guardsmen on duty in what was termed the first lighthouse stickup. In 1960, the MS *India Bear* plowed into the station grounds in a heavy fog. The freighter scraped over the outcrops and caused $70,000 damage to her hull. Destruction to the station buildings came to $7,500. The following year the attendant's dwelling was razed, the station automated, and closed to the public.

John Rankin, principal keeper of the Fort Point Light Station from 1878 to 1919. Photo courtesy U.S. Coast Guard

❊ Yerba Buena

Three miles southeast of Alcatraz Island is colorful Yerba Buena Island. In the lee of Yerba Buena, the brig *Alert* dropped her anchor in December of 1836. Aboard was a seaman named Richard Henry Dana, Jr., who was later to become famous in the literary world for his writings, the foremost being, *Two Years Before the Mast*. It was a story of the early hide trade from the California coast, and of the poor treatment of the men who sailed before the mast. Dana described San Francisco Harbor as "magnificent," and predicted that if California ever became a prosperous country that the bay would be the center of activity. Little did he know how right he was, for just 13 years later with the discovery of gold in the hinterland, San Francisco became for a time the world's busiest port.

When Dana first saw the island, a man named Richardson was the only inhabitant. From his clapboard hut he was trying to eke out a living by trading. Today the island is the nerve center of Coast Guard activities, the depot servicing buoy tenders and repairing buoys and other aids to navigation. Lights and fog signals are monitored at the site and it is the locale of the San Francisco Vessel Traffic Service Operation Center.

Since 1875, a Victorian-style lighthouse has stood on the slopes of Yerba Buena. The dwellings and outbuildings are located well away

Since 1875, this little lighthouse on Yerba Buena Island has sent its friendly glow over San Francisco Bay. The buoy depot is also on the isle, a place steeped in history.

from the tower, and all in all it is a serene setting. The fogbell at the location was in operation a full year before the lighthouse was completed, the bay ferryboats and steamers passing just offshore. The Lighthouse Service (12th) District, established its depot there in 1873, and three years before that the Army had a base on the 140 acre isle. There, the Costanoan Indians once roamed, coming by canoe to gather tule reeds, cut trees, and raise goats. The military put an end to the Indian haunts, but the goats remained. Land was set aside for the lighthouse in 1870.

The lighthouse station was conducive for families of the keepers, but the children had to go to the mainland by boat in order to attend school.

With the isle denuded of many of its trees, Joaquin Miller, poet and naturalist, began a replanting effort there in 1886 which marked California's first Arbor Day.

In 1939 with the construction of the San Francisco-Oakland Bay Bridge, a tunnel went entirely through the island as the mid-way link, and it was curtains for the huge ferryboat and commuter fleet that had so long been a colorful part of the San Francisco scene. Two decades later, in 1958, the lighthouse was automated and the dwelling became the home of a ranking Coast Guard officer. The island is off-limits to the general public.

❋ Other Lighthouses

There were many other lighthouses that marked the shores of San Francisco Bay and environs in earlier years but they have disappeared. Such unique structures as the Oakland Harbor Lighthouse, abandoned in 1966, was sold to a restaurant firm. It was established in 1890 and re-established in 1903. Then there was the Southampton Shoal Lighthouse dating from 1905, which in 1960 was sold to become the summer clubhouse for the St. Francis Yacht Club on the San Joaquin River. There was also an important light on Angel Island, established in 1900, at a place where a fog bell pre-dated the light by 14 years. John Ross was the first keeper there. A lady keeper, Juliet Nichols, serving at the station in 1906 tolled the fog bell for 20 hours manually when the clockwork mechanism failed to function. Minor lights were also displayed at Point Knox, Point Blunt, and Point Stuart on the isle of Angel.

Keeper Albert Joost, serving at the former Southampton Shoal Lighthouse, set himself on fire while trying to repair a radio antenna with a blow torch in 1936. His quick thinking wife rushed in with a fire extinguisher, dowsed the flames, then bundled him up and rowed him to Angel Island for first aid. He survived.

A lighthouse was built on Mare Island in 1873 and abandoned in 1917. In later years the structure was torn down, after a Navy ammunition dump explosion inflicted heavy damage on the structure. A minor aid to navigation replaced the old Carquinez Strait Lighthouse established on the north side of the strait near Vallejo in 1910. Its closing came in 1951, and it was sold four years later. The buyer, while attempting to remove the 150 ton frame building nearly lost his life in a fall. In 1961, it was towed to Elliott Cove, east of the Carquinez Bridge and converted into a marina.

Roe Island Light Station, commissioned in 1891, was seriously damaged by the powerful explosion at the Port Chicago Ammunition Depot July 17, 1944. In that catastrophe over 300 lives were lost. The cargo vessels *Quinault Victory* and *E.A. Bryan*, a train, and two Coast vessels were destroyed. The Roe Island Station, though a distance away, was in shambles and stricken from further usage in 1945.

❋ East Brother

The Coast Guard might well have abandoned the East Brother Lighthouse had not interested public servants and citizens gotten involved.

One might sing a ballad of lament—where have all the lighthouses gone on San Francisco Bay? It does appear however, that the survivors will be around for a long time. Perhaps the one that gets the most attention from the public is the East Brother Lighthouse which has been converted to a Bed and Breakfast Inn. East Brother, Alcatraz, Fort Point, and Point Bonita are the only active beacons presently accessible to the public in the bay area.

East Brother Lighthouse, like many of the old lighthouses is on the National Register of Historic places. Located on an isle off Point San Pablo, the vintage structure was built of redwood in 1874 and has held its Victorian appearance since that day. All of the original buildings remain and all have been restored. At this writing the fourth order lens was still in the lantern room. The former keepers quarters offer accommodations for overnight guests and there is always a waiting list.

From March 1, 1874, the light operated until 1934, when the lighthouse Service decided it was surplus to the needs of the day. The public rose up in its defense and forced its reopening. The question of closure arose again in 1968 when the Coast Guard decided that it was no longer needed. This time Joseph Picotte, officer—in charge of the station, mounted a campaign to save the lighthouse. With zeal, he prevailed contacting all of those who had been involved with the station including J. O. Stenmark, who put in many years of service at the facility and was its best known keeper. Picotte got the cooperation of the Contra Costa Shoreline Parks Committee and the Richmond Planning Commission. All eagerly joined in to save the last of the harbor family stations. The effort paid off in a big way and a piece of San Francisco Bay history has been preserved.

❋ Lightship WAL-605

Among the many historic vessels that have been preserved for posterity on San Francisco Bay is the *WAL-605*, a lightship built in Boothbay Harbor, Maine in 1950, and similar to the *WAL-604*, Columbia River Lightship which is part of the Columbia River Maritime Museum at Astoria. The *604* was the last lightship to serve on the Pacific Coast. Her sister, the *605* was saved from the scrap buyers by Alan Hosking who moored the vessel in Half Moon Bay and later presented her to the U.S. Lighthouse Society, headquartered in San Francisco. Serving most of her career as the Overfalls Lightship off the Delaware coast she was transferred to the Blunts Reef station in 1960, and nine years later operated out of Astoria as a Relief Lightship.

As earlier mentioned, the oldest museum lightship on the coast, dating from 1904, is the Relief Lightship, owned by the Northwest Seaport in Seattle.

Tethered by chain
and anchor tight,
The lightship rolls
with foghorn and light.

—JAG

❈ The *Shubrick*

The Pacific Coast's first U.S. lighthouse tender, which also served as a revenue cutter, was the venerable *Shubrick*. Her colorful career is covered by my earlier book, *Oregon's Seacoast Lighthouses*. Since then some additional information on that historic vessel has come to light, thanks to Peter Demarest of Glastonbury, Connecticut, model builder, who perused her logbooks in the National Archives. For instance, during December of 1862 the Sacramento River flooded dangerously and the *Shubrick* spent the better part of the week making repeated trips upriver and down river bringing hundreds of victims to safety. Captain Pease, her commanding officer, was apparently a southern sympathizer as the Civil War heated up, and five months later when the San Francisco-based vessel docked at Astoria, a nefarious scheme was hatched. For a considerable period of time Pease reported that his ship was keeping a vigilant lookout for Confederate raiders...even though his ship spent much of her time at her moorings. It was oral tradition that the ship commander had arranged for a Confederate takeover of the *Shubrick* at Astoria while the crew was ashore at a dance early in April 1863.

Aware of the sinister plot, Lieutenant Scammon and two crew members who had remained on the ship managed to get her out to sea. Though details are lacking, a two week gap in the *Shubrick's* log pretty much told the rest of the story. The crew was reduced to half the size, and Scammon had taken over as commanding officer when the log entries continued. No reference was made as to the fate of the southern sympathizers.

In earlier log entries in that time frame many disciplinary problems of loyalty and rebellion indicated that morale was low aboard ship, and among the crew were those who would have gladly joined in the Confederate takeover if it had not been foiled.

No less than remarkable was the history of the *Shubrick* which began at a shipyard in Philadelphia in 1857 and continued in a brilliant career of service and law enforcement on the Pacific Coast and Alaska. It all ended in 1886 when she was bugled out of service, sold, stripped, and burned on a spit in San Francisco Bay. For many years she had served as the Pacific Coast's only lighthouse tender, and her adventures were legion, including her near brush with total disaster off the California coast in 1867.

Engraved in the history of the Pacific Northwest maritime world is the name Shubrick. *Congress authorized her construction in 1856, and she came on the scene a year later. She was a steam powered buoy and lighthouse tender that served the entire Pacific Coast. She had a long and extensive history serving both the Lighthouse Service and the Revenue Marine, often acting as the official law in isolated areas.*

7. Southern California Lighthouses

The curse of the sea, its mystery,
is the silent fog and its misery.

—JAG

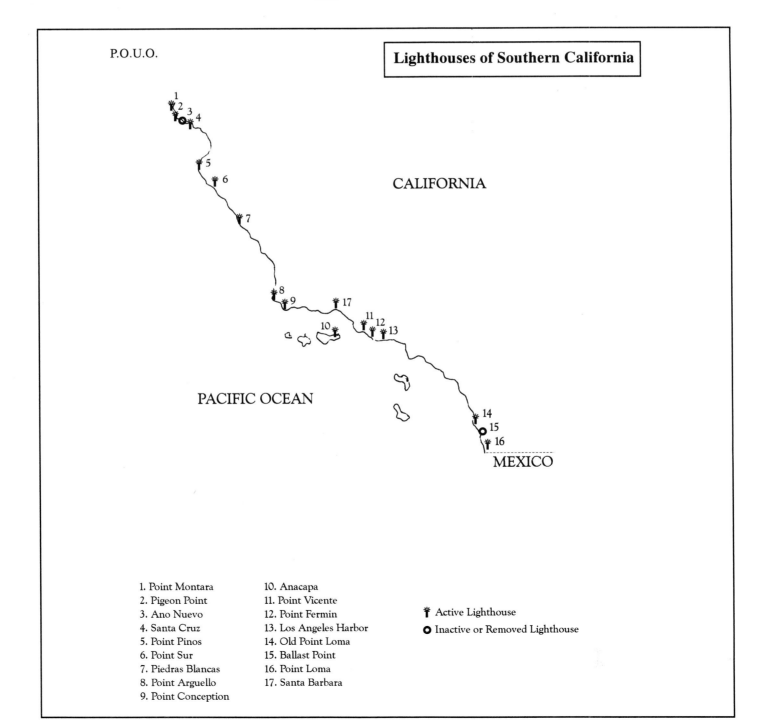

P.O.U.O.

Lighthouses of Southern California

CALIFORNIA

PACIFIC OCEAN

MEXICO

1. Point Montara
2. Pigeon Point
3. Ano Nuevo
4. Santa Cruz
5. Point Pinos
6. Point Sur
7. Piedras Blancas
8. Point Arguello
9. Point Conception
10. Anacapa
11. Point Vicente
12. Point Fermin
13. Los Angeles Harbor
14. Old Point Loma
15. Ballast Point
16. Point Loma
17. Santa Barbara

🕯 Active Lighthouse
⭕ Inactive or Removed Lighthouse

Point Montara

Point Montara is the seaward end of a spur from Montara Mountain and the northwestern extremity of the ridge forming Pillar Point. It terminates in cliffs about 60 feet high with numerous outlying rocks. Covered rocks and ledges lie 0.8 mile westward of the point and extend in a northwesterly direction for 1.5 miles. This is a dangerous locality in foggy weather and extreme caution is necessary when inside the 30 fathom curve. Point Montara Lighthouse sends out its flashing light over those waters and is shown from a 30 foot high white conical tower. The station was built in 1900, but a fog signal had been on the point from 1872. Located 25 miles south of San Francisco on Highway 1, the place is well known to the Youth Hostel affiliation which offers accommodations on the station grounds.

In light of the numerous ship disasters in the area it was strange that it took so long to get a lighthouse at the location but it was obvious that much of the problem was remedied by the installation of the fog signal and light. The present tower, sheeted in metal, was built in 1928 and replaced the original edifice. It sits at an elevation 70 feet above the sea, its former Fresnel lens replaced by a modern aero-marine type beacon in later years.

The same year the original fog signal was placed at Montara, the ship *Aculeo* of 800 tons, crashed on the outlying rocks spilling its $150,000 cargo of coal, iron, and grain into the sea. Captain McKay and his crew were saved but the loss was severe for the shipowners. Salvagers purchased the battered wreck for $3,000 but they probably did well to break even on their investment.

The fog-bound steamer *Colorado* was wrecked on the outer fangs of the point in November 1868, one of the earliest recorded wrecks in the locale, and it was that calamity that first generated public demand for a fog signal there.

Photographers find the Point Montara Lighthouse a good subject for their cameras, especially when the setting sun goes down immediately west of the tower. The lighthouse grounds are open to the public.

Pigeon Point

Certainly in California and probably on the entire coast, no lighthouse is featured more than Pigeon Point. Even though its auxiliary light on the gallery has been the aid to navigation for the past few years, the location and the easy availability in reaching the place attracts visitors like a magnet. These grounds are also utilized by the American Youth Hostels, developed in cooperation with the California State Parks and Recreation.

The 115 foot tower reaches skyward, tapering gracefully. The sentinel was first lighted on November 15, 1872, and still contains its first order Henry Lepaute, Parisian lens although it is presently being used only for display purposes for tower visitors. The giant cage of glass is composed of 1,008 prisms. The last keepers of the lens complained about the dust in the fields when the broccoli and brussels sprouts farmers were plowing.

A radio beacon is located on the grounds, with a 40 mile range.

Pigeon Point was named for the 844 ton clipper ship *Carrier Pigeon*, Captain Azariah Doane, which sliced her hull on the outlying rocks and became a total loss June 6, 1853. Most of her 1,300 tons of cargo were lost. The wreck nearest to where the lighthouse was eventually built was that of the British ship *Sir John Franklin*. That casualty took the lives of 12 seafarers including the captain, a tragedy that caused great concern on a dismal January in 1865.

One of the saddest incidents that occurred off Pigeon Point was when the 47 year old passenger steamer *San Juan* collided with the tanker *S.C.T. Dodd* on September 29, 1929. For a short while the ships were locked together but when the *San Juan* started to go down they pulled apart in the heavy fog. It took only three minutes for the 283 foot ship to take her plunge amid the wailing and crying of the passengers. An estimated 87 lives were lost in that tragic chapter in marine history.

Point Ano Nuevo

Point Ano Nuevo (New Year), 18 miles northwestward of Santa Cruz is formed by sand dunes, 20 to 100 feet high. Low black, rocky, Ano Nuevo Island is 0.3 mile off the point. It was the location of a lighthouse, but no more. Virtually all the buildings on the little isle have been razed and the place has reverted to a bird and sea mammal preserve. The dangerous shoreline and the frequent fogs made it mandatory for a light and fog signal there as early as 1872. The original light was a lens-lantern backed by a 12 inch steam whistle. As the years rolled on two different lighthouses were erected on the isle, the latter a skeleton tower, afforded its lantern house when the first structure was decapitated. By the 1940s the lighthouse had been terminated, and the isle was marked by the nearby Ano Nuevo Island lighted whistle buoy.

To give the reader an idea of the way life was on the tiny island during the days of the Lighthouse Service we turn to the personal words of Radford Franz Franke, who after a period on the San Francisco Lightship *No. 70*, got an appointment to Ano Nuevo Lighthouse. It was in April 1929 that he packed his suitcases and headed for his new assignment.

"I arrived at the ranch opposite the island, got permission from the rancher to pass through his property. This was the only access to the beach. It was about one half mile through the ranch and another half mile over sand dunes before reaching the beach; this was all new to me, with the wind blowing the suitcases between my legs, I was ready to go back. I left the wife in San Francisco as she had a job and I was uncertain as to what I was getting into. I finally reached the beach and signaled to the island so they could come and get me. Luckily it was calm enough for them to come over. The island is about one half mile from the shore, and the transportation was by an 18 foot dory. It can be a dangerous trip if the wind is blowing, as the seas come around both sides of the island and met right where the crossing is made.

"We had to buy all our food supplies in San Francisco, there was one special store that supplied us and they would see that it got to the pier and loaded on the lighthouse tender. We got our groceries every three months when the tender brought our coal supplies as well as fuel for the fog signal engines. We could not order any fresh food, maybe some hamburger, frankfurter, just enough to last two or three days, so it wouldn't spoil. The grocer would send the goods down on the stage and the driver would leave it at the ranch, where we had a small shack built for mail delivery. The only trouble was the stage didn't go by 'till afternoon and many times a storm would come up and we were unable to go after the food. We really didn't want for food, as we (the keepers) had our own chickens which kept us supplied with eggs, and occasionally a chicken dinner, besides all the delicious abalone and fish anytime we wanted it. We raised a few vegetables even though there was no real soil on the island. By cutting the bottoms out of cans after we used the contents, we placed a can around each plant, and watered them by pouring the water in the cans and that way it would soak into the sand instead of running off.

"We had real water problems on the island, the light tower was on a slight hill, and the hill sloped down toward the fog signal. The hill was graded and cemented, and at the bottom of the hill was a cistern. Our water supply was furnished by rainfall, which was caught in the cemented section and rained into the cistern. On the hill next to the tower there was a tank house which housed a 38,000 gallon redwood tank which furnished us with a gravity fed water supply to the quarters.

Another casualty of the Coast Guard austerity program was the lighthouse on Ano Nuevo Island in the 1950s. A small tower was placed there with a lens-lantern and 12-inch steam fog signal in 1872. In the Coast Guard photo, the skeleton lighthouse was the last sentinel on the isle, the lantern having been removed from the building to the right of it. A jolting earthquake on October 22, 1926 shook the lighting apparatus from its pedestal and sent it down the hatch to the watch room in a smattering of glass. A standby lamp was also shattered and a third had to be installed. The isle was put up for sale in 1958, the GSA awarding it to a state agency. It is now the haunt of sea lions, seal elephants and birds under the auspices of the Ano Nuevo State Park Reserve, off-limits to the public. Most of the buildings have been torn down and the mammals undermined the light tower and toppled it.

Unfortunately a new tank had been installed which had not been cured properly, so the water supplied to the houses was not fit for consumption. It could be used for bathing and laundry purposes. After we bathed, the water was dipped out of the tub into a bucket and carried down to water the vegetables. The water used for cooking and drinking was supplied from another tank beside the quarters and was kept filled by the rain off the roofs of the quarters and carried into the kitchens in a bucket.

"There were three keepers on Ano Nuevo. In 1929, I was second assistant; Oliver Berg was first assistant. He was married and lived in the single quarters. Jack Chambers was the (principal) keeper. He was single and lived in the lower quarters of a two-story dwelling and I had the upstairs quarters. The quarters were excellent—two bedrooms, bath, kitchen and living room. Because this was isolated duty, we received 96 days leave a year. There were only two men on board the station at a time. We stood watches around the clock—six hours on and six-hours off, seven days a week. In order to change watches once a week we would each stand a nine hour watch starting at 6 a.m. on Sunday. During the day we would turn to for the station maintenance.

"After I was on the island about two weeks I wrote my wife and told her to give up her work and come down. Life was not too exciting for a young fellow isolated as it was; there really wasn't much congeniality on a light station. During the day we worked together which wasn't too bad, but in the evenings you were either in bed resting for your next watch, or you were on watch at the fog signal watch room. The light had to be watched closely as it burned kerosene vapors and was prone to cooling and flaring up. We had an alcohol torch that we used to heat the small kerosene tank in the lens; it was similar to a Coleman lantern and burned a mantel like the Colemans do. Occasionally a moth would get in the lens and eventually fly into the mantel, breaking it, and it would have to be replaced immediately. There were very few dull moments, especially since the fog signal consisted of two distillate engines each running a large air compressor which in turn kept the air receivers filled with air for the fog sirens. The engines would be alternated in the event of a long fog run—the longest period of fog I experienced while there was ten days.

"The fog signal and light tower were reached over an elevated board walk extending from the quarters with hand rails on either side, for at times the winds would be so violent that one had to hang on or be blown away.

"Finally about ten days after corresponding with my wife Marie, she arrived and we started our long and happy life together in the lighthouse service.

"During my stay on Ano Nuevo the rocks on the North Island were inhabited by Steller sea lions, hundreds of them. The females stayed year round while the males migrated from Alaska each year for mating purposes, and then left after a stay of only a few months. After the young were born the adults would mate and then the males would leave. After the young were born they would have to be encouraged into the water by their mothers who in turn would teach them to swim. Many of the young would be washed from the rock and eventually wind up on the beach where they would die. The mothers never really tried to find them. This was an unhealthy time of the year because of the decomposing seal bodies on the beach. Another interesting experience was to watch the killer whales that would come around after the young were born. The small seals would be crowded along the edges of the rocks and the killer whales would swim close and sweep them from the rocks with their huge dorsal fin, and of course eat them. We also had to watch for the killer whales when we crossed in our dory. We were never threatened but we never knew for sure.

"We made a visit in 1978 to the beach to have a look at our old home (Ano Nuevo). The area was protected by California State park rangers, and they take visitors to the beach area under escort because since we left the island the elephant seals have taken over in great numbers. There are so many that they have spread out to the beach on the mainland and have to be protected. The elephant seals are in such great numbers that they were even in the old lighthouse buildings. The light tower (since torn down) which was a square pyramidal skeleton tower was undermined by elephant seals and had finally toppled over and was no longer visible from the mainland.

"My stay at Ano Nuevo lasted about 18 months. Finally I was asked if I would like to transfer to Ballast Point. Not knowing anything about Ballast Point I asked the office if I could call them back. I then asked the keeper (Jack Chambers) what he thought and he, being a real dyed-in-the wool old salt said (expletives deleted); "Get back on the phone and tell them Yes!"

Franke heeded the advice and left for Ballast Point. His tour of lighthouse service lasted well into the take over by the Coast Guard, from 1927 till 1957. He retired after 30 years of combined service, he and his wife married well over 50 years.

Several happy years were spent at Ballast Point by the Frankes and their son who also became affiliated with the Coast Guard. It was on Ballast Point where Juan Rodriguez Cabrillo and his crew landed over 400 years ago, in 1542. Viscaino came in 1602. The very first beacon on the Pacific Coast, other than American, was maintained on the point by the Spaniards as early as 1769. Though just a feeble oil flame it was a history maker.

As far as Ano Nuevo's beacon was concerned the worst accident there was during the October 1926 earthquake when the lighting apparatus was shaken from its pedestal and went down through the hatch into the watchroom, shattering the glass. The keepers installed a standby lamp but a later tremor destroyed it as well. The station suffered considerable damage but a second auxiliary light was finally put into operation through the tenacious efforts of the keepers.

⚜ Santa Cruz

Santa Cruz Lighthouse of today is sort of a memorial lighthouse. It replaced a former lighthouse in 1967, the newer addition built of brick with a white lantern house. Mr. and Mrs. Charles Abbott funded it in honor of their son, drowned while surfing off the point two years earlier. The Coast Guard accepted the light as official. The original government lighthouse at Santa Cruz was torn down in 1948 after serving during World War II as a coastal lookout for the military. It was replaced by a small wooden tower with a minor light until the construction of the present tower. The first lighthouse at Santa Cruz was erected in 1869. It was located on Lighthouse Point, and featured a 35 foot frame tower rising from the keeper's dwelling. The optic was a fifth order lens with a fixed red characteristic, first lit on New Year's Day in 1870.

The flashing white light in the tower today has a range of 17 miles. Many visitors come to see the edifice as it sits in a park-like setting on that scenic portion of the coast. Santa Cruz Lighthouse Park is located on West Cliff Drive in Santa Cruz and features a free surfing museum inside the lighthouse structure.

⚜ Point Pinos

Point Pinos Lighthouse on the point at the south entrance to Monterey Bay is rich in history. Today it continues operative as it has since 1855, one of the very first American lighthouses on the Pacific Coast. Perhaps the most unusual incident in the history of Point Pinos Lighthouse was the fact it had a socialite lady keeper, Emily Fish, that faithfully tended the light for 21 years, retiring in 1913 with a flawless record of service. She polished glass, cleaned the clockworks of the third order lens, and kept the prisms gleaming for her long tenure of duty. A marvelous hostess, she was loved in the community.

It was Commander Nichols, inspector of the 12th Lighthouse District, that inspired Emily to become keeper of the light in the wake of her husband's death. The opportunity came when keeper Allen Luce announced his retirement. During his tenure at the light, Luce in 1872, was host to Robert Louis Stevenson. The great poet and novelist was highly impressed with the neat little lighthouse and the many scenic attractions around Monterey Bay.

The lighthouse first became operative February 1, 1855, as Charles Layton, a veteran of both the British and American armies lit the oil lamp. After an unsuccessful try at gold mining he and his wife settled in Monterey in 1855 and eventually got his appointment as keeper, at an annual stipend of $1,000. Unfortunately his reign at the lighthouse was short. He joined a posse seeking out notorious bandit Anastasio Garcia. In a shootout, Layton was seriously wounded and shortly afterward died. As was often the case in a one family station, his wife assumed the lighthouse chores and was soon after appointed as keeper.

The lighthouse suffered serious damage in the 1906 earthquake while Emily Fish was its keeper. Cracks appeared in the tower and the flame in the lamp wicks flickered. One of the outbuildings was wrenched from its foundation and considerable other damage was apparent at the station. Emily and her hired help did what they could do to keep the lighthouse operative. She was also concerned about her widowed step-daughter Juliet, who in the interim had become keeper of the light on Angel Island in San Francisco Bay.

When the destroyer *Prible* arrived in Monterey Bay, she brought news of the terrible damage that had occurred in San Francisco during the earthquake. All communications between Monterey and San Francisco had broken down. Emily was at last informed that her daughter was all right, still at her keeper's post on Angel Island. In turn, Emily went about her lighthouse chores, doing what she could to help those who had suffered from the quake.

That zealous lady was later appointed head of the welcoming committee for the landing of Commander Sloat at Monterey marking the 50th anniversary of California's annexation. She was also involved with Monterey's grandest celebration and ball at the city's Presidio, given in honor of the officers of President Teddy Roosevelt's Great White Fleet when the armada of naval ships anchored in the bay in 1908-09.

Both Emily and Juliet retired from their respective lighthouse positions in 1914. The former died in 1947 at age 88, and was buried in Oakland.

In later years the fixed third order lens was fitted with clockworks to turn a brass plate known as an eclipser which revolved around the optic and changed the characteristic of the light. Though some of the early lighthouses were fitted with eclipsers, the revolving lens proved much more effective as the bullseyes in the panels gave a sharp flash of higher intensity.

In the aftermath of damage from the 1906 earthquake the station underwent a major renovation, all the cracks in the stone and brick masonry repaired. The rehabilitation of the station, plus its improvements, came to as much as the $26,000 it cost to originally construct the sentinel. Even at the earlier time (1855) there was a cost overrun, as the intention was to do the job for $15,000. First suggestion for a light at Point Pinos (Pine Point) was made by Army General Persifor Smith, of the Pacific Division, on his visit in 1849. Though the Spaniards utilized Montery Harbor as a place of refuge for its ships in early times there is no record of them having placed an aid to navigation at the location.

Today, the lighthouse is still in place and shining its beacon, but the surrounding area has greatly changed. A golf course comes almost

to the door of the sentinel in an area of expensive property. It is kept in immaculate condition and is open to the public on weekends. The Pacific Grove Museum has displays inside the lighthouse which is situated on Lighthouse Avenue between Sunset Drive and Asilomar Avenue in Pacific Grove. One can recognize the tower as being one of the original eight by its umbrella dome atop the lantern house. The light characteristic at this writing is occulting white every four seconds. The structure is 43 feet in height and stands 89 feet above sea level. A radiobeacon is nearby.

❋ Point Sur

It sits near the top of a large hummock, 96 miles southeastward of San Francisco Bay, 270 feet above the sea. Its name is Point Sur Lighthouse and it has been shining its light seaward since 1889.

In 1866 an examiner was sent out to research the point under the auspices of the Lighthouse Board. He returned the following findings:

"Point Sur is metamorphic sandstone, and has an altitude of 363 feet. It covers an area of nearly three acres, its general shape being that of a wedge with an indented edge. The north side and top of Point Sur are covered with grass, and the sides are very steep, making the ascent difficult. The extreme and western portions of this point of rock are almost vertical."

He went on to say that "the only way in which supplies can be sent to Point Sur is by water, for the only road is a trail almost impassable even for a horse. It must also appear that the erection there of a lighthouse, with the accompanying buildings, will be an expensive operation. As nearly as can be estimated with the data available, it will cost not less than $100,000."

The result of that report somewhat dumbfounded the Lighthouse Board principals, but the necessity of a beacon at the point was obvious, regardless of cost. The SS *Los Angeles* had scattered her remains over the rocky surf in 1873, and the SS *Ventura* was a total loss after skimming Point Sur too closely and going down about a mile north of Santa Cruz, two miles from Morro Rock. Shipmaster George Fake and his passengers were rescued but the ship's cargo washed ashore and citizens of the locale descended on the loot. In the *Los Angeles* tragedy, six persons lost their lives.

Such disasters prompted greater demand for a lighthouse on that important steamer route. After much agitation and debate, Congress finally coughed up an appropriation of $50,000 at the urging of the lighthouse authorities. Another $50,000 was allotted the following year, and the gears began to grind. Equipment for a quarry plant, and materials such as lumber, wire, boiler, and engine were ordered. In May of 1887, a 25-man force of laborers was on the scene to quarry stone at the site and blast out a road and trestle from Big Sur Valley.

The Report of the Lighthouse Board from 1888 told of the progress made, including a road blasted out of the side of the promontory on the seaward face, and a railroad track 480 feet long to the site of the lighthouse. Out of the calcified substance the workers created a site for the tower, oil room, boiler rooms, engine house and dwelling. The great need for water necessitated a cistern with a capacity of 53,000 gallons. In the interim, contracts were completed for the lantern and iron work, and for the boiler and engine to operate the fog signal. And already, a plea went out for an extra $10,000 if the station was to be completed.

The big first order Fresnel lens for the station was manufactured by Barbier & Fenestre of Paris in 1885. It came by sea to San Francisco and was installed at the lighthouse in 1889. Weight of the lens was 4,330 pounds, its height when assembled was eight feet 10 inches and its inside diameter six feet 3 1/2 inches. (That original lens was removed from the lighthouse in 1978 and placed on loan at the Allen Knight Museum in Monterey.) The replacement at the lighthouse was a

DCB-224 beacon, a low maintenance optic serviced by the Coast Guard every six months. It is backed up by a diesel generator in case of power failure.

The station was first opened for operation on August 1, 1889, alternating red and white flashes every 15 seconds, visible 20 miles at sea.

Originally, some $1,500 was paid the landowner of the property for a right-of-way to get into the lighthouse property. Some $6,000 was requested but denied for quarters for a fourth keeper. Already the project was well over the estimate.

Even though a crude wagon trail from the top of Point Sur to the county road existed, the keepers still depended on the lighthouse tender landing supplies at a landing platform at the bottom of the tramway from which they were hauled up on a cart, 280 feet. The supplies were brought in by the tender's boat. A steam engine to operate the tram car was at the top of the cliff. The old winch house was later converted to an additional keepers' dwelling.

By 1900, the road was widened and improved so vehicles could have easier access from the land side. There was even a horse barn and a school for the keepers' kids set up near the country road for a time.

At the summit of the hummock, in addition to the dwellings, was a carpenter-blacksmith shop. The lighthouse, built of granite, was west, and down the sea slope from the station residences, the fog signal portion and watchroom connected to the tower.

It wasn't a shipwreck, but a dirigible accident that caused concern on February 13, 1935. As the Pacific Fleet worked its way along the coast, the navy dirigible *Macon* flew ahead of the surface craft. When opposite Point Sur, keeper Tom Henderson watched in awe as the huge aircraft passed over. A squall suddenly hit the *Macon*, and before Henderson's eyes he observed the collapse of the tail section. Down went the airship with her 83 man crew, ker-splash into the ocean. Fortunately, an SOS had gone out and the surface warships rushed to the disaster scene. All were rescued except a radio operator and a mess boy who went down with the dirigible, a $3.5 million loss.

The station was automated in 1972, and most of the buildings boarded up. With increasing vandalism, the California Department of Parks and Recreation got involved and took over all the structures except the tower and fog signal house. In turn, they expended nearly a million dollars to revamp the former granite tri-plex head keepers' dwelling and other buildings.

Still a bit off the beaten track, the nearest large settlement is at Carmel. In 1989, Point Sur Lighthouse celebrated its centennial, the same year the former Lighthouse Service marked its bicentennial.

The lighthouse is situated off California Route 1 in Pfeiffer Big Sur State Park, the nearest town being Big Sur. Hiking tours are available for the hardy who wish to climb up the long road to the top of the hill where the station buildings are located. They are usually Sunday tours although plans are being formulated to give public greater access. In the meantime, the DCB flashes its white light every 15 seconds. The Point Sur radiobeacon is nearby sending out its three short dots around the clock.

It is of interest to note that when the 11th Coast Guard District, Alameda, ordered the removal of the original lens, under the direction of chief warrant officer Craig Bitler, he in turn enlisted his associates, and each prism was given to a volunteer to restore. Vandals had damaged some of the pieces which had to be fabricated. After six months, and 2,000 man hours of restoration work on the lens and its mechanisms, it was figured that with everything put together its total weight was 9,750 pounds, almost five tons. It is presently the star attraction at the Monterey Maritime History Center.

❀ Piedras Blancas

Until 1949, Piedras Blancas Lighthouse was one of the most imposing on the California coast. Gracefully tapering skyward, the 74 foot tower suffered when the Coast Guard elected to remove the lantern house and place an aero marine beacon on the flat metal base that once held the lantern housing and its first order lens and apparatus. That most unfortunate move was to turn a thing of beauty into a rather ugly tower.

Point Piedras Blancas is a low, rocky point projecting about a half mile from the general trend of the coast. The light stands 142 feet above the water. Piedras Blancas are actually two large rocks, 74 and 31 feet high, 500 yards offshore and 0.8 mile eastward of the point.

The lighthouse is at the half-way mark between Pigeon Point and Point Conception. It is located just off Highway 1, a mile north of the town of San Simeon. It would have been every bit as much a tourist attraction as the nearby Hearst Castle had it not been for the decapitation of the tower.

Not only was the removal of the lantern house unfortunate but the delicate lens was placed on the roadside at Cambria as a tourist attraction, nobody giving thought to its exposure to the elements. For many years it stood there unsheltered, and it was only in recent years that lighthouse enthusiasts realized that the optic was of tremendous historical value. Despite the damage that occurred it has in recent time been put under cover and restored.

The vital need to light the California coast prompted the construction of the Piedras Blancas Lighthouse, and it became operative in 1875. In 1906 it was joined by a fog signal. With an eclipser, at that date in history, it displayed a fixed light varied by a white flash every 15 seconds. The masonry structure was a popular destination for visitors in the days when it was operated by the Lighthouse Service, especially in the summer time when the weather was milder and groves of wild flowers were blooming in profusion. Most stayed away however, when the fog rolled in and the notoriously loud fog signal went into operation. It was one of those two-tone diaphone blasters that could shake the skin off a sea serpent. Too bad the signal wasn't located on the point when the British ship *Harlech Castle* was wrecked on the nearby outcrops August 31, 1869. At this writing the modern beacon atop the tower is capable of putting out 1.4 million candlepower.

A funny thing happened at the lighthouse in 1896, when assistant keeper James Marner resigned his post and then tried to cancel his resignation by claiming, "I was under the influence of grog at the time."

❀ San Luis Obispo

A lighthouse was established at San Luis Obispo in 1890. It was located on Point San Luis at the westerly side of San Luis Obispo Bay, near Port Harford. It was described in the early *Light List* as a "square, white frame tower attached to the southwesterly corner of a one-and-one-half story white, frame dwelling with lead colored trimmings, green blinds and red roof; lantern, black. A one-and-one-half story double-dwelling, painted like the above stands 150 feet to the eastward. Fog signal between dwelling and 150 feet to southward."

The fog signal was a ten-inch steam whistle.

The 1994 *Light List* describes the modern beacon as being on a cylindrical structure east of the old lighthouse, and a radiobeacon with a 20 mile range nearby. The area has been off limits to the general public as the facility is in the shadow of the Diablo Canyon Atomic Power Plant.

Port San Luis Obispo on the western shore of the bay is the seaport for San Luis which is ten miles inland. The port in recent years has featured an oil loading terminal and a base for commercial and pleasure fishing craft.

Early day activity in the bay was the reason for the lighthouse which originally displayed a fourth order lens that served as both an entrance light and a seacoast beacon.

In 1994, a group was formed to work toward the restoration of the old lighthouse. Former Port San Luis District officials Howard Mankins and Gerard Parsons donated materials for the restoration work.

✹ Point Arguello

There's not much glamour for lighthouse buffs at Point Arguello anymore. A powerful light on a single post flashing white every 15 seconds and a fog signal mark this important point along the Pacific Coast. There has been a lot of marine tragedy in the area, but ironically it was not one of the earlier considerations for a lighthouse. Even though meager funds were appropriated for a beacon at the location in 1888, it was not until February of 1901 that a station was established at Arguello. The beacon was a fixed white light of the fourth order situated on the extreme end of Point Arguello, 12 miles northwest of Point Conception. Undoubtedly it was the short distance from the Conception tower that made the authorities drag their feet so long on the construction of

the station at Arguello. The structure was described as a square tower with black lantern rising from a fog signal building. There was one double and one single dwelling for the keepers, 600 feet northeast of the tower. The frame buildings had red roofs and were painted white with lead colored trimmings. The height of the tower was only 28 feet, but the beacon was 91 feet above sea level.

Very much aware of the thick fogs that often obscured the coast, the government placed a 12-inch compressed air whistle on the point, and much to the chagrin of the keepers the whistle got plenty of exercise.

The first lighthouse at the site was decommissioned in 1934. An aero-marine beacon was eventually placed atop a skeleton tower at that time in lighthouse history, accompanied later by a radiobeacon.

Several faithful keepers served at Arguello. They were always alert to shipwreck along those rugged shores and none was more gripping than on a September night in 1923, at the nearby Honda when one of the greatest peace-time naval disasters occurred. A flotilla of 14 destroyers were enroute from San Francisco to San Diego in a heavy fog. Because of a mix-up in signals, and the fact that the lead destroyer was slightly off course, seven vessels piled up, one after another, on the dreaded rocks. Two others were damaged but managed to veer away from danger. The terrible grinding of steel against rock was to cost the lives of 22 sailors and a $13 million loss for Uncle Sam (big money in those days). The loss of life could have been much worse as the fleet represented a total of 770 officers and men, most of whom had to go through a nightmare fending for themselves in an effort to gain the inhospitable shore.

Captain Edward Watson, Destroyer Squadron Commander, a seasoned military man, was off on his dead reckoning and his future hearing had all the intensity of the novel, *The Caine Mutiny*. An otherwise brilliant career was badly tarnished. One thing in his favor was that there was a mix-up in radio signals with a merchant ship, the SS *Cuba*, in distress off San Miguel Island.

Keeper George Olson at the Point Arguello station made the following report:

Several light structures have stood at Point Arguello from time to time since the station was established in 1901. Those shown here have been replaced by a pole light and fog signal in an area where many wrecks have occurred. DCB lamps and aero marine beacons of different types have made the traditional lighthouse structure obsolete, all weather, watertight, exposed beacons rotated by small electric motors (by remote control). The Coast Guard has no choice but to use the latest hi-tech mechanisms, which in essence spelled the doom of the lighthouse keeper, not to mention many other electronic gadgets.

At Point Honda, three miles north of Pt. Arguello on Saturday night, Sept. 8, 1923, seven U.S. destroyers were wrecked by running on the rocks at 9:07 p.m., all running aground at intervals of two minutes. At 9:20 p.m. the last of the seven were on the rocks. High seas and heavy fog. Twenty-two lives were lost. Seven hundred and seventy men including officers were on the ships.

The keepers loaned what help they could in the aftermath of the tragedy, but the lead destroyer *Delphy*, followed by the *Lee, Young, Woodbury, Chauncey, Nicholas* and *Fuller* were totally lost. Their hulls have remained all these years and still offer pickings for the treasure-hunting divers.

It was keeper W.A. Henderson who was in charge of the station when the beautiful passenger liner *Santa Rosa*, Captain J.O. Faris commanding, ran aground in the heavy fog and broke up on July 7, 1911. In a dramatic rescue operation, he and others in the lighthouse service played a major role in saving passengers as they were evacuated from the steamer. The twin-screw iron-hulled vessel dating from 1884 was one of the favorites in coastwise passenger service, but her hull was unable to remain intact on the black boulders, and soon broke in half amidships.

Henderson worked several hours in the cold surf helping bring survivors ashore. Though there were several injuries, a joint effort of many willing volunteers and the crew of assisting vessels managed to complete a brilliant rescue effort. The Honda, however, had claimed another victim and salvage was negligible.

The Arguello keepers were also involved when another sleek coastal passenger liner ended her days on the outcrops of Point Arguello. The SS *Harvard* was ripped to pieces May 30, 1931. She and her sistership, the *Yale*, were the "darlings" of Southern California sea going tourists—fast, commodious, and graceful. The passengers were saved, the ship totally lost, breaking a popular overnight run between San Francisco and Los Angeles.

❀ Point Conception

Point Conception Lighthouse got off to a rocky beginning. As one of the first eight lighthouses contracted for on the Pacific Coast it was in one of the most difficult areas in which to build. Gibbons and Kelly constructed the sentinel on a plateau 133 feet above sea level, the tower rising another 52 feet. The difficulty of getting supplies to the site and fear of a cost overrun made it a bad deal from the beginning. The old saying that haste makes waste may have been in play at Point Conception. As the work progressed in 1854-55 and the tower took shape, lighthouse inspector Bache arrived and was totally dissatisfied with what he termed, "inferior workmanship." After a verbal confrontation with the builders, the tower was dismantled and a new start begun. This, of course, delayed the completion of the station, but it would not be accepted nor any money paid until the lighthouse met Bache's satisfaction.

Finally the lens and lighting apparatus, packed in several crates, arrived aboard the schooner *General Pierce*. While being brought ashore in the ship's boat, damage occurred to some of the components and the anticipated turn on of the light, set for December 1855, was canceled until replacements could arrive for the lighting apparatus. As the construction crew eagerly left the location with a unanimous "Good riddance," Head keeper George Parkinson arrived on the scene and not only found the station lacking the finishing touches but also several curious Indians pondering the merits of the place. He hated the lighthouse from the start openly describing his domicile as "This dreadful promontory of desolation." The lighthouse building apparently was on unstable ground as cracks began to appear. The keeper made repairs where he could but deterioration was everywhere. He was one discouraged man. And he wasn't alone, for when the inspector came in 1875, he was so alarmed by the wretched condition of the lighthouse that he immediately recommended its removal. Money was tight, however, and patches had to do for the next seven years. Finally, in 1882, a new lighthouse was constructed at a lower level on a seaward shelf below the other station buildings.

The new lighthouse featured a first order Fresnel that showed a white flash every 30 seconds with a range of 18 miles. The fog signal house was set apart from the lighthouse and blew a powerful diaphone horn that really shook the rocky cliffs. The keepers quarters were at the top of the hill. When the Bill Owens family moved to the station in 1931 they occupied a little dwelling at the foot of the exterior cement staircase. His wife had her hands full caring for five children and a dog. Two of the children were surprise twins. It was depression time, Owens' salary being only $1,140 annually as third assistant.

Until electricity came to the lighthouse, the five wick oil lamp like those at other major lighthouses, consumed 2,282 gallons of oil annually, compared to 685 gallons for second and third order lenses, and 243 for fourth order lamps.

The stretch of coastline between Conception and Arguello is very dangerous, especially when the weather closes down. The point has often been referred to as California's Cape Horn because of the fickle nature of the seas and the weather. From the sea it's a very desolate looking area and the beetling cliffs are prodigious.

The lighthouse is still active and a fog signal is operating continuously at the site today, but the place is off limits to the public, automated and overseen by Coast Guard remote control.

Cape Mendocino and Point Conception were the two main landfalls that the old Spanish galleon navigators searched for on return from the Indies back when Spain ruled the Pacific, but neither promontory had an aid to navigation until Uncle Sam came on the scene.

❀ Santa Barbara

The feminine touch was highly evident at the Santa Barbara Lighthouse, as it was at both Point Pinos and Angel Island in the early days. Julia Williams kept the light burning for a record 40 years, beginning in 1865. There were only a couple of nights when she wasn't on duty. She raised five children at the lighthouse, each of which became adept at tending the light as they grew up. It was her husband Albert Johnson Williams who was appointed as the first keeper of the light at Santa Barbara, and after nine years he turned the chores over to his wife so he could attend to other business pursuits. Julia took over like a duck to water and was still doing her thing at age 81 when she fell and broke her hip and reluctantly had to resign in 1905.

George D. Nagle was the builder of the station which displayed its light for the first time on December 1, 1856.

A devastating earthquake struck the lighthouse on June 29, 1925. Keeper Weeks tumbled out of his bed in the morning amid cracking walls. He managed to rescue his mother, sister, and brother, but the lighthouse was in shambles. A temporary light was set up. In 1935, a short 24 foot tower was built on the point, southwest from Santa Barbara landing, and was capped by a powerful aero marine beacon developing 1.2 million candlepower, which would have made Santa Barbara's original oil flame look puny by comparison.

The present structure has none of the personality of the original but the beautiful city of Santa Barbara makes most any feature look good.

❀ Point Hueneme

Point Hueneme Lighthouse was a pert frame Victorian style lighthouse built in 1874 on the north side of the east entrance to Santa Barbara Channel. It was razed in 1941 and replaced by a square tower on top of a fog signal building. The present structure is 48 feet high and 52 feet above the water. The light characteristic is five quick flashes followed by fixed white for 30 seconds. The foghorn is 296 degrees from the light and makes one blast every 30 seconds.

Port Hueneme doesn't get the accolades as do California's resort areas, but it has been of considerable importance to commerce through the years which was why a lighthouse was placed there originally in 1874 to act both as a harbor entrance and seacoast (4th order Fresnel)

The original Point Hueneme Lighthouse, sister to the Point Fermin Lighthouse. This beautiful structure was torn down in 1941, and replaced by a modern structure. Photo courtesy The Keepers Log

light. Sailing vessels, steamers, and fishing vessels have frequented the port through the decades. In recent years Port Hueneme, a basin inside Point Hueneme, protected by jetties, has catered to a number of off-shore drilling rigs and oil support vessels.

⚓ Anacapa Lighthouse

One of the least visited active lighthouses on the California sea-scape is Anacapa Lighthouse. It was one of the last to be built under the Lighthouse Establishment before the takeover by the Coast Guard in 1939, and is a fine example of a latter day lighthouse with traditional values. The structure stands proud on barren Anacapa Island, one of three isles in the Channel Islands National Monument. It was built in 1932, and shines its light from 277 feet above sea level. The fog horn is activated by a fog detector, human hands are no longer needed except for occasional Coast Guard checkups. The former keepers' dwelling is occupied by National Park rangers, the only inhabitants of the island.

Anacapa Island is located 11 miles southwest of Point Hueneme and is the last of California's offshore stations still in operation. Auto-mated in 1966, Anacapa Light Station previously had eight Coast Guardsmen in attendance on the isle. It was a 45 minute, 12 mile run from the Oxnard Coast Guard base on the mainland after which atten-dants had to scramble up 152 steps imbedded in the sheer basaltic cliff at the east side of the island, followed by a half-mile hike to the light-

house. (Point Bonita Lighthouse, in 1980, was the last of California's 32 Coast Guard lighthouses to be automated.)

Anacapa was fitted with a third order Fresnel lens on completion in 1932. The 600,000 candlepower light was electrically operated and the original fog signal was a powerful diaphone with a two-tone air blast.

Winds sometimes howl over the island but it doesn't stop the squad-rons of gulls and pelicans as well as numerous other varieties of birds from inhabiting the place. Seals and sea lions also like the beaches and off-island obstructions.

The first lighthouse on Anacapa was established in 1912, but it was only an unmanned skeleton tower with an oil lamp. Not until the new lighthouse was built was the isle properly protected from ship-wreck.

There have been scores of wrecks in and around the Channel Is-lands, one of the first being that of the sidewheel steamer *Winfield Scott* which went to her grave against the ramparts of Anacapa December 2, 1853. The 250 survivors had to eke out an existence on the lonely is-land until help finally came. Divers still dive on her remains even at this late date. Many relics have been recovered, but as far as is known none of the reputed treasure of gold.

In the summer of 1994, Channel Islands National Park archeolo-gist Don Morris and volunteer marine researcher, writer and diver Bob Schwemmer, spent several days on the island tracing the shipwrecks that have occurred there through the decades. Schwemmer traveled from his Valencia home to San Francisco and Washington, D.C., to tap in on the archives. The two men have come up with a list of about 100 vessels wrecked in the general area, and found the remains of several. Its easy to see why lighthouses and fog signals were needed in the past, and still offer comfort to the soul in our present day.

✸ Point Vicente

Point Vicente Lighthouse is Hollywood's beacon, not only because its near Hollywood but because it's been used in so many movie and TV films as a backdrop. Point Vicente is situated 6.3 miles from Point Fermin, in a northwesterly direction, and is a steep rocky cliff, 120 feet high, off-white and reddish in color. A dangerous rock is awash 250 yards southwestward of the point and a smaller 25 foot high black rock, pyramidal in shape, is close inshore, 0.3 mile eastward of the point. Point Vicente Lighthouse, a graceful 67 foot tower, stands 185 feet above the water on the southwesterly end of the point.

The lighthouse was built in 1926, and still presents a beautiful sight in a park-like setting, amid graceful palm trees. With a rock strewn beach, ragged cliffs and an ocean of azure blue with silver surf, it's easy to understand why it is so often featured.

The greater Los Angeles sentinel is located off Palos Verdes Drive north of the city's Marineland. Out of the path of most of the proverbial smog, the sea breezes keep the foul air at bay. Ocean shipping has long depended on the light and fog signal on the point to guide them in and out of San Pedro Harbor. Its powerful 1.1 million candlepower beacon is seen about 20 miles at sea, and sparkles like a jewel at night. When commissioned in 1926, the lighthouse was supplied with a third order Fresnel lens which at that time produced 900,000 candle power.

In the Lighthouse Service days the station was a "preferred location" and there was a waiting list of keepers, especially with families, wanting to tenant its dwelling.

Like all lighthouses it had its ghost. All traditional lighthouses had ghosts whether real or tongue-in-check. The Vicente ghost was created by the reverse parenthesis of the lights' beam.

The Vicente tower was very similar to the one on Anacapa, although taller. Despite its presence, an occasional wreck did occur on Point Vicente as well as at other nearby locations, most as a result of fog. The beacon and foghorn, however, prevented several other ship losses.

✸ Point Fermin

Point Fermin light today shines from a utilitarian pole, but the historic old lighthouse at the site has become one of Greater Los Angeles' top tourist attractions, having been totally restored to the way it looked when Los Angeles was just a small settlement, back in 1874. Typical of several of the early California lighthouses, it was Victorian in style and constructed mostly of redwood. In a civic endeavor in recent years the edifice was restored as a tourist attraction in a Los Angeles city park, and a caretaker is retained to keep the attraction pleasing to the visitors' eyes even though it is not generally open to public inspection. Located on Paseo Del Mar, west of Pacific Avenue, the grounds are inviting and the view spectacular, a good place to see the harbor entrance and the Los Angeles Lighthouse at the end of the jetty.

It's hard to believe when one sees the marine activity in the greater Los Angeles sealanes, that early on it was not even considered to have possibilities for a major seaport. According to history, the small sailing vessel *Lelia Byrd*, Captain William Shaler, of New Bedford was the first American flag vessel to enter the port, in 1805. The early Spaniards saw no possibilities of a harbor of refuge at that location. In fact,

through the years it's been the ingenuity of man that has turned the harbor of San Pedro and environs into a paramount seaport, especially in the transport of petroleum.

By comparison with the light stations in the Pacific Northwest, California, had many more women lightkeepers in early times, perhaps because the state was somewhat more populated and conditions more conducive. Point Fermin's Mary Smith brought her sister along when she was assigned as keeper in 1874. She claimed they wanted to find a place of peace and healthful living in what was then a quiet fishing village. Who ever heard of smog in 1874?

Directly off Point Fermin, on a foggy October day in 1888, the British ship *Respigadera* came to grief on the outcrops. The 2,583 ton vessel, out of Australia, draped her carcass over the unrelenting rocks, and was so badly damaged that salvers paid slightly over $1,200 for the ship and its cargo of coal. When the elements refused to break up her stubborn timbers, she was dynamited as a menace to navigation. There were several other wrecks nearby from time to time but none any closer to the locale of the lighthouse.

Inasmuch as San Pedro has long been an oil port, many ships have been subject to fire and explosion. A typical example was the T-2 tanker *Markay*, which on June 22, 1947, exploded and burned at Pier 168. In her tanks were nearly three million gallons of gasoline. The ship was destroyed, five docking berths were burned and 11 lives were lost.

What a sad contrast it is to see the pioneer Point Fermin lighthouse no longer showing an active light in her crown, while a minor pole light in the point's "front yard" is the aid to navigation in our present age.

✸ Los Angeles Harbor

What's this? An old lighthouse with a modern touch! Yes indeed, Los Angeles (Harbor) Lighthouse with its flashing green characteristic has gone solar. The unique 69 foot tower on the outer end of the San Pedro Breakwater has been passed by thousands of ships of every description since its establishment in 1913. On a concrete block, the white cylindrical tower with black pilasters was one of the first Pacific Coast lighthouses built to stand earthquakes. In fact, it was designed to get out of plumb and still be stable. Actually it is slightly out of plumb today as a result of a trembler some years ago, but it remains unscathed. Over the years it has become both a seamark and a "landmark" light, not only known to seafarers but to the many cruise ships sailing in and out of the harbor inbound or outbound from world destinations. Photo albums in great numbers contain a picture of the lighthouse.

In 1988, the third order lens which served in the lantern house from 1930, (replacing a fourth order optic) was in turn interchanged for a modern acrylic 190 mm rotating fixture operated by solar power. Where the former light utilized commercial power which sometimes failed, the new optic could soak up California sunshine in its solar panels, saving government money. The facility is on the National Register of Historic Places, and was manned until 1971 when automation knocked at the door. The 15 mile range of the present light was four miles less than the former. The third order lens had a range of 20 miles, the 1,000 watt quartz iodine bulb shining through a classic bivalve (clam shell) lens. That classic optic was consigned to the local maritime museum.

The present electronic fog signal is only audible for one mile. The diaphone two-tone fog signal once used at the station, according to the skipper of the SS *Talamanca,* of the United Fruit Line, was once picked up 33 miles at sea, which is perhaps an all-time record.

When manned by the Coast Guard, Los Angeles Light had four men who rotated on duty. Their isolation at the end of a two-and-a-half mile jetty was not necessarily popular, especially when the fog poured in through the Angel's Gate. In storms, the waves went over the break-

Keeper in the lantern room of the Los Angeles Harbor Lighthouse in the 1930s. The Fourth Order bivalve or clam shell optic has since been replaced by a modern optic and the old lens placed in the local museum. Photo courtesy The Keepers Log

water and drenched the tower, sometimes breaking the lower windows. In thick weather, ships have narrowly missed the concrete caisson on which the tower stands. Many years ago a battleship got slightly misguided and almost poked its snout into a place where it didn't belong. The station's diaphone horn snapped the helmsman to attention along with a strident command from his superior.

✸ Long Beach Harbor

Perhaps the first innovative switch from the traditional lighthouse to a modern counterpart was accomplished at the Long Beach Harbor Light in 1949. That seems like a long time ago, but even today it looks extremely modern in every respect. It is a white rectangular tower set on a square structure supported by four short columns, or legs. It was built to withstand earthquakes and high winds. It is even immune from seismic tidal waves, according to the architects. Immediately the name "Robot Light" was attached to the structure, and as effective as it is it would make the typical old lighthouse keeper turn over in his grave.

The location is at busy San Pedro Middle Breakwater. There were never any attendants from the beginning. It was designed to be self-sufficient with its 36-inch airway beacon, dual two-tone fog signals and radiobeacon. Such a monolithic creation certainly gets the attention of the curious and it has proven itself through the years. Also, it ushered in the age of automation with a capital A. Not much romance or drama revolves around a robot lighthouse—that kind of stuff is relegated to a time lost in the mists of progress. With it came the disappearance of the personal touch.

And so it is, we have come full circle with the lighthouses of America's three-state Pacific Coast. Its been an era unparalleled in the marine history of the west. From sail to steam to diesel along with steam turbine, diesel electric, and finally nuclear power in ships, the lighthouses along the way have seen it through to our modern automated radio and satellite controlled navigation. Such a variety of innovative electronic wonders have caused the sun to set on the traditional lighthouse. It is indeed twilight time, a period of reflections on the past.

Until the 1850s just about every lighthouse in the United States used Argand lamps and parabolic reflectors for illumination. Those lamps were placed side by side around the circumference of a circle, the number of lamps used depended on the arc of the horizon where illumination was needed. Though bullseye magnifying lenses were utilized on each lamp they were highly ineffective, and by 1840 the lenses were removed and the reflectors left on their own. It was known as the American System, not too expensive to operate but extremely inferior. What a break it was that Augustin Fresnel revolutionized the lighting of foreign and American lighthouses, one of France's great contributions in the field of pharology, and the fact that our country adopted the new optics just as the planting of lighthouses got underway on the Pacific Coast was of great significance.

Now we have come to the electronic revolution when most of the classic Fresnels are being put out to pasture. The traditional lighthouse keeper joins the ice man and the blacksmith and many others who have been ruled out as a necessary factor in the American economy. The fading memory and the written word are all that is left of the way it was. When one considers the fact that lighthouse keepers have been active for nearly 2,500 years in all corners of the world, soon there will be none, and it almost brings a tear to the eye. May the surviving lighthouses live on.

It might be fitting to end this epistle by returning to Ballast Point Lighthouse in San Diego to pay tribute to a fog signal. The lighthouse is no longer there, but the old Ballast Point fog bell came home to rest for a while on June 2, 1990. San Diegans were again treated to the deep resonance of the bell, an unrung hero for over 45 years. It not only signalled its own 100th birthday but also the 200th birthday of the U. S. Coast Guard. It was a part of the Coast Guard's bicentennial celebration. Though the one-ton bell, cast in San Francisco by Garritt & Company, was replaced by fog horns in 1928, it remained at the site as a standby signal until 1957, when the entire station was razed.

Radford Franke, who was a keeper at the facility from 1946 till 1957 last gave a warning with the bell while he was an assistant keeper there in World War II, after a naval vessel entering the harbor in the fog was in danger of running aground.

The bell was rescued from a Navy scrap yard in 1969 by Alva Oliphant, and was placed on loan with the Maritime Museum in San Diego.

Bits and pieces of relics of the heyday of the lighthouse keep turning up here and there, but most of the old keepers have been laid to rest, men who never knew such words as Racon, Omega, Anrac and LORAN, yet alone the fact that ships would ever be guided by satellite navigation and other electronic radio-oriented guides that can penetrate any kind of weather or sea conditions.

Paul James caught the spirit of the past when he wrote the following:

The scene was more beautiful far to the eye
Than if day in its pride had arrayed it.
And o're them the lighthouse looked lovely as hope,
That star of life's tremulous ocean.

In conclusion, a further word must be said about lighthouse ghosts. As earlier mentioned, it is doubtful one will find a lighthouse without a ghost, whether in truth or jest. It is however, one of the most asked questions by visitors to lighthouses. Even before automation, Coast Guardsmen, and earlier U.S. Lighthouse Service keepers talked about ghosts in their respective lighthouses, and to those who were superstitious the spirit world was real. Even when such phenomenon was scientifically and practically explained the keepers often refused to accept the explanation. To others it was just an accepted tradition. The mind can play tricks on those who tend to be vulnerable under certain conditions.

Do the ever changing lights and shadows play tricks on our minds? Is it the ever present wind soughing gently through the branches of nearby trees or is it the gale-force blow that tears branches off and roars down the chimney that brings ghosts to mind? Perhaps its the fog that creeps slowly across the ocean pointing its muted fingers toward shore, beckoning one to step out of the shelter of the warm cocoon of the lighthouse so it can wrap one in its cold, clammy blanket.

Perhaps one's favorite lighthouse isn't a warm place at all. Maybe its damp, impersonal, almost a prison because of its remoteness out on a rock or at the edge of a headland, alone far away from anywhere. When the winds find cracks in the window sills or whistle around the complex angles of the tower or scream up the spiral staircases, noises are created that chill the spine, and the mind conjures up all kinds of spectral things. Yes, it's true, every lighthouse has its ghost and usually when a lighthouse was abandoned, new ghosts took up residence and hung around until the edifice no longer existed.

There is something about the human mind that likes to delve into things that are not of this world. There are many mysteries our good Lord has not yet revealed to us in this present life. We're still flesh and blood, and until we become spirit we'll never understand many of those mysteries. There are good spirits and bad spirits just as there are good and bad angels. The keepers of old used to discuss such topics around the table in the lonely lighthouses when they were isolated from the mainstream for long periods of time, just as they discussed politics, religion, and other controversial topics. Sometimes arguments ensued and sometimes tempers flared, but on a rock station there was no get-

ting away when personality clashes occurred. Having served with some of the oldtime keepers I came to know that they were not too much different from those in common occupations. There were perhaps a lot more introverts than extroverts. The life of a light keeper did not interest the majority, as most people like to be around other people, but there were some keepers who turned out to be the life of the party, especially in mainland family stations. Others would spend their off hours in seeming meditation staring for hours at the ever changing sea around them.

Frederick Faber wrote the following words that captured such moods.

The sea, unmated creature,
tired and lone, makes on its
desolate sands eternal moan.

Yes, one can see that the oldtime keepers' life was different, especially on the rock stations where women and children could not visit. Some liked it, some tolerated it, some hated it and some went out of their minds from the isolation. Automation changed all that, but the ghosts remain at such places as Cape Flattery, Destruction Island, Tillamook Rock, Yaquina Bay, Yaquina Head, Point Vicente, and all the others. Some ghosts lost their homes like when old Humboldt Harbor Lighthouse collapsed, and at Point Adams when it was razed back in 1912.

As the lighthouses fall into their final chapter, the words of Longfellow come to mind, from his writing, *The Day is Done.*

A feeling of sadness and longing,
That is not akin to pain,
And resembles sorrow only
As mist resembles the rain.

Hopefully after reading the words and viewing the photos and illustrations in this book, the lighthouse lover will look upon the aging towers of light with a slightly different perspective. We can't go back and capture the past but we can look ahead to the future and still preserve remnants of the past in order to make the future brighter.

Long Beach Harbor Lighthouse is known as the "Robot Lighthouse," the first on the coast to use high technology. Erected in 1949, the cutaway photo shows the inner workings of such a self-sufficient aid to navigation. The ANRAC system, Aids to Navigation Radio Control, is used at the structure, controlled from a mother station.

Epilogue

For some unknown reason lighthouses have always left an indelible mark on the mind of man. Certainly those marks differ depending on the person involved. It is said that it was a lighthouse that had a profound effect on John Newton, an impious and tough sea captain who was changed from his role as a slave runner to a warm and loving preacher, a remarkable metamorphoses.

Newton's mother died when he was a child. He quit school and went to sea at a tender age and worked his way up the ladder to skipper of his own vessel. His basic trade was the devilish transportation of black slaves from Africa to America. During a furious storm at sea, his sailing vessel, caught in its grip, plunged headlong into one giant swell after another straining every timber in the ship's hull. In the thick murk as the vessel neared shore he searched for a light. As his eyes strained for the glimpse of a beacon, he could hear the mournful cries of the shackled slaves agonizing and suffering, and the terrible stench that rose from the bowels of the storm-tossed ship. At that moment God somehow found Newton, and his life was changed. In later years he wrote his own epitaph. It read: "John Newton, clerk, once infidel and libertine, a servant of slaves in Africa, was, by the rich mercy of our Lord and Saviour, Jesus Christ, preserved, restored, pardoned and appointed to preach the faith he had long labored to destroy..."

John Newton died in 1807 at the age of 82. That great English clergyman will be best remembered for writing the glorious hymn, "Amazing Grace."

No structure that man has ever built, other than houses of worship, so play on the mind as does the lighthouse. People find solace there; photographers, artists, writers, meditators, and the curious are drawn to these unusual towers.

It was a lighthouse that prompted Philip Paul Bliss, American evangelist, to write among other hymns, "Let The Lower Lights Be Burning," and Edward S. Ufford to pen, "Throw Out The Lifeline."

No matter what one might think of American light keepers of old they were often superior to their counterparts in foreign maritime nations, and generally worked under better conditions.

Take the case of the keeper of the lighthouse on Clipperton Island, in a dreadfully isolated location 1,500 miles from Central America in the vast Pacific. After Mexico sought to enforce its claim to the island in 1908 by settling 29 men, 13 wives and several children there, many problems arose. Six years later when Mexico was torn by revolution, the tiny colony was virtually forgotten. Supply ships failed to bring needed food and supplies. The following year, scurvy swept the settlement. Several died. The captain of the group, mentally disturbed, insisted he saw a rescue ship on the horizon and ordered all the remaining men, except the lighthouse keeper, to man the oars and row out in pursuit of the imagined vessel.

The women on shore saw the men arguing violently, apparently over the captain's hallucination. A scuffle broke out in the rough waters and the skiff overturned. Sharks gathered and one by one the men disappeared in the depths, never to be seen again. The witnesses watched in horror. A pall of doom fell over the dwindling colony.

As the dreary months dragged on, the loathsome lighthouse keeper hatched a nefarious plot and decided to take over the women as his own private harem by threatening their children. He literally made the survivors his slaves and gratified all of his personal desires. Things became so odious that on July 8, 1917, one of the exasperated women grabbed an ax and at the opportune moment crushed the man's skull. The lighthouse no longer had a keeper.

Ironically, the navy gunboat, USS *Yorktown*, approached the island the following day, after months had passed with no sign of any ship. The remaining three women and eight children who had survived illness, starvation, and abuse were taken aboard and eventually returned to Mexico.

A further irony came in 1930 when Mexico, the only nation to try and colonize Clipperton, lost its hold on the island. In a bid by England, France, and Mexico, each laying claim to the detached hunk of real estate, King Victor Emmanuel of Italy was asked to be the arbitrator. He gave the island to France.

The body of the offensive lighthouse keeper may still be moldering in his grave somewhere on the remote Pacific isle.

Clipperton, seemingly jinxed from the beginning, was named for mutineer John Clipperton, first mate of an English sailing vessel, who led 21 confederates in seizing the craft in 1704. They turned pirate and made the isle their stronghold for eight years until their leader was finally captured and duly hanged.

Then in 1897, a shipwreck cast 36 English sailors on the island. Their skipper quelled a brewing mutiny by spreading the rumor that the erstwhile pirate, Clipperton, had a vast treasure somewhere on the island. In turn, the men worked off their mutinous intentions feverishly digging for the booty until a British warship arrived six weeks later to end the castaways' occupation of the insular dot.

Down through the years many shipwrecked seafarers have become unwilling captives of the island. As late as 1964, ten survivors of the sunken San Diego tuna clipper *Monarch* reached Clipperton. For three weeks the marooned individuals held out until two small fishing craft removed them and eventually rendezvoused with the diverted destroyer *Robinson* which took the castaways back to Long Beach, California.

Interest in the nation's remaining lighthouses continues to grow even though their originally intended purpose has dwindled. Lighthouse lovers, especially volunteers, will go to great lengths to assist in preserving the old sentinels. For instance, in 1982, California's Crocker Bank donated $25,000 to help refurbish the light and keeper's dwelling which were leased to American Youth Hostels, marking the initial incidence that a corporation had made such a unique donation. Then when East Brother Lighthouse was turned into a Bed and Breakfast Inn, the

Coast Guard altered a long standing policy of granting only one year leases. It granted a 20 year license to the non-profit group undertaking the extensive project. With a $67,000 Maritime Preservation Grant from the National Trust and the National Park Service and through donations of material and labor, the Victorian style structure was totally restored and maintained. Oldtime keepers would have probably turned over in their graves at such a use for a lighthouse, but had it not happened, the structure might have been torn down.

Studies are still underway for the San Luis Obispo County Land Conservancy to get the San Luis Lighthouse more readily accessible to the public through a grant. In the Pacific Northwest citizens are lining up to adopt a lighthouse, and preservation groups are becoming legion.

Nadine and Jerry Tugel, who spent several years as caretakers of Battery Point Lighthouse, have spent hours in research on the historical edifice. The "Friends" of the Yaquina Bay, Cape Blanco, and Cape Meares lighthouses have made numerous improvements, and the list goes on and on.

It's a far cry from the days of the oil lamps lighting the Fresnels, the clockwork mechanisms with weights that had to be wound by hand every four hours, the chariot wheels that turned the massive lenses, the lamps using up to five concentric wicks: but the spirit of the lights is still there even with automation and many modern innovations.

And you, the reader, just how do lighthouses effect you? Back in 1839, a frightened Russian seafarer on approaching New Archangel Harbor (Sitka) where the Russians burned a feeble oil lamp in a lantern house above the government building declared it this way:

"There are no words to express the feelings that induce a sailor to offer fervent prayers when he sees this mark of sympathy expressed by his fellow men. Suddenly he sees that he is no longer alone in the midst of the ocean waves: He sees that people are caring for him with paternal solicitude."

In days of yore such sentiments were undoubtedly felt in the hearts of seamen and navigators searching for a landfall light or a harbor beacon along the treacherous shores of the Pacific Coast. It all belongs to another era, but may the old sentinels long stand in regal solitude, monuments to a thrilling and historical chapter in maritime Americana.

The world is getting overpopulated, but Heaven beckons the saved to a place where an eternal lighthouse displays the greatest beacon of all, a light which can never be extinguished.

Point Sur Lighthouse on a seaward loft of a giant hummock showing the nearby radio tower. The lighthouse is 270 feet above sea level, a 50 foot stone structure commissioned in 1889. Photo courtesy U.S. Coast Guard

Bibliography

Andrews, Ralph W.; *Redwood Classic,* Schiffer Publishing Ltd., Atglen, PA, 1985.

Funicane, Stephanie; Heceta House, *A Historical and Architectual Survey,* Waldport Ranger Station, U.S. Forestry Dept., Waldport, OR, 1980.

Ehlers, Chad and Gibbs, Jim; *Sentinels of Solitude,* Graphic Arts Press, Portland, OR 1981.

Davidson, George; *Pacific Coast Pilot,* U.S. Government Printing Office, 1889.

Gibbs, Jim A.; *Lighthouses of the Pacific,* Schiffer Publishing Ltd., Atglen, PA, 1986.

Gibbs, Jim; *Windjammers of the Pacific Rim,* Schiffer Publishing Ltd., Atglen, PA, 1987.

Gibbs, Jim; *Pacific Square-riggers,* Schiffer Publishing Ltd., Atglen, PA, 1987.

Gibbs, Jim; *Peril At Sea,* Schiffer Publishing Ltd., Atglen, PA, 1986.

Gibbs, James A.; *Pacific Graveyard,* Binfords & Mort, Portland, OR, 1950, 1964, 1990.

Gibbs, James A.; *Tillamook Light,* Binfords & Mort, Portland, OR, 1953.

Gibbs, James A.; *Tillamook Light II,* Binfords & Mort, Portland, OR, 1979 and 1995.

Gibbs, James A.; *Sentinels of the North Pacific,* Binfords & Mort, Portland, OR, 1955.

Gibbs, James A.; *Shipwrecks of the Pacific Coast,* Binfords & Mort, Portland, OR, 1957.

Gibbs, J.A.; *Shipwrecks off Juan de Fuca,* Binfords & Mort, Portland, OR, 1968.

Gibbs, Jim; *West Coast Lighthouses,* Superior Publishing Co., Seattle, WA, 1974.

Gibbs, James A.; *Oregon's Seacoast Lighthouses,* Webb Research Group, Medford, OR, 1992.

Gibbs, James A.; *Oregon's Salty Coast,* Webb Research Group, Medford, OR, 1994.

Guthorn, Peter J.; *U.S. Coastal Charts 1783-1861*, Schiffer Publishing Ltd., Atglen, PA, 1984.

Hebert, Gerald A., Jr. EM2 USCG; *Lighthouses of the Oregon Coast* (U.S. Coast Guard booklet). Aids to Navigation team, Coos Bay, Oregon.

Holland, Francis R.; *The Old Point Loma,* Cabrillo Historical Association, in cooperation with the National Parks Service, San Diego, CA, 1968-78.

Holland, Francis R.; *America's Lighthouses,* Stephen Greene Press, Battleboro, VT, 1972.

Jackson, Walter A.; *Doghole Schooners,* California Traveler Inc., Volcano, CA., Mid-Cal Publishers, Fresno, CA, 1969.

Kaplan, H.R. and Hunt, LCDR James F., *This Is The Coast Guard,* Cornell Maritime Press, Cambridge, MD, 1972.

Lubbock, Basil; *The Down Easters 1869-1929,* Brown, Son & Ferguson Ltd., Glasgow, Scotland, 1971.

Marshall, Don B.; *California Shipwrecks*, Superior Publishing Co., Seattle, WA, 1978.

Mason, Jack; Point Reyes, *The Solemn Land,* DeWolfe Printing, Point Reyes Station, CA, 1970.

McNairn, Jack and MacMullen, Jerry; *Ships of the Redwood Coast,* Stanford University Press, Stanford University, CA, 1945.

Nordhoff, Charles; *The Lighthouses of the U.S. in 1874,* Harpers Magazine, New York, NY.

Osborne, Ernest L. and West, Victor; *Men of Action,* Bandon Historical Society Press, Bandon, OR, 1981.

Peterson, Emil R. and Powers, Alfred; *A Century of Coos and Curry,* Binfords & Mort, Portland, OR, 1952.

Putnam, George R.; *Lighthouses and Lightships of the U.S.,* Houghton, Mifflin Co., Cambridge, MA, 1917 (Boston).

Riesenberg, Felix Jr.; *Golden Gate,* Alfred A. Knoff, New York, NY, 1940.

Roberts, Bruce and Jones, Ray; *Western Lighthouses*, The Globe Pequot Press, Old Saybrook, CT, 1994.

Shanks, Ralph C. Jr. and Shanks, Janette Thompson; *Lighthouses and Lifeboats on the Redwood Coast,* Costano Books, San Anselmo, CA, 1978.

Shanks, Ralph C. Jr. and Shanks, Janette Thompson; *Lighthouses of San Francisco Bay,* Costano Books, San Anselmo, CA, 1976.

Snow, Edward Rowe; *Famous Lighthouses of New England,* Yankee Publishing Co., Boston, MA, 1944.

Stears, Mavis; *Two Points of View,* Tacoma News Tribune (sponsor, Browns Point Improvement Club) Tacoma, WA, 1986.

Stevenson, D. Allan; *The World's Lighthouses Before 1820,* Oxford University Press, London, England, 1959.

Swan, James G.; *Indians of Cape Flattery,* Collins Printers, Philadelphia, PA, (Smithsonian Institution) 1869.

Wall, Dorothy, *Yaquina Lighthouses on the Oregon Coast,* Webb Research Group, Medford, OR, 1994.

U.S. Coast Pilot (Pacific) for various years, Department of Commerce, NOAA, Washington, DC.

U.S. Government Light Lists under both the U.S. Lighthouse Service and U.S. Coast Guard for various years.

U.S. Lists of American Merchant Ships for various years, U.S. Government Printing Office, Washington, DC.

Index